# World War Two Simulated

# WORLD WAR TWO SIMULATED

## Digital Games and Reconfigurations of the Past

**Curtis D. Carbonell**

UNIVERSITY
*of*
EXETER
PRESS

First published in 2023 by
University of Exeter Press
Reed Hall, Streatham Drive
Exeter EX4 4QR, UK

*www.exeterpress.co.uk*

https://doi.org/10.47788/DRBM3952

A CIP catalogue record for this book is available from the British Library

ISBN 978-1-80413-060-5 Hardback
ISBN 978-1-80413-061-2 ePub
ISBN 978-1-80413-062-9 PDF

Cover image: istockphoto/breakermaximus

Typeset in Adobe Caslon Pro by S4Carlisle Publishing Services, Chennai, India

# Contents

# Introduction

This book argues that in today's technological societies, computer-game simulations do more than entertain; they allow players to reimagine the past, encouraging an involuntary form of learning through a dynamic that blends gameplay and the interpretations of a variety of historical and gaming texts. It takes World War Two (WWII) as a case study, focusing on core aspects of how this complex event is simulated within challenging computer games.

With a focus on flight and tank simulators, as well as first-person shooters (FPSs) and grand strategy games (GSGs), it covers a wide range of player experiences from the subjective personal frame of sitting in a cockpit or crouching in a foxhole to the broadest, such as managing national economies, armies, and policies. This book proposes the *simgame–simtext dynamic* ('simgame' meaning a computer simulation game and 'simtext' a digital or analog text) as a core part of the process whereby players often begin with simgames, such as a flight simulator, but then turn to simtexts as they investigate how to play a historical game. The more demanding the simgames, the more prevalent the dynamic.

Even if success in the game is the goal, an awareness of the past gradually emerges, one that often leads to traditional forms of study. When players search through these simtexts, hoping for a better understanding of how to play a simgame and maybe posing an intriguing 'what if' scenario, they confront the complexities of a past that, while distant enough that many people view it without trauma, is still close enough to directly affect lives today. This book is being finalized as the conflict in Ukraine refracts Russian memory politics of its May 9, 1945 victory over Nazi Germany as a spurious justification for its current invasion, a clear sign that the memory politics of WWII can still have a devastating effect. In this context, remembrance is being used to further political and even military action, another clear sign that the symbols within computer games do more than entertain—they reflect real-world political action.

This project is grounded in an interdisciplinary approach to interpretation that primarily engages historical game studies. It crosses into literary and film studies, media studies and (digital) game studies, as well as digital humanities and theories on how to manage large archives of texts. It works beyond but acknowledges the well-trodden fields within military history, with its focus on strategic theory and its application of real-world policy, especially sidestepping how simulated computer games can be used for training scenarios. The project also recognizes its marked differences from important work in the history of war-gaming and its intersections with military history.

Exploring war-gaming as a broad genre in military history and gaming reveals how WWII-based simgames differ from other categories. Historians of war-gaming have noted that by the time of Georg von Reisswitz (1794–1827), who created *Kriegspiel* (1824), war-gaming as we now consider it was emerging as a codified structure with sophisticated rules and charts that represented the movement and activity of recognizable units, using dice to add degrees of randomness, together with time-limited turns, a referee, and so on. It could be easily packed into a box and carried from one table to another. The referee adjudicated games that could be highly imbalanced to replicate specific scenarios. The history of *kriegspiel* as a genre of war-gaming is rooted in the Napoleonic Wars, with the education of the rising Prussian warrior class and an interest in simulating the battlefield. According to Martin van Creveld, war games as training, rather than mere playing, continued in the decades that followed, even in the years leading up to, and during, WWII, with the Germans taking them most seriously (2013: 162).

Such war games as those staged by the Germans during WWII itself, according to van Creveld, work in a more expansive category that is not limited to playing with figurines on a table for entertainment. He sees them as just one of the various instances that have emerged in different cultures and even in other species in which war is mimicked. Following the culture-defining approach of Johan Huizinga (1872–1945) to games and play (Huizinga, 1949), van Creveld situates play as integral both to human culture and to other species, finding the roots of war games in our evolutionary past. For him and other scholars, human culture has always presented play in the form of sophisticated games, such as the Olympics or even deadly gladiatorial fights. Combat, tactics, and strategy emerged on a larger scale, according to van Creveld, in a number of different forms such as medieval tournaments, eventually evolving into broad-scale mock battles (for his full argument, see van Creveld, 2013).

I find this comprehensive approach helpful in explaining how we arrived at a place where boardgames as simple as *Risk* (1957) and computer games such as *Civilization* (1991) that simulate contests between civilizations continue to be developed alongside a newer, digitally based approach, with serious simgames that provide an experience of the past as simulated historical configurations. This compelling gameplay is similar to other modes of representation that are considered to be part of a fantastical impulse within the broad tapestry of human creative history, which Kathryn Hume argues has challenged a dominant mimetic impulse (for how these two impulses define representation in Western literature, see Hume, 1985). This touch of the imaginative (what we might consider to be part of Hume's pervasive fantastical impulse) constructs the past as reimagined configurations, blending the what-has-never-been within a historical context of what-was.

My study focuses on the mimetic much more than the overtly fantastic, even though WWII games cross genre boundaries in any number of ways, such as often having a 'zombie mode' in FPSs in which a player can gun down undead waves of enemies. A direct crossover into the highly fantastic in historical computer games can also be seen as early as the initial entry into the *Castle Wolfenstein* series (1981), and can thus be situated within Hume's mimetic–fantastic frame. In such a way, history and fantasy are entwined for entertainment, rather than to provide a serious approach to the past. This fantastic-history genre retreats from serious simgames that attempt to simulate aspects of WWII into other forms of entertainment; I find it interesting but less compelling when explaining the simgame–simtext dynamic that can be seen in serious simgames. If anything, adding zombies or occult forces to a WWII game might point players to other fantasy works, rather than historical ones.

However, for the case studies in this book, I argue that mimetic and fantastic digital simulations should be considered unique in that they offer unparalleled historical agency to players beyond their analog counterparts. If we focus on digital (war) simgames, rather than on analog, we can see that computing systems are flexible beyond their initial abilities to perform calculations far faster than human cognition, to store information, to facilitate communication between systems, to provide artificial intelligence (AI) opponents in the form of bots, and so on. The visual and aural fidelity that has increased dramatically since the arrival of the first personal computers in the early 1980s means that simgames are increasingly able to capture specific aspects of the past, especially 'simulators' and 'shooters' within close-subjective frames.

This is not to denigrate the importance of analog war-gaming, and Philip Sabin offers an exemplary and scholarly approach that shows how analog war-gaming theory can help us understand history (Sabin, 2012). This indicates, however, how my thinking pivots in a different direction, even though a point of similarity exists when he moves from the common notion among military theorists that simulation is armed forces engaging in mock conflict, based on prescribed scenarios, to the concept of simulation as an actual 'war game' within functioning militaries. He recognizes that the traditional way of thinking about such war games has been challenged in popular culture, at least, by a "less well-known form of modern war-gaming" (Sabin, 2012: xvii)—that is, commercial tabletop war-gaming. Sabin spends considerable time examining the relationship between these two, even as he argues how the mechanics of tabletop war-gaming have been overlooked by the academy. He disputes this dismissal, insisting on its importance as a tool of knowing history.

I find affinity with such projects because I worked in a similar vein in my previous book on tabletop role-playing games (RPGs), arguing that a massive archive of published materials in science fiction and fantasy has been overlooked as foundational texts by professional literary scholarship (Carbonell, 2019). Sabin mines the many published (and often forgotten) analog war games that are increasingly being superseded by computer games. He even recognizes that simulation, within the context of war-gaming, no longer references the analog versions; instead, it more often references the digital types that I now explore.

Sabin's preference as a military historian for analog versions centers on his use of simulations as teaching tools, within which he designs his "own specially tailored simulations" (2012: xxi) that students can play through to learn about the past. A war-gaming theorist such as Sabin thus carves a space that defends gaming in the face of simulation as a serious and important way to model the real world. He prefers the term "military simulation games" (2012: 5) to describe the sorts of commercial war games he analyzes. A point of departure for my study begins here. I combine simulation and games into simgames as a signifier for my focus on complex digital military simulation games that are a starting place for players who may find themselves within a dynamic that points them toward simtexts as learning tools that explore the past.

My terminology channels the popular computer game *The Sims* (2000), a series of games about the provincial, domestic lives of digital persons guided and shaped by players. Although our context here is WWII, this dynamic can be extrapolated to other areas. For instance, an investigation into how science-fiction simgames are experienced and how they point to key science fiction simtexts would be a fruitful project. This could also apply to how racing simgames direct players to simtexts, and even to embodied experiences, such as buying time in an actual race car at a track.

Sabin's work demonstrates how 'what if' scenarios can present real-world dilemmas to students who are thinking through conflicts in the past, as well as potential conflicts today. These imagined scenarios act in a similar fashion to mathematical models in the sciences, yet instead focus on the roles of key figures, such as generals, and their strategies and tools, such as maps and figures, to simulate these conflicts. My project departs from such strategic historical analysis, asking a question closer to the heart of literary studies that explores how we engage with fiction today: How do players encounter the imagined and reconfigured past in these games? They form a space I call the *simulated imaginary gameworld*. Such imagined (or reconfigured) historical spaces are a core part of our literary past, and even comprise a popular subgenre of science fiction, alternative history. Using the imagination to model the world (and the past) may stretch the concept to its limit, but with our powerful digital tools we are creating reimagined history as experiential spaces in a way that demands further comment.

I also have a strong affinity for the material tools within war-gaming and how they both represent and simulate. The analog and digital therefore emerge as two modes with fundamentally different engagements. The digital far surpasses the material/analog in its potential to simulate complex environments and their elements with increasing fidelity, while the material keeps us grounded in embodied experience.

Such a dichotomy in how we experience today's technologized world and its past leads us into a conversation rooted in the genesis of digital game studies and its insistence on disciplinary differences from other core humanities, such as literary studies or history or even philosophy. The personal computer, gaming consoles, and even hand-held devices are now allowing simulation to create experiences of a different kind, moving beyond the representations found in novels and films, through a new gameist mode of cultural consumption and its primary mechanism—play. I find such a shift thrilling, especially in how this offers agency to players.

A military historian such as Sabin, however, is more interested in how analog war games teach, rather than in the experience of agential play, as I am. He finds computer war-simulation games less fruitful in approaching the past than their analog counterparts, and this is convincing if your didactic purposes require the pedagogical flexibility of the tabletop experience, with a classroom, students, and so on. I, on the other hand, ask how the player of a complex computer simulation game experiences imagined/reconfigured history, often involuntarily and sometimes with surprising depth. It is this intriguing latent form of learning (and awareness) that informs this book, and is the core feature of my primary mechanism of analysis. Serious computer simgames enact the past, be they analog or digital, and players learn of the past through curated experiences.

To that end, this book works through three major types of simgames, each with a dedicated chapter: shooters, simulators, and strategies. The first two chapters are dedicated to how to theorize the simgame–simtext dynamic and what is meant by these terms. The dynamic that leads a player to look outside a game is the core process under examination. It sees a process of latent interpretation happening as players encounter a variety of media (simtexts) that either explain how to play a simgame or provide information on the past. These initial chapters also clarify how simulation in this book is used. Rather than as a scientific model of the world, or even as an abstract but helpful tool for training, simulation here provides a type of curated experience that approximates aspects of (but never captures fully) the lived experiences of the past. In this sense, it offers necessary (and limited) scope, rather than sufficient (and full).

An important question is how well these serious simgames provide historical accuracy. I find this goal to be central to the developers of the simgames studied here, especially how historical accuracy is approached as degrees of curated authentic simulation rather than in a comprehensive manner that would capture the full lived experiences of historical agents. In particular, we see this drive for simulated accuracy in how care is given to the meticulous simulation of aircraft, weapons, classes, maps, kits, and so on. What makes these historically authentic and accurate gameplay elements? My insight is that degrees of curated authenticity add to a particular gameist experience, rather than a direct correlation with history—and yet, critically, aspects of lived history often emerge inadvertently through the simgame–simtext dynamic in a search by players for clarification of both history and gameplay. A hint of the lived past becomes known through play and study.

Historical game studies, rather than military history or war-gaming, provides the most relevant discourse, especially in how counterfactual scenarios emerge in simgames as both forms of entertainment and ways to reconfigure the past; it also, critically, reveals how simgames present lacunae for the most difficult subjects related to the war, especially those that are often ignored in gameplay such as the Holocaust, the use of nuclear or chemical weapons, terror and war crimes as strategic military options, and so forth. These unplayable elements reveal the potential pitfalls of the often limited experience of simgames; that is, players learn little of the most difficult parts of the war until they look beyond gameplay.

In such a way, this book frames simgames along a continuum of scope from the narrowest (the first-person perspective of an infantry soldier looking down the barrel of a rifle or a pilot sitting in a cockpit) to the broadest (the god-like perspective of directing a nation at its highest level). To this end, the critical issue of how games and war intersect is addressed in Chapter 1. Rather than provide a critique of 'milsims' or how the military industrial complex and entertainment have a long history, I shift the focus to individual players and how he or she experiences gaming aspects related to a historical understanding of WWII. This does not negate the link between war and games; rather it foregrounds how players come to know the past through the particular experiences provided to them by developers (and modders) of computer simgames.

Chapter 2 addresses the most flexible concept in the book, which is simtexts. It begins by recognizing a deep connection between our humanistic disciplines and the categories they share in critiquing texts. The interpretive activity some players inadvertently adopt when looking to understand both gameplay and the past is analyzed. This interpretation works because of the massive digital archive of materials about the war that is accessible to players with an Internet connection—an archive that augments gameplay.

Defining a simtext beyond a game manual or in-game information expands the reach of gameplay to that massive archive. The chapter offers a few examples of the types of simtexts curious players might encounter. Popular histories are the most common and accessible, while those for professional academics are at the far end of the continuum. In between are memoirs, novels, cinema and TV series, technical descriptions, YouTube videos, and so on, all of which refract the past through particular lenses. The dynamic between player and the past that emerges in these games can point to any of these texts depending on the player's interest, the past forming as a reconfiguration through the simulated imaginary of a player's study coupled with gameplay.

A description of the three primary simgame types analyzed in this book begins with FPSs in Chapter 3. This examines in detail two of the most serious WWII FPSs, *Hell Let Loose* (*HLL*) (2021) and *Post Scriptum* (2018), which distinguish themselves from the many more casual FPSs. These are often less demanding in players understanding historical context or even in relating historical tactics to gameplay. In so doing, the chapter analyzes a few key categories, such as how game-time and game-space are simulated, especially in how players experience these in curated maps. With the additional categories of the military roles a player chooses and the equipment offered, such FPS simgames allow players to move through maps and experience critical 'snapshot' moments of the war. These have traditionally been located in battles consistent with the narrative of the triumphant Allies, with touchstone cinematic examples being *Saving Private Ryan* (1998) and *Band of Brothers* (2001), while those on the Eastern Front have been underrepresented until recently. These map-focused, serious simgame shooters therefore provide a type of playable memorial—in a way, a type of digital reenactment that combines play and learning.

Chapter 4 focuses on simulators such as *IL-2 Sturmovik: Great Battles* (2013) (*IL2:GB*) and the WWII modules and assets of *Digital Combat Simulator* (2008) (*DCS*). It does so because the interior of an airplane or a tank condenses the experiential space for players, thereby even more approximating the lived experiences of pilots and tankers than games do of infantry. While this book notes that so much fails to be simulated, the formidable connection between how a simgame curates the past and an experience in the present is revealed here. These powerful but curated player experiences are fueled by memoirs or other simtexts such as fictional cinematic accounts, many of which attempt to capture the heroism, danger, and tragedy of such conflict. The chapter examines how new technologies such as virtual reality (VR) are enhancing the immediacy and presence of such experiences, separating serious simulators from the casual and arcade-like.

Chapter 5 finishes the case studies with a close examination of a GSG that focuses on WWII, *Hearts of Iron IV* (2016) (*HOI4*). It works through the simgame's national focuses as a way to show how curated history emerges as gameplay. Rather than just military tactics and strategy, the choices players make when directing their nation speaks to these abstracted forces, suggesting fundamental causal mechanisms for what happened. The scope here differs from the tighter views of the shooters and simulators.

This widening perspective opens players to more abstracted forms of war, wherein the most damaging effects of 'total war' are erased. Such removal of the Holocaust or playable Nazis is expected, and in many ways welcome—although they prove problematic in their erasure. These missing pieces create glaring lacunae that the chapter argues become known outside gameplay. The sensitive and important nature of how to frame (or not) such difficult elements as war crimes is recognized here. Historical game studies works these concepts into its discourses as 'fantasies of control' or 'dark play' (Chapman and Linderoth, 2015; Salvati, 2020). These lacunae are real concerns that developers face because of the need to avoid gameplay that fetishizes the horrors of war.

Chapter 5 also unravels a thread mentioned in the previous two chapters, which is a trend in gaming that reveals the importance of the European Eastern Front as a critical yet overlooked aspect of the war in the West's popular memory. This study argues that the dominant narrative of Western triumphalism (expected in WWII computer games) is challenged in the popular sphere by other important narratives—especially the German-Soviet War on the Eastern Front—both in terms of European history and WWII computer gaming. It ties this to the most glaring of lacunae in both casual and serious strategy simgames, that of Germany's terrible 'war of annihilation,' and just what this meant for Jews, Slavs, Communists, and others. To ask that a simgame addresses these issues with the same care as do literature, cinema, and philosophy may be to ask too much. But this book examines the nature of the experiences that such simgames provide players, as well tries to understand what is ignored.

In such a way, this book appears to refract its audience to those interested primarily in the Eastern European theater of conflict, as well as its later cultural effects on those most impacted by that part of the war. However, this focus on the German–Soviet War works within the larger case study of WWII. The dynamic that players encounter can just as easily be applied to other theaters, such as the Pacific, and to how particular experiences of the war are erased but can be approached through play. This book, then, admits that narratives of the war are very much culturally located, with stories told about the Pacific bearing their own inflections in contrast to those told in Europe, North Africa, and the Middle East. Yet the most dominant narrative for popular culture (i.e., cinema and computer gaming) has been Allied triumphalism, and that has been challenged by a refocus on the European Eastern Front in the last two decades in both history and computer gaming, as well as a number of other narratives, especially cinema.

# 1 Theorizing Simulation

## The Simgame–Simtext Dynamic

In centering simulation computer games as its primary area of investigation, this study foregrounds a curious dynamic that emerges when we observe how games point us to texts for historical or gameplay clarification, a phenomenon similar to the one that occurs when someone encounters a work of art, a piece of literature, or a film. This demands some engagement outside an initial experience to better understand the interpreted object. When someone reads a novel as a guide when visiting a new place, the relationship between the actual world (the place) and the representation (the written or screened text) becomes apparent, with interpretation (the clarification of the place) providing significance for the experience. This also works when one tries to understand a film, a novel, a work of art, or even the past.

To take an example from a simgame that this study features, *IL2:GB*, I argue that playing it points players to a variety of media about WWII, and that areas within the game become clearer through study, many of them demanding analysis and practice—a type of active interpretation. In this way, a 'poetics as technics' of military aeronautic engineering emerges, a phenomenon that in this case clarifies the particulars of aircraft and their uses through play. Other elements also emerge in this interpretive process, broadening the game's range through traditional humanistic practices. These elements are often anecdotes about pilots, their stories, their fates, and so on, written in simplistic and obvious hero-worship memoirs, but they can also reveal the complexities of the human condition—an example being a German Luftwaffe pilot who, while flying a fully armed Messerschmitt Me 109 fighter, escorted a damaged

American B-17 bomber back to the Atlantic (Makos and Alexander, 2012). I do not mean to suggest, however, that such investigations always reveal human beings demonstrating admirable ethical behavior; they can also expose quite the opposite.

In confronting such unlikely events between enemy combatants, players become a kind of interpreter, confronting apparently conflicting elements and parsing them into some form of understanding of their motivations—for example, what life was like for such people, how they operated their machines, how they survived, or not. This path may even lead to more serious study of professional historical discourses that will also confront players with difficulties, such as differing Allied and Soviet narratives of the war, the myth of the 'clean' Wehrmacht, the cultural logic that led Germany into a war of annihilation, and so on.

To theorize this complex gameist mode of historical awareness, the core concept of the simulated imaginary gameworld is predicated on the primary process, the simgame–simtext dynamic. A further clarification of terminology will help explain my use of this term and why I have chosen to apply it to a very narrow, specific category (i.e., WWII simgames), even though it can be applied more broadly.

Unlike the focus applied by military historians who are interested in analog war games, my use of the term 'simgames' can be applied to a wide range of simulated experiences from casual games such as *The Sims* (2000), which allows players to manage a small domesticated modern world, and the earlier *Sim City* (1989), which allows for the creation and management of cities, to all sorts of more intensive and challenging games, to be found on PCs and consoles (rather than on mobile devices). These have been categorized with enough distinction that real-time strategies such as *Star Craft* (1998) are distinct from turn-based games such as *Civilization* (1991). The latter have developed into the more complex and challenging genre of GSGs, which have their origins in tabletop war-gaming, such as the popular *Diplomacy* (1959) and the later *Axis and Allies* (1981). The *Total War* (2000) franchise by Creative Assembly approximates some level of this detail, while Paradox Interactive's simgames such as *Europa Universalis* (2000) and *Hearts of Iron* (*HOI*) (2002) best exemplify the depth and challenge required. Moreover, the first FPS fantasy/science-fiction simgame *Doom* (1993) has morphed into a variety of different sub-categories, such as the tactical *Counter Strike* (2000), or today the immensely popular cartoon-shooter *Fortnite* (2017) (among others). Massive online RPGs such as *World of Warcraft* (2004) have a long pedigree, reaching back to tabletop RPGs such as *Dungeons and Dragons.* These RPGs are another major category with complex subcategories, and there are many examples.

Simgames, in this broadest sense, offer a way into the imaginary that moves beyond the discursive boundary of the written analog text into the digital world of visual, aural, and haptic virtualized reality, as well as beyond the short story, novel, and film into a hypergameist mode that would simulate the real as the virtual. The promise of these digital environments can primarily be found in 2D computer games on monitor displays, and also in computerized VR, as well as augmented reality (AR) and mixed reality (MR). Granted, VR has been overhyped and has failed before, yet it is continuing to gain traction within entertainment, enough to garner attention in both the professional/academic and popular spheres. VR, even more so than 2D simulation, is becoming a powerful new mode beyond representation, in that it refocuses representation into experiential and agential simulation—that is, the playable. This can be used for a variety of means, from education to indoctrination, but also for entertainment and for approaching curated configurations of the past.

Simulation, as I understand it, is thus located in the power of new digital platforms to create the experience of aspects of imagined and reconfigured reality. For example, the history of war can be approached as romanticized adventure experienced in a safe game environment, or the player can be confronted by a more focused view of the details and specifics of machines and conflicts, and their effects on individuals or entire societies. Regardless of whether entertainment or learning is the focus, the simulated imaginary offers a curious dynamic that frames simgames as containing assemblages of simtexts that augment a game. This dynamic also asks us to consider simgames as more than simplistic games, which is how players might consider casual FPSs set in WWII, such as the *Battlefield* (2002) (*BF*) or *Call of Duty* (2003) (*CoD*) franchises.[1]

When we foreground this dynamic and apply it to the most demanding of simgames, though, we recognize that an interpretive process is embedded within gameplay. To play complex WWII simgames also recognizes that they exist in a wider arena of game-informing media, such as the traditional literary or cinematic texts about this monumental and disruptive period.[2] As players investigate further, they begin to recognize that these multimedia simtexts are critical to their experience. If one wants to play a simgame with anything more than casual involvement, one is driven by the dynamic toward simtexts. For example, as seen in Chapter 4, a demanding simgame such as *IL2* presents attacker and bomber aircraft that must be mastered, such as the lend-lease American P-39 Airacobra used by the Russian VVS, the RAF's effective Lancaster or Wellington bombers, the infamous German Junkers 87 Stuka dive-bomber and its terrifying siren, and so on. These each require different combat tactics, which in turn are different from those needed by the fighter aircraft offered, which themselves also have marked differences in tactics, from energy fighting to turn fighting. Associated simtexts offer a wide range of content that explains these differences, some of them opening windows into the realities of the event beyond aviation tactics and strategy.

For example, in learning about level bombing techniques used by the United Kingdom's Royal Air Force (RAF) against Germany, one will see debates about defining legitimate military targets as opposed to those that would kill civilians, and how this proved problematic for the Allies. An interpretive posture thus begins to form. Attacking communication lines, railways, factories, depots, airfields, and so on at first glance seems appropriate in war, if difficult to implement without civilian casualties. Yet the historical record is clear that non-military targets were deemed acceptable, if controversial, during Allied late-war bombing runs. This type of reasoning led to a factory worker who made AA shells becoming a valid target. One can continue such logic, and conclude that anyone working in a military factory could be a target, women and children included. Continuing along this line of reasoning, it is possible to see how the RAF openly justified carpet-bombing cities by viewing its inhabitants as part of the enemy's support system. (The morality behind Allied fire-bombing in Germany or the use of nuclear bombs by the USA in Japan is a critical area for moral philosophy, and is still relevant in a world where drones can target anyone, anywhere, at any time.) The complexities involved in 'total war' resist any simple answer. What becomes apparent in any close investigation is that an encounter with WWII simulation games often encourages consideration of such topics.

Simtexts are the second part of this dynamic, which typically begins with simgames. When looking at WWII in this way, a new form of practiced understanding emerges beyond the common genres of war histories, its fictions and films, and even outside overt texts or ideological or political proselytiza-tion, such as *Mein Kampf* (1925) or the earlier *Communist Manifesto* (1848). It is located deep within an appreciation of reimagining the past through simulating aspects of its events, with a primary focus on gameplay. One might think that such simulations would valorize, say, a Marxist-Leninist ideology, or be a haven for Neo-Nazis who are in favor of glorifying the economic and political successes of prewar Hitler. Although games can attract those interested in fetishizing the wrongs of the past because of their prejudiced thinking today, simgames for a popular audience include mechanisms added by devel-opers and communities that self-regulate and/or ban egregious activities.

Rather than simgames turning games into arenas of political indoctrination (which can be achieved through modding), those relating to WWII more often reinforce myths of nationalist pride for the winners (such as the nimble Spitfire for the British, the sturdy IL-2 for the Russians, the dominant Mustang for the Americans). We see this myth-making in screened texts as well and their often heroic war representations, such as Tom Hanks as Captain Miller in *Saving Private Ryan*, dying on a bridge he must protect after firing a useless handgun at an approaching Tiger tank. A critical awareness emerges as players encounter these myths, and as the curious begin to peek behind the veil of their construction.

A particular aspect of this project that needs clarification is why I am interested in the dynamic between WWII simgames and simtexts. This may appear to be an odd or even obscure phenomenon, with no broader impact on how most people engage with digital media or historical games. I admit that such digital experiences as flying WWII aircraft are niche; in terms of popularity, they are far behind other types of digital experiences. But WWII as a context for digital games is not niche: it has been flourishing within digital game culture for over two decades. This allows me to explore how traditional media (i.e., simtexts) continue to inform and shape the experience of these new digital forms. It is more complex than just saying that with the internet and the democratization of knowledge (and history), informative media continue their growth even as the more popular forms of social media distract from serious study. All these points are valid. Yet my interest has a larger goal—to understand how the simulated imaginary of the past continues to expand both its domain and its mechanisms, especially when this allows us to imagine what might have been; and, critically, to enact these new understandings.

This agential element with the dynamic speaks to both imaginary and reconfigured aspects of simulation, but also to how we learn about the past. Imagining a counterfactual victorious Axis that was successful in taking Leningrad, Moscow, Stalingrad, and the oilfields in the Caucasus, or imagining what would have happened if... finds a different inflection beyond real-world scenarios or fantastic alternative-history novels because we can experience simulated aspects of the event in what Tom Apperley calls "counterfactual imaginations" (2018: 1). This allows for history to be scaffolded by the imaginary, a type of reconfiguration of the past (made up both of that which happened and that which did not). I see continuity with traditional storytelling, from the written poetic forms that led to the novel, to screened texts such as cinema, and to played versions of the imaginary in analog and digital games. This allows the power of the fictive to blend mimetic and fantastic impulses into powerful gameworlds (Hume, 1985).

When we see the imaginary flourish in games, we also see many variations that far exceed the scope of this book. By focusing on what most people consider to be simulations within the context of WWII, I challenge the standard description of digital computer games as simple simulations of driving a tank, flying a plane, or managing an army, when they actually offer an approximate experience of those past activities that encourages interpretation, especially when attempting to understand what is not simulated.

The simulated and imagined reconfigured world of 1939–1945, then, is the central focus of this book, one that grounds my theoretical approach and its primary dynamic. From this analysis, I hope to show why simtexts remain important in today's world of digital games. I foreground the simtext concept because of my interest in the continued theorization of how we consume the imaginary, whether the past or the present, and the continued importance of virtualized media in our modern lives.

This may seem like a traditionalist's posture, especially in my move from literary to media studies, but my interest stems more from the phenomeno-logical importance of the dynamic rather than a disciplinary need to justify my field in the academy. In fact, by giving game elements from WWII the same valorization as, say, literary characters, I place myself squarely within a camp that appears to deny the primacy of literature and would rather focus on non-literary elements or processes situated within science, technology, and engineering. I find, though, that interpretive practice is flexible enough to adapt to the results of our digital turn and that its methods still flourish, especially in the spaces between games and texts.

Of importance throughout this book is the distinction between the imaginary and the configurative. Imaginary in the broadest sense reflects that what we have with serious simgames, even though we encounter degrees of historical accuracy, is a reimagined environment that has been scripted, programmed, and designed by 'developer-historians,' as Adam Chapman notes, to simulate a digitally contained world (2018). The reimagined, then, is part of our fantastic impulse that runs counter but parallel to a realistic-mimetic mode; in this widest sense, the reimagined is what happens when we approach the past through the mediation of representation combined with simulation so that we have a particular experience of the past—one that is curated, but also provides degrees of accuracy with enough fidelity to both convince and encourage understanding (Hume, 1985).

However, a more refracted, focused approach takes these imaginary, mediated world-building elements to frame a simgame's constructed environments, spaces, and maps, as a staged 'place' that is reconfigured for players in which to play, but where they also encounter some aspect of history—a reconfiguration. And what is curious is that this scaffolded configurative mediation functions in a similar way to a map in a high-fantasy world, say that of Tolkien's Middle Earth; it grounds a reader/player who is encountering the virtual world, thereby creating a sense of connectedness to the setting (Saler, 2012). In digital simgames, this connectedness is directly related to the demands of immediate gameplay mechanics, as well as locating a player in a simulated, reconfigured/imaginary gameworld.

## What is a Simulation?

A route into the professional conversation about history, simulations, and games can be found in the journal *Simulation and Gaming*. Through more than five decades, it has covered a wide range of topics, but prominent has been how simulation works within training scenarios or for educational purposes. A pressing issue has been how authentic, or real, these simulations are. In contrast, my project seeks something other than pure accuracy of facts or authenticity of experience; rather a type of curated simulated experience that emerges from an engagement with the past through play (Copplestone, 2016). Even so, as I detail in subsequent chapters, serious simgames regard accuracy as critical, with key categories increasingly being rendered with greater accuracy, such as aircraft flight and damage modeling, the specific classes of key military roles, equipment used, and gameplay maps.

Deciding how best to conceptualize the broad category of 'simulation' is difficult. A variety of disciplines that span the sciences and the humanities use this term in different ways, with different applications. The fruitful examination of core concepts such as theory versus model versus simulation within the natural sciences reveals that these primary conceptualizations function at cross purposes because they provide different forms of knowledge, yet we can observe that they all challenge the fundamental ways in which we understand the world, in particular the fact that "models and simulation both pose essentially philosophical problems about the nature of representation" (Humphreys and Imbert, 2012: xiii).

This claim can be found in an anthology of philosophical debates on how to consider simulation within key contexts, such as modeling in biology or theoretical physics. Not only the sciences, but also education demonstrate the term's reach, especially into the social sciences. A common issue is how well computer simulations function as experiments, with difficult concepts such as complexity and emergence complicating this approach. This even reaches into linguistics, where phenomena are considered to be modeled within the mind, another mysterious space that provides more questions than answers. My use of simulation, as I will show, is rooted in a literary understanding of the imaginary, along with how we experience it through digital and analog tools.

Thus, thinkers outside these disciplines might take for granted questions such as "What is a simulation and what is the difference and the relation between a model and a simulation?" (Hartmann, 2005: 1), asked in an article that offered a way to think of simulation in its broadest sense as a process that imitates another process. Such a starting point values working simplicity rather than acknowledging the complexities of competing approaches that dominate discourses outside the sciences.

Openness to a flexible form of the concept is expected within the humanities, since they rely on discursive techniques that explore differences and varieties. Yet simplicity has its merits. In this book, I begin with imagined representation (a type of fantastic mimesis) before moving to reconfigured simulation, grounding my approach in a reworking of core concepts with the humanities, such as those found in the visual arts, literature, philosophy, and history—all disciplines with their own particular approaches to representation.

We may then ask what happens when we not only construct a representation, but also enter its world through simulation and become an agent. At this point, we have moved from standard notions of static representations of the world to the creation of virtual spaces and activity, and simulated versions of the world (actual or imaginary, present or past). At this point, my approach steps outside the simulation versus representation debate (Crawford, 1984: 4–5, for an early look at representation versus simulation). Instead, it finds its most contentious area as encompassing understanding and play and how the latter encourages the former. I argue that through the imaginative process of play we gain understanding, albeit often inadvertently. My approach works alongside foundational ideas within the cultural theory of games, such as those of Johan Huizinga, who argued for play's centrality in human affairs, rather than as a childish activity (Huizinga, 1949). As my case study of WWII shows, play through an engagement with simgames and simtexts provides an impetus for deeper understanding of such an event.

I acknowledge that these many articulations of the simulated once-real past are 'virtualized' phenomena, a concept of Deleuze's that he argued emerge from the actual world as flows of energy we experience as the 'virtual' (Deleuze and Parnet, 2007). For Deleuze, philosophy was an activity that creates concepts to explain the unconsidered, those hidden processes that work around us as reality. The humanities provide nuances, tones, variations on these concepts so that, like an artist's brush, the freedom to explore allows for a multiplicity of expression.

I admit that I work outside the well-mined field within postmodern studies that sees simulation as a type of delusion, counterfeit, simulacra, supplement, misrepresentation, or misapprehension of complex reality. French critical theory has explored this terrain in detail. Thinkers such as Jean Baudrillard (1929–2007), for example, offered the 'hyperreal' as a way to rethink the 'real' as inherently fantastic or imaginary, a still-intriguing concept but one that works against common notions that the world can be known in a reliable fashion (unless the imaginary can also be known in a reliable fashion). As virtualized, digital imaginary worlds increase, the type of fantastic world that Baudrillard offered as being true reality, such as Disneyland, is becoming increasingly more prevalent as lived places (at least for those living in technologized societies). Rather than debate the simulated real versus virtual versus the fantastic, my approach asks that the simulated imaginary remains a core category of how we experience the world rather than differentiated from other spaces. This upsets Baudrillard's thesis that separates actual reality (the hyperreal or an empty simulacrum) from the imaginary (somehow more real because it is inherently fantastic), while at the same time reworking it by taking from the analog/material/real world its inherent fantastic impulse and placing it within a digital context.

With this in mind, I collapse how we experience a simulated historical context (e.g., WWII aviation, the cockpits of airplanes, navigating between airfields, etc.) into an imaginary gameworld (e.g., a reconfiguration of such an event within a simulator such as *IL2*, which allows us not to simply fly virtual airplanes but to experience this historical phenomenon so that the simulated imaginary emerges as the core experience—a reconfiguration of the simulated, the virtual, and the imaginary within a historical frame). This reconfiguration thus reimagines the past for an experience in the present.

Continuing at this level of critical analysis, I recognize a difference between an imagined or reconfigured simulation and a training simulator. Training simulators prepare a user for action in the actual world. Action leads us beyond reading or viewing into the category of training rather than play, whereas simgames offer players experiences of the simulated imaginary rather than preparing them for real-world activity. Complications exist in this categorization for modern simgames that provide both play and training, such as *DCS*; while WWII simgames focus more on a recreation of the past rather than providing training in using WWII weaponry in modern war. Action, though, demands careful consideration because of its problematic nature. What is being enacted when we simulate a past like WWII? Training for an activity in the actual world or an experience with an imagined or reconfigured past? I suggest the latter.

With WWII as my case study, many authentic aspects of being a pilot or infantry soldier are not simulated because they would provide boring gameplay or because such experiences are impossible. For example, in a dogfight combat simulator, activities such as sitting through real-time debriefing meetings (rather than those cursory mission briefings in virtual squadrons), or reviewing ground-crew procedures in detail, or waiting to take off while strapped in would make games tedious at best or ridiculously hard at worst. And imagine the simulation of sleep deprivation while being stuck in a cold cockpit at 20,000 feet by forcing the player's screen to remain darkened and by reducing the effectiveness of the control surfaces because the virtual pilot is suffering lethargy or numbness.

Degrees of authenticity are expected and framed within gameplay contexts, ultimately for fun, but also for challenges (as can be seen in the different types of servers and squadrons, some that allow for casual game play with all player aids, and others restricting in-game aids and demanding a seriousness that encourages role-playing virtual pilots). But, more often than not, only selected aspects (such as dogfighting tactics, flight and damage modeling, and weapon capabilities) have increasing authenticity, which both curates and foregrounds the past in specific ways.

Here, I would like to comment on an approach by Alexander Galloway. This helps because it frames digital video games as those that try to replicate reality accurately and those that construct imaginary worlds, but also points toward a way in which we can think about the complexities involved in understanding these configurations. Galloway unpacks the categories expected within video game culture as those that are "generally realistic or fantastical" (2006: 72), yet recognizes that some fantasy games can be presented with high graphical fidelity that mimics what we would expect to see from, say, someone walking on the deck of a starship or sneaking down a dungeon corridor (what he calls "realistic representation") (2006: 72). Yet if these actions take place on purely imaginary worlds, they are not part of the 'realistic narrative' of our daily lives (since none of us live on interstellar starships). They are fantastic, or imaginary, while still realistic.

This schematizing of 'realisticness' into two disparate areas is helpful. I am interested, though, in turning this on its head by asking what happens when we have increasingly convincing graphical and aural representations of the past, as well as improved physics, haptics, and so on, coupled with historical contexts outside our daily lives, or 'narratives' in Galloway's terminology. In essence, what happens when we have realistic simulations of the imaginary/ reconfigured past that treats the realistic narratives of the past with care, but are still outside what we experience in our daily lives?

This complex aspect of representing-through-simulating the past becomes a process of re-reimagining into curious configurations, as postmodern thinkers such as Umberto Eco (1932–2016) have argued about how we reconstruct past eras. Within postmodern critical theory a book such as Umberto Eco's *Il Nome della Rose* (1980; *The Name of the Rose*, 1983), recreates the medieval world within a contemporary novel. In this vein, I see the imaginary as an important solvent between the mimetic and the fantastic—a type of agent that overlaps and catalyzes these categories into a variety of configurations that provide experiences and understandings. Galloway complicates this relationship in his own way, stating that "realisticness is important, to be sure, but the more realisticness takes hold in gaming, the more removed from gaming it actually becomes, relegated instead to simulation or modeling" (2006: 73). Galloway references Jameson as one of many thinkers who demand a separate space for 'realism,' that slippery concept with such a varied and heavily mined historiography in critical theory and cultural studies.

At stake here is the argument that realism ranges further than mere realistic representation in articulating complex phenomena, especially with the artifacts of the humanities, beyond holding up a mirror to nature; that is, the real world. To take one often-used example, realism allows art to do more than present that mirror; it teaches, as well as allows for the expression of the creator (or artist) (Abrams, 1958). This loaded aspect of realism separates it from naive realism or simple realistic representation. What binds philosophic, literary, artistic realisms in their resistance to any flattening of the real is the focus on subjective experience—in this instance, historical game studies and WWII.

For Galloway, the core question is how we should think about social realism in the context of 'realistic' games, and if this is even possible. Social realism finds its home as the expression of artists, writers, and philosophers, who attempted to articulate the lived experiences of the burgeoning working and middle classes in the nineteenth century. A common thread was a resistance to aristocratic norms in art, culture, and thought; the focus, instead, was on common individuals, with all of their troubles and supposed defects. This shift created a new awareness that had been ignored, thereby allowing for much-needed consciousness raising. The idea is that (social) realism provides this grounded gaze, through which we better understand the actual real world (with all its problems).

Galloway recognizes a dangerous potential when he writes that "video games reside in a third-moment of realism" (2006: 84), a loaded space where one can see that a causal relationship between video games and action in the real world is complicated by more than the congruence between the two; yes, a relationship exists, but it is contextualized by the individual (maybe, in a dangerous case, by someone with mental illness who might mimic action based on continued repetitive play in FPSs) and by social context (e.g., Palestinians playing resistance games such as *Under Ash, 2001*). Considerate thinkers such as Galloway and others, though, recognize that this relationship is predicated on the sort of action that may develop from the engagement with these simulated realistic worlds—imagined or lived, or both?

## Historical Game Studies

My approach finds common ground with the examination of narrative and play in a few foundational texts within historical game studies, one of which (Kapell and Elliott, 2013) is an anthology that mines historical game studies in how to inform the present by looking at the past. The editors and contributors work within the discourses of both professional historical analysis and digital video game studies, with the former focusing on understanding the past, while the latter foregrounds the ludic qualities of play.

The editors theorize ways in which agency for players does more than provide a type of assembling the past; it reconfigures as well. They consider the implications when historical digital video games misrepresent the past, a type of inaccuracy. They write:

Such a paradox might thus lead us to conclude, resignedly, that when it comes to digital games, the possibilities of engaging with history seem to be at best incompatible with playing the games, and at worst downright impossible, since even the most accurate simulation of the past on the first level (the level of details) is potentially doomed to failure by granting players the freedom (agency) to explore, expand, contradict, or subvert the historical realities. (Kapell and Elliott, 2013: 13)

Their answer is that these complex ludic aspects of gameplay provide not just agency but understanding—sometimes through alternative views of history. This critical function is a second part of how I theorize the simulated imaginary, beyond the core mechanism of the simgame–simtext dynamic detailed in Chapter 2.

The use of 'what-ifs,' often now referred to as counterfactuals, in rethinking history through alternative historical scenarios demonstrates the power of this process. Rather than focusing on narratology, or the importance of stories, I foreground a method of interpretation that reimagines the past into a variety of reconfigured, historical gameworlds. Reading history, or interpreting and experiencing it, emerges as a critical aspect of this dynamic. Rather than focusing on new historical approaches to culture or texts, my study sees in the thinking about counterfactuals a fitting example, within the discipline of history itself, of how we rethink the past into the future along lines that span from what may have been possible to the impossible (for a relevant comment from within historical game studies, see Apperley, 2018).

Niall Ferguson argues that such speculation has importance for the study of history, especially in its ability to challenge determinism. He calls this "chaostory—a chaotic approach to history" (1997: 89) and sees a benefit in asking 'what if' events had transpired differently and changed history. Two chapters in his collection focus on WWII, asking questions such as "What if Germany had invaded Britain in May 1940?" or "What if Nazi Germany had defeated the Soviet Union?" (Ferguson, 1997: vi; and for more on 'what if' as a way to learn history, see Black (2008) and Cowley (1999, 2005). He also provides a final, comprehensive afterword that begins with the Stuarts' survival to the assassination of JFK as a move through Western history. Speculating about a living JFK or the Luftwaffe's success in the Battle of Britain often feels natural within the public sphere, as well as in speculative literature, but Ferguson spends the bulk of his introduction defending the practice against the perceived resistance of professional historians, a sure sign of a discourse at work to disrupt.

As an academic whose research areas often push up against the field of history, I feel comfortable with these sorts of questions because they admit that a persistent fantastic impulse exists. In this conceptualization, the imaginary plays a critical role in the fictions that arise out of a dominant mimetic impulse running through the stories of human history. We see such imaginings even in the alternative history subgenre of science fiction, a form of popular writing that constructs such common scenarios as a victorious Germany in WWII, or the many novels and films that imagine modern society ending in a nuclear winter and the fallout its survivors must endure. Even literary-fiction writers such as Cormac McCarthy have ventured into this traditional science-fiction space; see his *The Road* (2006).

Such scenarios also dominate gaming. The hugely successful PS3 exclusive *The Last of Us* (2013), which was released as an HBO series in 2023, explored such post-apocalyptic landscapes with more depth and character focus than most video games of the time, as has the PC game series *Fallout* (1997). The majority of WWII games, from shooters to simulators, also allow for a wide range of historical scenarios to be played, some with the intention of repeating the past within the game, but most allowing players to change the outcomes. Again, the focus is not necessarily on a recreation or revision of a detailed narrative of the past; it is rather in the construction of a setting that allows particular elements to be simulated and experienced. Ferguson would have counterfactuals theorize history through speculation, as offered in a game that he worked on: *Making History II: The War of the World* (2010). Within most simgames, though, such speculation often occurs outside gameplay, once the dynamic has encouraged the interpretive process and a movement toward simtexts.

In historical game studies, the past can be counterfactually simulated in ways that teach beyond a student in a classroom poring over a textbook. When looking at this process interdisciplinarily, we spiral upward from modeling aspects of the material world into active forms of literacy, pedagogy, gameplay, subject formation, and so on. This takes us toward rarefied areas in which core aspects of the humanities return, from philosophical debates over the nature of play within Plato's *Republic* to how empire is reconstructed in the *Total War* (2000) or *Civilization* (1991) series. Intriguing conversations follow, critiquing war and empire, exploring the roles of such strategy games in reinforcing soft forms of colonialism, and considering the resistance to this continued neocolonial ideological effect in the form of 'indie' games. From gameplay to interpretation, we see the dynamic in action.

My approach here, though, looks at historical games through the refracted lens of WWII to pull to the surface the inherent imagined impulse that couples with historical elements to create something other than the expected educational aspect of learning facts about the past (which also occurs). Instead, in foregrounding the simulated imaginary and its many reconfigurations through the intriguing simgame–simtext dynamic of WWII, something other than traditional history emerges. Rather, we see a safe version of the imagined past form through gameplay that is devoid of any physical danger. The dynamic thus emerges as a curious and unexpected by-product of players encountering digital war games: In allowing them to imagine/simulate what could have happened, they are pointed toward texts for clarification, especially in aspects of the war that are ignored and not simulated.

What we see in these fruitful spaces emerging from historical game studies is that history, as a professional academic pursuit, parallels thought within the popular sphere—a type of playable public history in which non-professional historians rethink the past with the technological tools of the present. A quick look, for example, at YouTube channels dedicated to WWII tanks, planes, or battles reveals independent knowledge-building beyond peer-reviewed mono-graph or article publication as a dynamic and fecund form of information and analysis. These varied new forms of 'knowing' the past are emerging in bulk within the popular sphere, although parsing the serious and worthwhile from the casual and problematic poses its own challenges. What is required to parse them effectively is a constant and steady form of interpretation, one that becomes sharper through use—especially when bolstered by gameplay.

'History' known in this manner finds cohesion within the context of democratized simulated historiography, with the available record, in all its digital and analog forms, offering a field for the interpretive process. This way of understanding reinforces the disciplines of history, alongside literature and philosophy, as valuable keystones within the humanities, along with the visual arts, providing various types of understanding from simulated experi-ences. Of course, such cross-disciplinary entanglement often proves as problematic as it does helpful, but it allows me to keep the concept of the 'text,' in all its multiplicities, at the center of my theorizing. (I am using 'text' here as any arena that demands interpretation for some form of understanding to emerge.) I have resisted collapsing everything into textual analysis, another common expectation within literary studies; instead, I look to historical game studies to ground the conversation in a ludic approach to the past through agential play.

An obvious fact to note here is that these historical simulations are happening outside professional gate-keeping discourses, with little concern for its terminologies, debates, or specializations. With mass-market fiction, film, and computer games, the popular sphere is a juggernaut of production. Many of its artifacts are ephemeral kitsch, the detritus of modernity's continued reproduction of objects. Others, though, do more than titillate with distraction; they have depth, and they have their own platforms of articulation outside the academy.

I embrace this independence from the dominance of the professional sphere to determine what history is, or what literature is, while I foreground how we learn through simulated experience aspects of a crucial event within modern studies such as WWII. And while one might expect a focus on narrative or story from a literary studies thinker, I find that less helpful (although present) than a focus on the interpretive process required to form an understanding of gameplay and the historicity of game contexts, as well as on an exploration of the simulated past that emerges through these experiences. This fore-grounding of both literary hermeneutics and a philosophical approach to subjectivity inspires how I theorize this book's contribution: the 'dynamic,' as I call it in Chapter 2.

I recognize this places my approach outside a main theoretical current within digital game studies that would see us focus on games as objects of study with their own mechanics, rather than lugging in baggage from other disciplines (Aarseth, 2004). But my primary interest is one that reaches the broadest scope within modern studies and one that asks questions within the historiography of humanism: how are we framing what it means to be a human (or, as some would ask, trans-or-posthuman) in our technologized present? Game studies alone, though, enacts an anti-humanistic disciplinary step (which I avoid) that focuses on game mechanics as formalistic properties of gameplay. Granted, it does so to form a coherent academic discipline, and is often very informative. In a spirit that recognizes the messy complexity that is our current moment, I opt for a disciplinary blending to see what emerges from messy concoctions rather than drawing discreet differences.

Because of this inclusive acceptance, my approach can be viewed as a response to a foundational article by William Uricchio (2005). In it, he structures historical computer games at two poles: one detailing moments, the other eras. He sees moments as corresponding to particular events in history that can be simulated, thereby providing constraints for gameplay, such as when an event begins and ends. Eras correspond to larger processes, akin to major historical, structural abstractions such as the impact of agriculture, politics, resources, and so on. The scale is one of a narrower versus a broader focus, the former exemplified by, say, a particular event such as WWII, or even one of its major battles, such as the Battle of the Bulge (to use Uricchio's examples), while the broader view views large processes involved in nation-building or the creation of civilizations: Sid Meier's *Civilization* (1991) is a prime example often referenced.

My approach utilizes these scales in its particular focus in foregrounding experiences of WWII through simulation, which explicitly places players within contained spaces such as cockpits, usually in specific historical battles, or allows them to play as infantry soldiers in specific battles (snapshot moments), yet also provides the scale that allows players to manage the strategic war at the highest national level. The more rarefied view of the historical grand strategies allows for this much wider focus. Taken together, my approach covers these two poles theorized by Uricchio, and allows me to analyze the differing experiences afforded by the differing perspectives.

Uricchio also helps beyond this initial schema, his thinking being concerned with theorizing within modern studies over the nature of representation, and its crisis, as well as how simulation problematizes (or alleviates) some of these concerns. Uricchio writes: "I want to complicate the relationship of computer games to history, suggesting a fuller set of interactions with the process of historical inscription, that is, with the ways in which human subjects encounter textualizations of the past and are 'written into' the past" (2005: 327). In the constrained frame of particular events and moments, I place the experience of these player-subjects as critical to understanding how such simulations function. For example, the phenomenologically curious thrill of flying a WWII fighter in simulated combat encourages a latent textual encounter; in this case, the gameplay experience (or 'textualizations,' as Uricchio says) emerges as a drive outside the game's cockpit and into the wider world of books, films, and articles, where the past is reimagined, or 'rewritten,' to use Uricchio's terminology.

Uricchio's probing question over the nature of simulation helps us conceptualize the difficulties inherent with simulation as a new form of both cultural consumption and knowledge building beyond representation. He asks "What happens if we push the notion of mediation beyond language, to the domain of game, enactment, or simulation? Does this allow us to slip out of the well-critiqued trap of representation? And if so, where does it land us?" (2005: 332). This 'mediation beyond language' has inspired critical theory and its drawing (and erasure) of the subject for some time now, decentering that subject into a wide array of influencing factors from culture to the invisible (yet ubiquitous) text itself. What we find in historical game studies, though, is a recentering of an imagined player-subject as a simulated agent. The player-as-subject is predicated on constraints within game play, even as modding or other forms of player-agency allow for forms of resistance.

In this vein, Uricchio asks, at the end of his article, "Where might we look for future developments" (2005: 336). I hope to offer an answer to this question about where the simgame lands us—that is, a place with feet in both the digital and analog worlds where degrees of simulated accuracy increase the experiences of powerful gameworlds. The dynamic encourages this constant crossing, with games and texts in a collaborative dance, hinting at where we are heading.

At the most subjective and personal scale of VR, we find technological developments encouraging more authentic, accurate, and realistic experiences, already quite convincing in simulators. Yet the scale will widen from contained cockpits into the actual world with AR and MR (augmented reality and mixed reality). Realistic strategy games that will use these technologies are also emerging, yet these are in their infancy. One can imagine, though, full vistas displayed within a virtual environment, allowing for a comprehensive perspective of battlefields on the scale of nations. Such games will continue to grow more complex and challenging; and with them the past will come alive as convincing reconfigurations in the present.

## Distance, Games, and War

A specific focus on WWII through the lenses of simulated gameplay clearly overlooks important aspects of the war, especially any detailed analysis of its destructive effects. I am in no way attempting an exhaustive analysis of these powerful and destructive forces that reshaped the twentieth century and still have an impact today.

Professional historians have worked through many of these complex areas, with a growing consensus that the importance of the war in the East has been recognized by the West, and in particular the costly role the Soviets played in damaging the Wehrmacht's ability to win the war (see Chapter 5). I highlight this emerging narrative as increasingly important in simgames of WWII, a viewpoint much more prevalent now than twenty years ago. My study also admits that games and war have a contested past, one that peppers any broad-scale view of history with a continuous parade of conflicts, many of which find themselves simulated on tabletops or on computer screens.

The continued articulation of technologized modernities, of which WWII was but one major moment, is important within key critical areas of inquiry, especially the geopolitical, in that it sees the fallout of WWII, the Cold War, and the post-Soviet breakup as still critical in key parts of the world. As I revise this chapter in the late winter of 2023, Putin's army continues its invasion of Ukraine. My book is ultimately rooted in an interpretive exercise that examines how our fictive artifacts work today through practices of representation and simulation, and how understanding the past also helps us make sense of the present. In asking how these methods allow us to experience simulations in new forms of communication, beyond novels or films, it admits that a form of consciousness-raising can occur, such as the war's devastation or how it marred modern societies with an unmistakable blemish.

This field of inquiry crosses difficult terrain as we rethink the past through the present, although this is not my primary focus. Contemporary memory politics demonstrates how sensitive such a topic as games and war can be once a niche area, such as WWII military aviation or infantry and armored-vehicle weaponry, is viewed geopolitically as a tool of contemporary nation-building. Within the influence of the simgame–simtext dynamic, a player may confront subtle but deep-rooted issues that are still present today, such as national guilt over wartime aggression or constructivist stories of national pride that play into romanticized nostalgia for the victors.

For example, the concept of the British Empire still carries much weight as a prime example of colonial injustice (as do others). The discourse of cultural imperialism by Edward Said and others has recognized sophisticated and subtle forms of knowledge production that propagate (or not) through our cultural norms (1979, 1994). In this light, the dialog and cultural objects that describe a pugnacious but prescient Churchill, or the Battle of Britain with its perceived role in saving Britain so it could continue its struggle to resist National Socialism act as foundational myths.

The Battle of Britain as a foundational myth has emerged primarily in memoirs and simtexts aimed at the popular market. Hitler's Directive 16, which detailed his plans for a possible invasion of England, has been read as less than confident. Historian Stephen G. Fritz summarizes a number of historians when he writes:

"Hitler issued Directive No. 16, 'Preparations for a Landing Operation against England,' a document that contained so many qualifications that it convinced many of his top commanders that he never seriously intended an invasion. Indeed, Hitler told Goering in confidence that he never meant to carry out the operation. In order to launch an invasion of Britain, Germany needed control of the Channel both by air and by sea. To those around him, it seemed clear that, given the strength of the British navy and the crippling of the already weak German navy by the Norwegian operation in April, Hitler regarded the risk of invasion as unacceptably high. Instead, he would put his hopes in his peace proposal" (Fritz, 2011: 34).

These dialogs can also be used to construct an exclusionary British national identity, rather than understanding the past in a way that views an imperialist Churchill as a flawed military strategist or the Battle of Britain as less critical than imagined. The simgame–simtext dynamic works within this popular-history crucible. In it, paths are crossing between simplistic traditional views of heroism and hagiography (as well as demonization) and those of sustained critique, such as the postcolonial discourses in which various types of cultural imperialisms still exist today.

The mythology of British resistance complicates the dynamic even today. Russian understanding of its own survival in WWII has been consistently used by Putin to build national pride. The USA has its own way of framing

WWII, with this rhetoric of the 'Greatest Generation' driving films such as *Saving Private Ryan* and series such as *Band of Brothers*. One can pick and choose, based on the differing national histories, which myths of the war are most convincing. Again, the USA has been at this since the 'Golden Age' of Hollywood produced so many films. Most recently, Christopher Nolan's *Dunkirk* (2017) and the WWI film *1917* (2019) have provided glimpses into the struggle over the Channel, as well as a personal account of trench warfare.

One key aspect to the dynamic is how it reimagines this particular conflict, one that was horrifyingly devastating to millions of people. It works within a larger process of continued technologized modernity, as do the difficult terrains of memory politics, soft and hard imperialisms, and the traumas of actual war. Many individuals across the globe still feel the effects of the Cold War, such as those who live in the Baltic states of Eastern Europe, in Ukraine, China, Korea, and other parts of the world in which liberal democracy ran up against Stalin's version of Marxist-Leninist communism. Others within technologized popular culture feel the effects less directly, such as many younger North Americans, who view the distant events of WWII as primarily represented in film or TV, or from within safe arenas in video games. They view such an event (if they view it at all) as something in our past that now provides entertainment, while others with closer ties approach it as something to be honored, feared, mourned, or remembered.

Yet today, the stakes on how to consider the event remain high. Geopolitical jousting still occurs, such as when Putin generalized in public about events during the war to lay blame at the feet of the Poles, while responding to a tweet about Russia's culpability (Walker, 2019; Applebaum, 2020). 'Memory politics' ranges even more widely in places such as Germany where guilt and memory collide over ways to understand the past, another example being Japan, where its history is often taught without reference to WWII. And, of course, the May 9 Victory Parade in Russia has been a yearly blend of Russian pride at defeating Nazi Germany and Cold War Soviet military power.

This book recognizes that these deep-felt and complex issues mean players will differently experience the simulated imaginary of the event. What is risked in this approach, though, is justification of the sanitizing that occurs when casual players who may have only a passing interest in WWII play a simple game such as the original *CoD* (2003) with its curated history, and never think twice about the past. The more serious player's potential encounter with real history (and likely failure) challenges this.

Simulation as a mode of engagement increases the potency of encounters, sometimes opening a door to the interpretive practice for curious players. It may be preposterous to expect a casual player to learn how to parse history, war, and games from playing an FPS. But with more complex forms of simulation, even a casual player may be confronted with the need for a latent form of critique that considers the human condition, even if ever so subtly. The dynamic's nature as something subsumed within the simulated imaginary is part of the ironic barrier that provides degrees of safety. In many ways, the removal of actual horror encourages the imagined elements that have driven the various modes of fictive popular culture, cushioned as they must be by irony.

This protective barrier occurs as a necessary ingredient. A major aspect of WWII aviation (as seen in the example used throughout this book of a simulator such as *IL2*) was learning the proper technique of taking off in powerful 'tail-dragger' fighters such as a Spitfire or BF 109, both of which were challenging because of their narrow undercarriages. Landing such planes also meant that a novice pilot risked his life every time he took off or landed. (This was a major reason for the deaths of quickly trained Luftwaffe pilots near the end of the war.) A huge list of other potential dangers existed, such as high-altitude oxygen hypoxia, to engine fires engulfing cockpits, to bailing out of spinning aircraft and slamming into part of the abandoned plane (or maybe just as traumatic, like seeing an enemy you shot down struggling to open the canopy of his plummeting and burning aircraft). Such a simulated imaginary experience must admit the absence of these lived threats that speak of the actual horrors of war as developers foreground playable aspects such as combat aviation strategy and tactics.

The simgame–simtext dynamic is not blind to the complexity outlined here, or to another disturbing aspect: The dynamic as I theorize it may point players in the direction of simtexts that detail the most difficult of subjects, including the Holocaust, Japanese and Soviet war crimes, Allied fire-bombings, and the USA's nuclear attacks on Japan, among much else. We find these, of course, in the detailed accounts of the war's varied and important historiography. We also find them in the most complex of simtexts.

This book ultimately confronts how something as actual and horrific as violent conflict between nations, cultures, groups, and individuals functions in a simulated gameist mode, its players safe behind the unreality of games rather than faced with actual danger—as individuals in conflict zones today who live (and die) with the ever-present fact of violence. Thus, the observation that curated and sanitized versions of 'war' are simulated in a variety of mobile, console, and PC games in an arcade-like fashion is not my focus. Such highly visual and aural games have advanced in processing power but are not that different from their predecessors that were played on 2D-video monitors, such as the Atari 2600 games *Combat* (1977) and *Space Invaders* (1978). Even if successor games today are much more complex visually, they often ignore sophisticated simulation mechanics for ease of gameplay. In such cases, gameplay precedes simulation.

But, when we look beyond arcade games to complex simgames as increasing visual or aural verisimilitude, we see a move away from accessible toward complex gameplay, even as it fails to simulate the true difficulties of real war and its horrors. No one playing a simgame and holding a joystick or wearing a VR headset is experiencing actual war, regardless of the degrees of simulated reality in flight mechanics or damage modeling. (I am referring here to individuals playing games, not military personnel who remotely pilot drones or other semi-autonomous aircraft.) Even more so, the curated experiences of such simgames contain glaring lacunae that gameplay development mostly avoids.

We must be cautious as we embrace this necessary but problematic distancing aspect of the simulated imaginary. The critical component that must remain stable is a strong sense of constrained distance—that what we are experiencing is simulated, coupled with an awareness that the imaginary provides another buffer, one that protects and, in so doing, distorts. Simulation as training or indoctrination shatters this barrier because it drops the imaginary. As mentioned earlier, when we step closer to a type of full simulation, popularly called 'deep dive' or 'full dive,' we will have reached a critical ontological shift that will require a new type of theorizing. We can remain sensitized to the dangers of such latent modes, if we maintain that the simulated imaginary should always be experienced as distanced, and also that play should be decoupled from any encouragement to transfer damaging behavior from gameplay to actuality.

What we see with digital war games that provide realistically simulated training environments, even if they are not truly training 'games' in the way of

*America's Army* (2002), is that the safety cushion of knowing one plays a game may be complicated when the digital experience (imagined) encourages a material experience (lived). This might be as simple as learning about gun handling in a VR game such as *Hotdogs, Horseshoes & Hand Grenades* (2010) or actual room-clearing tactics such as those found in *Onward (2016)* (another VR game), and then buying a physical weapon and possibly translating in-game experience into real-world action. Of course, the trajectory from the digital screen to becoming an agent in the real world occupies much thought, the fear that FPSs leading to Columbine or other mass shootings is still part of a conversation that simplifies two complex phenomena (i.e., video-game culture and gun violence) into a direct causal relationship. Such concerns will only increase as the simulated imaginary becomes more convincing, especially with war and games.

Alexander Galloway (2006) calls for 'countergaming,' possibly through the fact some games can be modded, with the hope that this will provide agency for players as a form of resistance. What we must encourage and maintain as a focus is this crucial, yet nebulous relationship, in which reality affects the creation of the simulated imaginary, which can then affect reality. For example, anyone who learns to race cars in a game such as *Project Cars* (2015) or *iRacing* (2008) must be aware of how dangerous it is to drive at such speeds in reality. As another example, the antisocial activities encouraged in a series such as *Grand Theft Auto* (1997) must be kept within the gameworld rather than encouraged in the actual world (even though today we are seeing more and more examples of police chases, or 'public freakouts,' that mimic such activity). In these cases the simulated imaginary becomes part of reality, with the potential for unfortunate consequences.

This book seeks to understand how these new experiences are emerging as 2D gaming becomes more sophisticated thanks to its extended networks, especially with devices that extend play into areas such as computerized VR. It recognizes, though, that even more difficult terrain emerges when we ask how much of an event such as WWII should be playable. For example, VR encourages the creation of experiences rather than just the creation of gameplay. What happens when a market emerges for 'experiences' that are illegal in reality or that simulate the horrors of the past?

An entirely new set of discussions will be needed to address issues such as victimless crimes, thought crimes, future crimes, past crimes, and simulated crimes. It recognizes a gray area within game studies between abstracted violence, such as Pacman battling with ghosts over digital food-dots, to more intensely realistic FPSs such as the *Arma* (2006) series or highly fantastic ones such as *Doom* (1993) in which violence is sometimes simulated in a graphic fashion. Such games, though, are traditionally played in a secure environment in which a person stares at a 2D monitor, a separation that provides decontextualization. With the rise of VR, a convincing imaginary gameworld is simulated visually and aurally, and with increasing momentum toward sophisticated haptics, this will lend itself more to breaking the distance barrier for potentially dangerous psychological immersion.

As this type of experience becomes more 'realistic,' questionable games may emerge, such as murder or rape scenarios, or entire gameworlds that are constructed for the experience of engaging in genocide. If we ever arrive at this unfortunate place, we will have to confront how to address such problematic issues. This book condemns any such experience that replicates or encourages the fetishization or enactment of dehumanization through violence. It recognizes that some aspects of simulation are already used for conflict training, such as military scenarios, which one might argue justifies real-world violence in its simulation of warfare. However, they are also used in medical training, engineering construction, and advertising, for example, and even in preparation by professional drivers in motorsports such as Formula 1.

This study ultimately does not fully address these wide-ranging aspects of simulation. In focusing on the simulated imaginary as a reconfigured past affected by the simgame–simtext dynamic, it asks how we can theorize its positive use for persons within our technologized present; in so doing, it also seeks to understand the past as playable. It ultimately argues that along with the desire to experience a touch of excitement in our modern lives, simgames provide encounters with the past in a type of reverse engineering that encourages players to look to the actual world for understanding of and engagement with such games. Again, such a process might very well encourage a negative form of engagement with the actual world if such scenarios direct players to translate what they play/experience from the digital to the analog world. In such a way, it encourages us to examine these artifacts of the past through their digital simulations and accompanying texts.

# 2 Simtexts: Reimagining the Past

This chapter seeks to connect a few overarching ideas, in particular how players of simgames move from simulated experiences to simtexts for clarification. As detailed in Chapter 1, it finds this synergy working through serious computer gameplay that crosses boundaries into simulation modes mediated by digital technologies of the twenty-first century. Such simulated mediation refocuses a gameist 'historicism' beyond written language or screened texts. What emerges from this, like a swirling cloud, is the reimagined past in an archive of simtexts, today augmented with analog and digital game devices in curious reconfigurations.

The chapter is organized around a few theoretical concepts that relate to simtexts, followed by examples of types. It begins with the idea of how the popular memory of WWII is referenced in standard media such as literature and film, while ignoring games. It seeks, instead, an intersection for the player between serious simgames and related simtexts in massive digital archives that represent, and now simulate, aspects of the war. This digital archive also contains many traditional types of texts—especially written and screened—that remind us of the earlier primacy of core humanistic disciplines that ask questions about the human condition. It sees the challenge to literary studies, in particular, as being less a displacement of an older mode and more an augmentation. To the imaginary representations of fictions that we see in literature, even when they are historical, we may add simulations and player agency.

And it is to this agency that this chapter foregrounds the importance of player experiences, especially in how they work in the spaces between the virtual, digitized past and the actual, material world. Such experiences emerge as a type of immersion in a virtual past through the mediated spaces of simgames.

This chapter sees in such a dynamic a renewed need for interpretation, especially in players' engagement with a technologized 'gameworld' that is given to players. It ends with an examination of exemplary simtexts as something other than just game manuals or in-game information designed to guide players through a simgame. It provides examples from histories, fiction, technical works, and scholarly works, across a variety of media that represent typical types of simtexts a player might encounter when moving from simgame to simtext.

To embrace the history of this particular book's case study, WWII, and to read the bulk of its material or even just the professional monographs produced in the last decade alone, is overwhelming even for a serious student of history, much less a simgame player. Players who approach such massive archives today must also contend with the addition of the simgames themselves. When thinking of the games and WWII together, we can observe the rising prevalence of this curious simulated experience and the dynamic that follows. This occurs when digitized texts are used to enhance the simgame experience, especially when these prove accessible because they are increasingly visual and aural rather than only written.

The historical simtext, then, is firmly embedded in this relationship of history, players, games, and texts as an overlooked part of gameplay. I found, among the engineering culture at my university, a fitting place to begin with aviation simulation, a gameist/training mode that seemed at first to have very little to do with traditional humanistic learning but actually encouraged a type of deep engagement with simtexts from technical manuals, to history books, to YouTube videos, to films. From it, a 'gameworld' emerges that evokes the imaginary worlds of fiction, although now reconfigured with elements from a lived past.[1] While fictive literature may for some scholars be "the privileged medium when it comes to staging the playfulness of the self" (Alber, 2011: 13), broadening the idea of 'literature' into a digital archive of texts allows for varied media elements to emerge that demand interpretation. Today, we are faced with a massive archive of analog-and-digital media—for this study, simtexts that support simgames. The archive is an ever growing and expanding assemblage made of many units that we can engage with to clarify gameist experience and come to know a reconfigured past. By examining parts of this archive, within the context of a history of WWII approached through gaming, we see that its interpretation becomes a core practice that is in need of theorizing, both for scholars and for players.

Defining a simtext more narrowly than its broadest conception (as a piece of information within a computer game) asks us to consider how these various texts are encountered for players within the dynamic. There is a risk that players, games, history, and texts will become confused, and jumbled together in an indistinguishable mess; the trajectory, though, is towards the continued development of more complex relationships wherein players are foregrounded as a new type of 'player-subject' who engages with texts and play in novel ways. (Player-subjects are henceforth referred to as players.) The complexities will only continue to grow; thus the need to focus on the primary relationship of the simgame–simtext dynamic.

One can argue that the clearest use of the concept of simtexts refers to analog-or-digital information that directly relates to a simgame, such as an official manual published by a developer, game narration or cut-scene descriptions, maybe even a squadron 'history' written by the developers coupled with videos, graphs, statistics, and so on. These in-game paratexts are not simply scaffolding for gameplay but act as the first steps a player takes in traveling along an interpretive dynamic toward more demanding simtexts outside this narrow context. Beyond these in-game elements that require initial understanding, simtexts that look outward are critical to the core dynamic and to how such digital games are part of a larger archive. In the context here, these are the varieties of gameplay elements that encourage gameplay and also the experience of simulated configurations of the past.

Historical simtexts in this fluid context operate as core components within game-oriented arenas that players might encounter when moving beyond their simgames for clarification on gameplay, for general curiosity, or for a serendipitous encounter with new historical knowledge. A continuum works from accessible (sim)texts such as basic reference documents including game manuals and online reference sources toward more complex materials, such as written or screened memoirs and documentaries, general histories, books in the popular sphere that capture a small (or large) part of a specific event; these prepare more intrepid players to encounter the most demanding written and screened texts by professional historians or even novelists and film makers. Text in this context is an arena that demands interpretation, one that works along two axes—toward clarifying successful gameplay and toward an understanding, even if limited, of the past.

## Cultural Memory, Literature, and Games

Popular memory in its variety of forms has emerged as an important sphere of remembrance for events such as WWII, something that concerns Erll and Nünning (2005). The interdisciplinary discourse of that volume argues that one form of popular memory works within institutions, while another works outside them and their specialists, allowing for a less formalized way of remembering that acts through the many means of communication channels continually opening up to us in our technologized society. While today we can perceive that history has become an industry across mass media in both the professional and popular spheres, it has traditionally worked alongside literature and philosophy as pillars of the humanities, charting the human experience. The historiography of such humanistic forms of remembrance is embedded in poetry and later novels and films, intertwining the mythic and the everyday with a historic awareness that goes beyond that found in historical documents. Today, these pillars' gate-keeping roles have been challenged, for better or worse, by the massive archive of non-professional material that is being generated within the popular realm.

One idea that supports the ubiquity of this humanistic imperative to increase the archive is that truths and fictions of the past have power because they can represent real stories, and thus become memorable because of their power to enliven facts (the domain of history) with human experience (the domain of literature). Such fictionalized stories of the past and its representations, be they written or screened, have proven to be powerful mechanisms of historical awareness.

Anne Rigney writes:

> More research needs to be done on the relation between memorability, aesthetic power, and cultural longevity. But there is already evidence to show that "inauthentic" versions of the past may end up with more cultural staying power than the work of less skilled narrators or of more disciplined ones who stay faithful to what their personal memories or the archive allow them to say. (2005: 347–48)

Rigney continues by referencing Tolstoy and Spielberg, without reference to games; she thus reinforces the power of literature and cinema as remediating sites of the past, while not acknowledging the power of gaming as a new player in this field—as it translates representation into simulation. Rigney's insight is helpful as it clarifies that the ability of inauthentic fictions to reassemble the past within a fictive story may be more memorable than less narrative-focused descriptions of the past, but the absence of a gameist agency for such stories reveals a lack of recognition of this new mode.

Another important argument in this anthology directly relates to literature and history, also without mentioning the power of games. One of the editors, Astrid Erll, writes that "fictions, both novelistic and filmic, possess the potential to generate and mold images of the past which will be retained by whole generations" (Erll and Nünning, 2005: 389). A major goal of the editors is to understand how digital media within popular culture facilitate the impact of such impactful cultural memory; in essence, how they "create and mold collective images of the past" (Erll and Nünning, 2005: 390).

Erll approaches her examination by arguing that such fictions become powerful tools of reconfiguring the past when they become collective. She uses WWII as her example, referencing films such as *Der Untergang* (*Downfall*) (2004) as a powerful form of this collective, communicative memory. For Erll, the extraneous "network of other media representations" (2005: 396) endows such a film with its power to be memorable. Although games are not mentioned in this vast archive of media, as expected, I find in them not only a missing element of understanding history, but also a critical new agential-based experience that emerges when simgames, simtexts, and players intersect.

Recognition of the power of gameist remediation as detailed throughout this book points to how gaming is a primary site where simulation supersedes representation—a new mode that thus outperforms old ones. In the following chapters, we will see how shooters and simulators remediate key elements from memoirs and cinema by adding the critical element of player agency. This movement toward the simulated experience is grounded in a variety of media, creating synergy between them in a powerful dynamic that this book argues reconfigures the past through a combination of players, simgames, and simtexts.

## Digital Archives

As already mentioned, the concept of an archive of simgames and simtexts is helpful for approaching the simulation of such an event as WWII, its historiography containing media that, taken together, provide understanding through experience on particular topics. The digital as the primary substrate for such a phenomenon proves to be a central topic in need of examination.

My approach has a wide range of potential focuses beyond WWII that I leave unexplored, from the narrow subjective way in which one might simulate the role-playing of a Nordic-like barbarian in *Skyrim* (2011) and the other deep-story-driven RPGs such as those found in the *Witcher* (2007) series; or, moving to a larger scale, how one might simulate living in a contemporary family, such as in the *Sims* (2000) series. Continuing this broadening of scope, we can see in GSGs a focus on dynastic families, such as in Paradox's *Crusader Kings* (2004) franchise; on nations, such as in their *Europa Universalis* (2000) series; and even planetary systems, such as in *Stellaris* (2016). Yet we can also shift the subjective scope: Rather than thinking of it on a continuum from the personal to impersonal, we can think in terms of how the simulated imaginary provides experiences, such as driving a racing car or flying jumbo jets.

In avoiding data fetishism, or an uncritical acceptance of the increasing dominance of data-focused trends in the digital humanities, this chapter sees in the digital not only the structure of how these archives are encoded and consumed, but also the core dynamic of how players approach the past. Such a dynamic of players, games, texts, and simulation may appear to enforce anti-humanist trends in the digital humanities that threaten traditional modes of inquiry, but this study takes from both and offers a mixture wherein the player is enriched through both play and understanding. In its focus on how players experience new forms of simulated history across several disciplines, this chapter thus elevates the digital while resisting the tendency of data-driven knowledge to be perceived as the only worthwhile form. It sees in the interpretive posture a way to offer humanized significance to our world of distributed data by theorizing gameist perspectives that lead to understanding.

Following Jean-François Lyotard (1924–1998), Alan Liu recognizes (2004: 7) the momentum that might erase all non-information-based knowledge. Liu reverses the lament of Kafka that modernity will turn us, like Gregor, into horrendous insects. A reversal of such ignominious ends is in order, but Liu would locate this in a method of resistance rather than in a phenomenology of personal experience, as I argue. Liu sees cultural criticism, of which the literary proves to be a ground, as a type of hacking process. This "future literary" (2004: 8), as Liu calls it, following its hacker ethos, is to accept it is no longer in the service of creativity, but of recovering history. It is to be a "dark kind of history" (2004: 8), whose role is continually to mine those things that have been subsumed within the greater impulse of technological culture. I find this far too pessimistic.

Within the digital humanities, significance continues to be found at the myopic level of word frequencies, in the depersonalized application of algorithms to texts, and in simulation viewed simply as modeling or training. Simulated gameworlds of the past offer a way out of this constrictive revolution. They encourage the experience of engaging with historically based imaginary worlds, an experience that began when humans heard their first stories, or later heard (or read) heroic epics and tragedies, and continued with the first novels, then films, and now analog and digital games. Except now, players can act rather than just contemplate or observe.

In such a complex process, we can certainly still use, if we choose, digital tools to examine core data through algorithms. History, for example, can be understood (almost inadvertently) by mining computational texts, but it can also be used to engage the imaginary (for better or worse) through gaming. Thus, the focus in this chapter is on a reworked interpretive method of simgames and simtexts through gameplay, as well as on theorizing how players now experience such imagined worlds beyond reading or viewing; that is, through the use of computer games.

The digital ecosphere, then, is the primary space that supports these new ways in which we engage with simulated history. With the digital, the importance of the experiential subject returns. Some thinkers in the interdisciplinary digital humanities have suggested that the 'computational subject' emerges to usher these new digitized experiences into current technologized modes of being and understanding. But I find myself asking what if the experience of this digital subject has no practical ability to understand code or to write, read, or manipulate computer language; moreover, and especially relevant to this study, what if he or she has very little understanding of history beyond what is presented during gameplay? 'Code,' in this sense, disappears for most subjects, while 'history' is curated into highly scripted scenarios that have specific gameplay experiences.

The digital is also what an organization such as The World Economic Forum ('The Forum') considers to be the foundation of a fourth industrial revolution (Schwab, 2017). It drives what some digital humanists see as a way to organize a modern university that has lost its central referent (Berry, 2012: 8). The increasing ability to simulate the analog world demonstrates the power of applying algorithms to the humanities. My project does not deny the power of such algorithmic uses (see Ramsay, 2011); however, it seeks a way to situate computation within a framework that bolsters our understanding of simulated experiences. Within the digital humanities, the building of tools to create archives of digital texts, as well as tools to analyze them, speaks to the traditional focus on texts and their functions. Yet the computational turn in literary studies encourages us to follow our interpretative noses into arenas beyond the written word—those within media and game studies.

This digital ecosphere thus foregrounds the challenge for players in approaching its massive archives and how to understand them; that is, it demands a variety of techniques for analysis outside encoding and querying, daunting as they may be for non-coding players. These demands placed upon players remind developers that tools should be empowering. The challenges for developers are intriguing, but less helpful for my approach because they often shift the focus from the phenomenological subject to the script. Rather, in legitimizing a gameist process that accepts the importance of new media forms such as games and simulations, archives of texts recast gameplay for players, especially as a way to approach the past.

## Imaginary Worlds and Literary Studies

This dynamic between players, games, and texts raises a question about the reliability of such reconfigured pasts, especially when it appears to undermine the past with fiction. A suspicion follows that there appear to be cracks in the traditional humanistic disciplines, something that is also seen in the shift away from their 'first culture' status, as they are superseded by the upstart sciences and most recently engineering and digital tools.

This chapter admits that recovering what is valuable in traditional approaches remains critical, while still acknowledging the exciting and fruitful opportunities that these new digital tools bring to our humanistic practices by reconfiguring the past, all the while recognizing how the imaginary fits in. The effectiveness of the dynamic is therefore predicated on the idea that how we represent and simulate the past has been complicated by our computerized, technological artifacts in a movement that augments (and often replaces) traditional written representation with new forms of player agency, something that Uricchio notes as a way to "slip out of the well-critiqued trap of representation" (2005: 332). We saw a similar shift with the rise of cinema in the twentieth century as a powerful new medium of storytelling that repositioned spectators.

Traditional written literature and history are primarily analog forms of representation that articulate the vagaries of a complex world and its past through material substrates, from stone to parchment and papyrus to paper, and so on. Within the constraints of such analog media, these core humanistic practices have constructed reality through the literary and historical imaginary. Novels abound, as do histories. Within such recognizable media, both individual and collective subjects have formed. And with imaginary subjects as protagonists within imaginary worlds, even those with historical contexts, we have seen literature and history intersect in powerful configurations. Our greatest fictions attest to this.

To understand Napoleon or the history of the Russian monarchy, we might look to biographies or histories of the period, or even primary sources, but we might also take note of representations of persons and places within dramatized moments, such as the characters and setting of Tolstoy's *War and Peace* (1869) and its wide canvas from Czarist Russia to the battlegrounds of the Napoleonic Wars. This type of humanistic understanding now augments professional histories, with novels, films, and series dramatizing spectacle. What empowers this transmedial mode of encountering the represented past is a curious form of interpretation—a combination of entertainment and study.

While such traditional forms, from poetry and theater to the novel and cinema, exist on a long continuum of how human beings have represented the world, the appearance of digital simulations provides stark differences, and also affects elements of continuity. Viewing cinema within the frame of gameplay still proves valuable and popular, as does the literary search for characters with dramatic tension and conflict; however, rather than mining for narrative, story, or spectacle, player agency emerges in the following chapters as a core mechanic within this new gameist mode. Agency, then, is embedded in the simulated imaginary as a world-building mechanism, thus providing continuity with how fictive worlds have been drawn in literature and cinema.

Yet the traditional discipline of literary studies now lurks like a suspicious outsider, so full of complex subjects within imaginary worlds. Already displaced by cinema as a popular form, it seems also to be outmatched by the juggernaut of gaming. This has occurred because of a new agential relationship between players and texts that works by using aspects within literature far beyond the mode of reading. The new mode of simgames takes from literature its fully imagined worlds and histories, such as those full-bodied descriptions related to fantasy settings with their own complex lore, from Tolkien's Middle Earth to the Marvel Universe, to that of Star Wars. The imagined 'histories' these contain can inspire heated debate over canonicity by fans, as genre-readers once did over earlier favorites such as the virtual worlds of Sherlock Holmes or Tarzan. See Saler (2012). It then adds the ability to act, and to affect the gameworld itself.

When the past is reconfigured rather than the fantastic fully imagined, we see configurations of what happened parsed with complete fictions. A key distinction should be made between the representation of a fictional world (imagining) versus the simulation of a historical world (reconfiguring). Whereas the former is fully located in a frame as imaginary, the latter has roots in a lived past with elements of the imaginary. This distinction points to how fiction can contain completely imaginary characters alongside those who may have once lived and fully realistic characters who never were or are completely impossible, all in a realistic setting. This combination of the literary and the historical with simulation is enhanced through the dynamic of player, simgames, and simtexts, and works just as powerfully when the past is of concern as it does for the shared intellectual properties of popular-culture fictions. The digital continues to encourage this literary displacement by far exceeding what earlier analog writers were able to represent in their novelized world creations.

From a critical perspective, complex literary elements are often set aside, such as narrative, plot, character, conflict, drama, setting, the author, the reader, and the audience; just as disciplinary differences between American, British, Russian, French, and German literatures are ignored. Likewise, from a historical perspective, important arguments about the nature of history are often set aside, as they are best understood through universal methods of abstracted forces, or alternatively those particulars that are often overlooked but comprise so much of the lived experiences of individuals.

This use of a playable reconfigured/reimagined past allows developers to rework history within simgames. It reveals how players engage with the past through in-game challenges, certainly, but also how they understand the past so that their experiences are more engaging. It could be suggested that such simgames, even the most narrative-driven ones, fail to present the same depth as our most complex literature; but we might acknowledge that, by adding agency over literary demands, such simgames create completely new and uncharted territories for players to explore, as well as for theorists to consider.

In this sense, reimagined worlds in the form of configured history are presented, in a very similar way to how imaginary worlds in fiction are offered. Yet value can be found in the project to rework textuality beyond traditional literary studies and its written objects of study (and its most complex critiques), to add player agency as a gameplay requirement together with the powerful new experiences that extend what earlier media afforded (see Aarseth, 1997 for the key text that asks for a separation from traditional humanistic disciplines). Such a refocusing jettisons demands from story, or from what we typically consider as a traditional written text, so we can regard games as a new form of player activity.

What emerges in this book is the simulated imaginary gameworld. Within this set of contexts, it continues what literature provides in its ability to imagine worlds and subjects, yet now in a historical gameist mode that is scaffolded with entirely new forms of agential experience located within reconfigurations of the past. This may appear to move beyond 'literariness,' but books of fiction and history are here to stay even as we encounter their contents through mediated elements beyond the written word. In fact, the amount of written analog-and-digital content being produced today is on such a scale that it can create anxiety in individuals who desire comprehensive understanding (such as literary scholars).

How, then, can the traditional humanities such as literary studies, history, and philosophy help us to understand the phenomenon of engineered digital simgames and texts? In sidestepping twentieth-century debates in critical and historical theory, debates that saw traditional theoretical approaches give way to the new criticism, from structuralism to reworkings of modernism and historicism, some elements remain from literary studies, history, and philosophy that augment this new gameist mode of cultural activity; that is, the phenomenological experience that player agency affords.

## New Player Experiences

Such agential elements as have been introduced here converge in technologized experiences for subjects/players that are grounded in the imaginary (or the reconfigured), a process that leads us to the past through the present. This central process, so well articulated in a variety of humanities disciplines, takes us forward into the twenty-first century where new modes of simulated history are proving powerful in capturing our attention. We are carried far beyond traditional forms of narrative representation such as those found within the novel and film into procedurally generated worlds, simulated experiences, virtual economies, and so on, into the simulated imaginary and reconfigured past in its proliferating forms.

The risk exists that if we foreground games we may appear to dismiss traditional literature or historical analysis, with their detractors calling for their erasure as forms of serious study. Rather than doing this, we need to examine how digital computer games offer new experiences of the past beyond direct representations. And rather than highlighting differences between games and traditional humanistic fields, more fertile ground awaits if we discover how they are engaged, especially in how digital computer games rework particular aspects of literature and cinema, two often diverging forms of immersive media. Much can be found that overlaps between these forms and simgames, especially when we take into account the connective tissue of the simulated imaginary, the world-building mechanism that we find in literature and cinema, as well as any fiction making, even when it is scaffolded with historicity.

Scholars have sought connections between these new media forms in that they are both virtual and real, that they are core ways of experiencing reality and its simulations within popular culture. However, there is also anxiety over virtual fiction's potential to distract readers from reality, a phenomenon that has passed on to digital computer games, which have much more power to influence. Also of concern is an uncritical belief that readers and players will be so seduced by the virtual worlds they encounter that they will not be able to discern the real from the imaginary. Timothy Welsh offers the controlling idea of "mixed realism, or the synchronization of virtual and material realms" (2016: 164). He challenges the most extreme forms, especially in sensitive topics such as gun violence and video games: rather than assuming that one is contingent on the other, he argues that mixed realism reflects how a culture of gun violence will also produce video games with gun violence.

Seeing the digital and analog at work in tandem demonstrates how we are embedded in our digital devices and their accompanying mediated experiences. A constant critique is needed if we are to understand this relationship, something this chapter argues works in the form of digital agency. However, while critics of the simulated imaginary fear that fiction or video games so immerse a reader or player that he or she becomes ontologically confused, I would ask what sort of experience of the past occurs when we use digitally mediated, fictional pasts from literature, or cinema, or any fiction-making media.

We can answer this by foregrounding player agency as this new mode. Whether through story or game mechanics, a powerful player experience emerges from both a reconfigured and imagined past. And here a continuum exists with other media, from reading a novel to watching stories in a cinema to playing games that utilize degrees of narrative and story, but critically do something more. By adding the past to this concoction of agential play, we are confronted with a powerful mode of historical consumption that begs interpretation.

In avoiding a definition of what is literature or what is history, or even what is play, a gameist type of experience emerges for players with simtexts as a core aspect of simgames. In particular, traditional modes (as I have tried to clarify in this chapter) take on a new significance when framed within gameplay. These are enlivened when a playable experience leads to understanding through simulated experiences of the past. Gameplay is the core impetus of this new dynamic. In serious simgames, this may lead to an engaged (yet involuntary) form of interpretation that generates meaning through play.

One major challenge for anyone encountering a simulated historical gameworld with player agency is how to operate within it. Players do so through casual praxis (i.e., play), of course, but also through encounters with simtexts, an interpretive process similar to notetaking, sketching, casual or focused study, organizing, fictionalizing, and composing. This process can be daunting. Trying to learn about a certain part of a simulated gameworld, or historical moment, often proves difficult, even though online reference tools exist (e.g., game manuals or walk-throughs), with communities of experts eager to offer guidance. These provide entry-level information, and even directions for efficient gameplay. More high-level tools also exist if someone wants to find a specific playing technique or a simgame's context. In such cases, interpretive knowledge emerges as a dynamic process similar to parsing a source and its commentary and then applying that knowledge in a context. It is a process of piecing the material together through study and in-game praxis.

At this point, it is helpful to think of the player as embedded in a complex relationship between simgames and simtexts, and thus as experiencing a type of historicized gameworld in need of interpreting. We can translate this to the experience of simgame players as being a new humanistic category of simulation that cuts across cultural and academic boundaries. With simulation as the primary impulse beyond representation, we see that simgames separate themselves from other forms of digital games such as Tetris-inspired puzzle games or even from traditional decontextualized strategy games such as chess (even if elements of these can be found in simgames)—to do more than just entertain. They offer gameworlds in which the virtual past becomes known to a certain degree.

Interpretation of such gameworlds, though, must continue to be rethought within fields such as historical game studies, with distinctive processes being used to analyze games as generators of the simulated historical imaginary. This distinction reveals a rich experience of the imaginary as a primary phenomenological activity of our technologized gameworlds, while other elements such as the demonstration of skill or the process of discovery also emerge as critical.

While I agree with ludologists in seeking to theorize games, be they digital or analog, within their own discipline and separate from other humanistic forms of inquiry, I find in the study of simgames a resurgent discursive imperative that points us back to correlating simtexts—those novels, memoirs, films, documentaries, biographies, histories, even technical materials that illuminate simgames by adding meaning and significance to their afforded experiences, rather than just illuminating successful gameplay. A fertile middle ground now exists between the earlier disciplinary row in game studies wherein ludologists

Espen Aarseth, Gonzalo Frasca, and Jesper Juul, along with others, originally argued for games to be considered as games alone with challenges to be overcome for rewards, rather than the approach by narratologists such as Janet Murray, who saw in computer games key aspects from fiction, such as story, world building, character creation, and so on (see Murray, 1998).

The momentum away from these polarizing positions is encouraging, especially when we consider these gameworlds as always, according to Juul, "half-real" (2011: 1). Games require artificial rules to engage their imaginary and reconfigured worlds. They are always burdened with some degree of unreality. The focus on such mechanisms, along with elements from traditional storytelling, are both helpful, especially in how the past is simulated, rather than viewing them as discreet. While the case studies in this book have less to do with presenting stories of the war, they do offer 'world-building' fictional elements through reconfigurations and, sometimes, reimaginings of the past. It is at the intersection between the reimagined and reconfigured that this study firmly rests.

What is seminal here is a focus on how simplay provides perspective, understanding, and significance by looking outside the simgame. This is an interpretive process at work, grounded as it is in engaging with made things and their correlating elements. We see this when we begin to look at the different types of simtexts, especially those that directly relate to complex simgames.

## Types of Simtexts

Here, I examine representative examples from the broad categories of screened and written simtexts, several of which are popular histories that often situate players within narrow understandings of the past. Some are foundational works of scholarship that have captured particular inflections on how to understand the war based on the time of their writing and publication, who wrote them, and their particular rhetorics. These extend today into contentious areas in which the memory politics forged by the war still shapes thought. Others are works of fiction that capture the war through film and novels in ways that have inspired computer games and also demonstrate the power of combining fiction with history. This list is not exhaustive but exemplary; it represents categories that have similar simtexts.

## Histories

A fundamental benefit of the dynamic can be found when players seek historical documents for clarification on game elements. Here, a massive archive of WWII content confronts interested players even if they only want to know more about how to play a particular simgame. Some players come to these games with a historical foundation, maybe grounded in actual study, or possibly just through encounters with popular-culture texts such as films or TV shows or other games. Key works such as Winston Churchill's Nobel Prize-winning memoir *The Second World War* (1948–1953) or any of the biographies of major figures may have been read or skimmed by those who are interested in more than a basic understanding, even if they do not appeal to most players.

Instead, players of simgames often opt for specific accounts of battles or technical books about the machinery of war. These wide-ranging technical books also cover the history of the militaries involved, especially the tactics used by planes, tanks, and ships. Such histories detail the arms race that led nations to continually outdevelop each other. These weapons-focused simtexts also act as gateways into the era, leading players into an archive of other material that expands far beyond weaponry.

This archive reflects the complexities of categories that are rooted in the major humanities disciplines beyond history, such as philosophy and literature, and into the social sciences, including economics, political science, sociology, and psychology. General histories or even descriptions of particular battles may be unexpectedly encountered, showing how, for example, the Spitfire first became known to the Germans in the 'Phony War' and later in the Battle of Britain, or even why the Soviets disapproved of it. But there are also questionable memoirs written with skewed perspectives that justify the experiences of the author (see the description of Hans Ulrich Rudel's autobiography in Chapter 4). And at the opposite end of simtexts that present blatant hagiographies or that mythologize the war are encounters with more demanding texts that seek difficult answers for the war, such as Hannah Arendt's *Origins of Totalitarianism* (1951) or, more recently, Daniel Jonah Goldhagen's *Hitler's Willing Executioners* (1997).

The war as an event embedded in a reconfigurable past is often approached by players in much more simplistic contexts than thinking about totalitarianism or how deep National Socialism spread into the thinking of common Germans. Instead, players encounter gameplay elements as basic as a terrain map showing where particular battles occurred. These mundane mechanisms act as a game aid to orient players within gameworlds, but they are also used in most simtexts to ground an understanding that the event affected actual lived places where real tragedy (and, at times, villainy and heroism) occurred. A new player who encounters a focused but seemingly fragmented simgame mechanism such as a curated map for the first time will be overwhelmed by learning how to navigate it, not to mention the historical contexts of the charted terrain.

As detailed in Chapter 4, the first version of *IL2:GB* was originally released in 2013 with a focus on the Battle of Stalingrad, its map stretching from the west of the Volga River and the city to the area of Tatsinskaya, over 250 km from Stalingrad. This version of the series was followed by an earlier event, the Battle of Moscow (2016). Later versions featured other key moments on the Eastern Front, with a shift south to the Battle of Kuban (2018) region and then to the later part of the war to the west, and the Battle of Bodenplatte (2019). The online digital maps corral players into flyable areas that present key landscape features, from mountains, valleys, rivers, and coastlines to cities connected by roads and railway lines, while leaving other important areas of the war unmapped. In such aviation simulators, flight management is the first in-game hurdle, with the move from an airstrip to an altitude where the critical mechanism of surviving becomes important; this is followed by combat tactics.

If players choose some of the more demanding multiplayer servers or decide to limit any aids during a single-player game, they will find that navigation is a challenge in itself, with the map again proving to be a major component of learning the game. Flying without the aid of GPS means players must learn to read the environment, finding waypoints, judging time in the air, the speed of travel, and so on. A player will quickly learn that the western part of the Stalingrad map near Karpovka is a key rendezvous point for lost pilots, the easily identifiable three fingers of rivers pointing east toward the city of Stalingrad. From the sky, these function as landmarks. But curious players might move outside the game and encounter simtexts that explain the battle that occurred here, and learn they are flying over the area in which the Wehrmacht's Sixth Army was encircled and captured, the fateful major disaster for the Germans that solidified their descent toward defeat in the East. This may lead to other histories or even questions of motivations of the leaders, the soldiers, the citizens. The path to serious investigation has begun.

Players thus learn that other types of simtexts paint a broader canvas beyond military tactics, or even one particular nation's way of remembering the war. The literary record is filled with stories, accounts, narratives, and histories that record this human experience of loss and suffering, heroics and villainies, victories and defeats. These range from memoirs of soldiers such as RAF pilots who survived to write about their time flying Spitfires, Hurricanes, Mosquitos, and Lancasters to memoirs by defeated generals who survived to justify their roles in the war.

This required interpretive posture becomes clearer through a wider encounter with such simtexts, revealing that such 'histories' demonstrated a marked softening in the West toward postwar Germany, especially in its need to combat the Soviets as a competing world power during the Cold War, even as more detailed examinations into the crimes of National Socialism formed their own discourse. With the fall of the Soviet Union and the opening of its archives, the narrative shifted from a perspective that was primarily American and British to recognizing the importance of the German-Soviet War in the East (see Chapter 5). The wide range of texts covering subjects from particular battles to general histories reflect a growing awareness of how the war remains with us today as a key point of memory construction, with remembrance still being used to valorize the past as well as to justify actions in the present.

Written forms, of course, have been published alongside an entire archive of screened texts, many of which now prove just as foundational and mythmaking. The British *World at War* documentary series released in 1973–1974 provided an intimate look into the images of war, along with interviews of still-living participants, even if it was very much skewed by a Western perspective. A long list of WWII-centered documentary screened texts have been made, the internet now hosting a wide range of new media forms beyond those of the traditional documentary film or series.

While filmed documentaries such as *Apocalypse: The Second World War* have been released as recently as 2009, novel new genres are also emerging. Netflix has begun releasing a hybrid genre of historical programming that blends fictionalized narrative of the past with interviews and voice-overs by respected historians that place the narratives in proper contexts. They have addressed the times of the Romans, the Ottomans, even the ending of the Romanov dynasty. With *Hitler's Circle of Evil* (2017), they center on Hitler and those around him, focusing on these prime movers within Germany rather than the common soldiers and officers, administrators, and citizens.

Along with such creative new ways of addressing the past, video-streaming platforms such as YouTube have provided historians in both the popular and the professional spheres with new ways to examine WWII. These are varied and often very specific, exemplified for tanks by the Bovington Tank Museum and its YouTube representatives, such as military-historian David Fletcher, whose videos focus on all aspects of the tanks used during both world wars and after. Fletcher, though, is but one individual, and YouTube's history channels form an archive far beyond the scope of this project. Bovington is just one example of a museum that instructs through its physical space and material objects, along with its digital extensions. Such channels by serious historians are increasing, along with those from the popular sphere dedicated to WWII.

Either through gaming or just an interest in general history, players encounter these streaming channels that demonstrate the degree to which the past is being addressed outside the academy. And while these channels may be as simple as a player using a virtual video stream to talk about tactics while streaming a game, many are fully produced series by legitimate historians working outside the academy, which are funded through advertising. Granted, historical accounts must abstract their information so that analysis can be clear. This analysis proves invaluable as a doorway, offering a chance for eye-opening awareness in the dynamic from simgame to simtext. But it fails to capture the lived experience of the event: No material representation or simulation can ever fully do so, even if some approach to differing degrees.

The most challenging simtexts are found when players encounter works that fill lacunae ignored in most simgames (see Chapter 5). These often reflect the horrors of war avoided in gameplay, especially its most egregious forms such as war crimes or the massive destruction of loss and life.

Vasily Grossman's work is exemplary of this type of difficult simtext, as is his journalistic/novelized telling of Stalingrad. His accounts act as a corrective for viewing Stalingrad only within a tactical or strategic military frame. With Grossman as a source, the Battle of Stalingrad can be mined for any number of elements outside tactics and strategy. In detailing the horrors that happened in Eastern Europe and the Soviet Union, his work is exemplary of the most challenging type of anecdotal simtext, which moves beyond gameplay into nuances of the human condition in distress. Players who stumble upon Grossman are confronted with challenging simtexts—both the earlier book *Stalingrad* (1952) and the later *Life and Fate* (1959)—that attempt to recreate the depth and complexity found in a literary work such as Tolstoy's *War and Peace* (1869), with early twentieth-century Eastern Europe as their focus.[2]

No simulation exists that even hints at the degradation experienced by human beings on both sides of the conflict. Disease and starvation were as terrible, if not worse, than the actual fighting. Grossman writes of the many diseases, such as typhus, dropsy, diphtheria, and dysentery, and even of the cruel instances such as when mice nibbled away frostbitten toes. The extreme cold, coupled with the destruction from artillery and air raids, created an environment so far beyond imagining that history as a professional discipline fails to capture it unless it crosses into the literary and philosophical.

Stalingrad is the core setting, even though the canvas is wide enough to encompass universities, villages, and small towns, along with battlefields and its combatants from Western Russia to Ukraine. The cast also ranges widely enough that Stalin and Hitler are represented, along with the common people ensnared in the war. The themes in *Life and Fate* seek both the provincial and the lofty, the primary one set right at the beginning of *Life and Fate* when two Russian officers, Chuykov and Yeremenko, speak on the right bank of the Volga as the Germans assault Stalingrad. "Another moment and it seemed they might begin the one conversation that really mattered—about the meaning of Stalingrad" (Grossman, 2006: 40).

Through the account, the dates of 1937 and its purges feature prominently, along with 1941 and the disaster of how Stalin's armies allowed the Germans to invade the Soviet Union with such ferocity and devastation. But it is on Stalingrad that the key question focuses. Instead of ruminating on the symbolic nature of the battle, Yeremenko asks his superior officer about reinforcements and supplies. "The one conversation that could have had meaning failed to take place" (Grossman, 2006: 40). In *Life and Fate*, interested players are asked to take into account the moral (rather than strategic) importance of this battle, and also a larger question about the early German successes and Soviet failures as they encounter historical and fictional characters who experienced the war. The weightiest questions are asked, rather than specific concerns over armies, logistics, and maneuvers.

Some themes reach far wider than the concerns of most players who are interested in WWII simgames, such as the new philosophies within science that have been spurred by relativity and quantum physics or the new ideologies that have emerged alongside them. Grossman situates these within the modern problem of materialism as a prime culprit in technological determinism and its effect of dehumanization. These complex themes point interested players toward fundamental conversations in the humanities, directly relating to the largest causal mechanisms that explain the war.

Through the character of the scientist Viktor Shtrum, Grossman equates fascism with the ultimate process of removing the human (what he calls 'man') from any equation of happiness. "Man and fascism cannot co-exist. If Fascism conquers, man will cease to exist and there will remain only man-like creatures that have undergone an internal transformation" (Grossman, 2006: 78–79). And later, Viktor despairs over what is happening; he says to his wife Lyudmila that the culture of Goethe and Bach has led to the slaughter of babies. For Grossman, National Socialist fascism, rather than the earlier Italian form, comprises the ultimate fascist inflection because of the incredible horrors that spread from Germany and into Eastern Europe, from death camps to the war of extermination.

These "cruelest designs against human life and freedom" (Grossman, 2006: 179) emerge throughout the novel as moments of unthinkable inhumanity, some-times seen as iconic symbols of "silent horror" (Grossman, 2006: 183) such as humans crowded into cattle trains or prisoners marching toward ditches or gas chambers. We see this in the thoughts of a Ukrainian doctor, Sofya, now packed with others in a cattle car, who despairs at the inhumanity around her:

> Sofya learned that there were many things in human beings that were far from human. She heard about a paralysed woman who had been frozen to death by her sister; she had been put in a tub and dragged out onto the street on a winter's night. She heard about mothers who had killed their own children; there was one in this very wagon. She heard about people who had lived in sewers for months on end, eating filth like rats, ready to endure anything if only they could stay alive. (Grossman, 2006: 183–84)

The cattle car is for Grossman a symbol of bureaucratic organization wedded to inhuman practice. It is the mechanism of treating human beings as animals to be slaughtered. It is also another mechanism that is not simulated in simgames, such as *HOI4* that is examined in Chapter 5, a perfect example of a lacuna encountered by players that only becomes clear through simtexts such as Grossman's.

Along with this murderous symbol of modern transportation and industry as a glaring gameplay lacuna, the turbine is also used by Grossman to represent modern technology applied to the destruction of people. When the German officer Liss must follow Himmler's orders to inspect the "special measures" (Grossman, 2006: 455) being constructed for the extermination of the Jews, and then report to Eichmann, Grossman compares this project with "that of any other gigantic construction of the mid-twentieth century" (2006: 457), a recognition that the power of technology, coupled with ideology, can lead to mass-organized genocide. The gas chamber, along with the cattle car, is detailed here as an assemblage of mechanisms fitted together for one inhuman purpose. "And in this building the principle of the turbine was combined with those of the slaughterhouse and the garbage incineration unit" (Grossman, 2006: 458). The hallway leading into the gas chamber is compared with "supply canals" (Grossman, 2006: 458), another form of industrial transportation. We see people, through the eyes of Liss, reduced to "organic matter" (Grossman, 2006: 459) to be reused as chemical components. Like the cattle car, the gas chamber finds no simulation in complex simgames, and rightly so, even if its absence points to different problems of forgetfulness that may undermine the impact of its remembrance.

We also see Liss as someone upset by the requirement that he visit such a place. He would rather have read some philosophy while sitting in an armchair, comfortable and unperturbed. When he meets Eichmann, it happens to be at a table set with hors-d'oeuvres, in a gas chamber. Here he learns the inhuman number of Jews who are expected to pass through such a chamber— millions. Ending the conversation, Eichmann makes the argument that exterminating the Jews is a problem that hasn't been solved for centuries. It is to this supposed 'common good' the Nazis have set their aims. Grossman's account in this scene demonstrates how his writing reflects the delusions that warp philosophy in the service of ideology. Such fallacious arguments were used, of course, another being that National Socialism was fighting for Western civilization, setting itself up as a bulwark against 'Asiatic' Bolshevism. These echo the arguments that were used to form the "bonfires of the Inquisition [along with] the bonfires of Auschwitz" (Grossman, 2006: 470). We are told of Sofya's journey to the gas chamber and its harrowing end as she attempts to protect a child, David, from their fate. The passage ends: "Her heart, however, still had life in it: it contracted, ached and felt pity for all of you, both living and dead; Sofya Osipovna felt a wave of nausea. She pressed David, now a doll, to herself; she became dead, a doll" (Grossman, 2006: 538).

The power of a literary, historicized novel such as Grossman's can be seen in any number of finely drawn scenes. However, one in particular demonstrates that this kind of fictionalized account differs from other types of written simtexts, such as biographies or direct histories, and that a player reading such a simtext is faced with elements that are outright ignored in current simgames. This fictionalized type of memoir crosses literary forms, finding its most powerful effect when we read about such an event as the burning of bodies, which is recounted by Naum Rozenberg (Grossman 2006: Part 1, Chapter 44). He is an old accountant, also in a cattle car, mumbling numbers to himself as he recalls the loss of his wife during her pregnancy and how he was forced to be a '*brenner*,' someone who dug bodies out of massed graves with hooks and ropes, who cut timber the size of a human, who burned the bodies.

Throughout this process, Rozenberg counted the bodies but refused to think of them, as a German squad leader did, as items. Instead, he spoke to them as people as he exhumed them, humanizing them as individuals with stories. Such a close and subjective point of view (POV) exemplifies the power of fiction over gameplay and the freedom of the novelist to fictionalize an event that captures lived experiences, allowing us to see into the agony of someone who recalls such lived horror. This allows Grossman to foreground his theme of why Stalingrad mattered so much, with "two hammers, one to the north and one to the south, each composed of millions of tons of metal and flesh" (2006: 622) falling upon General Paulus's entrenched army—and the Germans suffering a critical defeat.

The unimaginable loss of life in Eastern Europe leads to even more difficult topics, many of which have been accessible since the war ended, such as excerpts from the Nuremberg trials and, not long afterwards, more personal accounts by Holocaust survivors such as Raul Hilberg's foundational *Destruction of the European Jews* (1961). Again, like the horrors of Stalingrad, these elements are rarely simulated, if ever, for various reasons.

Today, these difficult simgame lacunae have been foregrounded by many historical thinkers outside gameplay across both the professional and popular spheres. When players encounter mysterious lacunae in game, they may realize they are no longer just experiencing a simulation of flying a fighter, driving a tank, or outfitting armies and deploying them in strategic warfare; no longer are they just reading about battles or last-minute communications between diplomats, the historical moments that comprise battle tapestries or the political events leading up to them; no longer are they just playing a game for an immediate reward. Rather, they find themselves confronted with reconfiguring the past through an interpretive process in which they have to recognize that war causes mass destruction.

Numerous simtexts that detail the lived experiences of individuals who suffered at the hands of oppressors have been written since the 1990s. The historiography of the Holocaust is an example of this, with these simtexts across media focusing on the human condition at its most aggrieved rather than on tactics and strategy. Cinema reveals the power of the medium, with films such as *Schindler's List* (1993) finding large audiences. Adding in the novels, plays, memoirs, and biographies that illustrate how the Jews suffered under the Nazis' war of annihilation opens the war into broader categories beyond history, into moral philosophy and even theology.

These most difficult topics may never be approached by incurious players who see none of this in most simgames. Instead, the most common types of simtexts beyond technical descriptions of war machines, the specific and general histories, biographies, memoirs, documentaries, fictions, and so on, fill lacunae with differing degrees of focus but often in baby steps rather than in full strides. Each of these genres within the mega-archive of WWII historiography is represented in a variety of publication forms from volumes published by vanity presses to personal websites to streamed videos. Those offered for publication by respected publishers or studios compete with each other for sales as much as for consciousness raising, with it being difficult to parse what separates quality histories from those that are unreliable.[3]

Biographies form one of these difficult nexuses between the many forms of popular histories and those by professional historians. As noted in Chapter 4 on simulators, biographies of airmen and women become almost required reading for the most serious flight-simulator players. These are the most personal of accounts, often telling only a small portion of the war's potential experiences and often arguing that pilots' experiences were fundamentally different from those of other branches of the armed forces.

The most significant biographies often describe the leaders of the major nations, examples being Stephen Kotkin's monumental two works (eventually to be three) on Stalin, Ian Kershaw's trilogy on Hitler, or the many written about Churchill (see Kershaw, 1999, 2000; and Kotkin, 2015, 2017. One of the more interesting approaches to Churchill can be seen in the demythologizing by Charmley, 1993). These stand at the opposite pole of the individual memoir of a common soldier or even from comprehensive histories of particular battles or the larger event itself, with its often huge cast of individuals, of which many have been written (for a popular example, see Beevor, 2014). Between biographies and general histories exist the many stories told in an inevitably incomplete but massive archive of texts.

The personal memoir provides detailed portraits that can often offer a highly reflective type of representation for players, with memoirs and biographies being a middle-ground between fiction and history. Players might encounter key foundational memoir-histories on the broadest scale, such as the previously mentioned six-volume set by Churchill, or its abridged version of eight-hundred pages (Churchill, 1990). This central account by one of the Allied leaders offers a unique perspective and rare insight by one of the war's chief decision makers, recalling in detail, and from Churchill's particular perspective, many of the events, incidents, betrayals, and heroisms that spanned the time from the end of WWI to the end of WWII.

What is curious is how gameplay elements still emerge in a personal work, counterbalancing other texts that attempt a distanced perspective, such as technical books that explain the nuances of the machines of war without addressing larger motivating factors. When encountering such a series as Churchill's memoirs, reader-players find themselves in a curious position in which the dominance of the simgame recedes, while gameplay insights for simgame strategies are still offered, perhaps, for example, in imagining counterfactual scenarios in which Britain mobilizes early for war. Churchill's broader rather than narrower focus separates it from the memoirs of less prominent individuals, of course, with his account ranging across both military and political canvases and giving insights from someone who was in a position of power.

One might be skeptical that such a prominent memoir-history would be of relevance to someone who, in the case of *IL2*, only wants to fly simulated WWII aircraft or even play a GSG such as *HOI4*, or much less run around as an infantry soldier in *HLL*. And while Churchill's memoirs mention the air war, reveal his role as the prime minister, and detail infantry and naval battles, his broad description provides far more than a frame for gameplay. It provides his own particular perspective—for better or worse.

Unexpectedly, the simgame–simtext dynamic reveals that the simulated imaginary reconfigures playable history. To take an example from simulators, this relationship is catalyzed by flying WWII aircraft within a computer game, an activity that points to the wider event in which such aircraft flew (see Chapter 4). This trajectory begins for a player in the simulated cockpit of a Spitfire, perhaps leading to simtexts that explain the workings of the aircraft, then its use by leading RAF pilots, such as Douglas Bader (also Chapter 4). Questions about what happened in the Battle of Britain may lead to specific memoirs, or even to detailed histories. Finally, the broadest questions begin to be asked and general histories become relevant. Fictional accounts add clarity to all levels, whether the broadest, such as Churchill's grand justification for his role in the war as a staunch enemy of Hitler, or the narrowest, such as Grossman's personal account of brutal life in Ukraine and Western Russia. Documentaries and films play their role too.

The most important element in a player's encounter with such a work as Churchill's is the significance of his particular experience (and whether aspects of it can be simulated), since he was such an integral figure. Such a memoir can then be juxtaposed with biographies of Churchill that form a more critical and possibly different approach (Charmley, 1993).

What I find curious is how the memoir as a literary and historical genre serves a latent critical function, subtly demanding interpretation. A curious player will recognize that with such an account we are confronted with a layer of interpretation, in this case Churchill's perspective, or with a biography that recounts the same events but is filtered by the biographer's perspective.

Here we are in the perplexing area of texts speaking to other texts, a core process within the humanities' methodologies in which analysis is demanded and we understand through interpretation.

By foregrounding the importance of the memoir as an exemplary simtext of WWII that a player might eventually encounter, we return to a traditional search in the humanities that looks for unquantifiable factors within history, such as motivations, which are rooted in deep problems of determining causation. These can be expressed in generalized questions: What led to the rise of fascism in the form of National Socialism? Why was Germany allowed to rearm itself? Why didn't the Allies stop Germany before it was too late? It is not possible to find primary sources that answer these questions, so the process is rather closer to understanding a piece of fiction, or describing a POV as it applies to a series of events.

## Fictions

Another common type of simtext that players may encounter is fiction. This appears in a variety of forms that can be defined as popular culture: written and screened texts such as traditional novels, 'Hollywood,' international, and independent films, TV shows, documentaries, short films, webisodes, mashups, video-game introductions, and cutscenes. WWII has been reimagined in numerous fictional forms.

Literary fiction has mined WWII as well. In the English-speaking world, this applies a variety of postures and views. Satire is the lens in Joseph Heller's *Catch-22* (1962) and Kurt Vonnegut's *Slaughterhouse Five* (1969). The detailed perspective of Norman Mailer's *Naked and the Dead* (1948) is a precursor for James Jones's *The Thin Red Line* (1962) and its Pacific focus. Hemingway's *For Whom the Bell Tolls* (1940) reflects his time as a journalist during the Spanish Civil War. *A Farewell to Arms* (1929) recalls his time as an ambulance driver during WWI, establishing him as a major American literary voice beyond a correspondent who covered WWII. These types of serious literary simtexts are on the far side of a continuum that begins with reference documents, then proceeds through technical descriptions of planes, to memoirs and battle histories. The most important respected fictions are wide and global, and thus a potential area of interest for some players.

The event has proven to be more than its world-spanning settings and time period, reaching far and wide into other genres. Orwell's dystopian *Nineteen Eighty-Four* (1949) and its representation of authoritarian socialism proved prescient in its critique of Marxist-Leninist inspired Stalinism, written just after the war from a vantage point that saw clearly what was happening in the Soviet Union. Thomas Pynchon's *Gravity's Rainbow* (1987) is another example, this one published a generation later and looking back at the event through the complexities and disruptions emergent in postmodern culture.

Translations broaden this canvas even more, such as Günter Grass's *Tin Drum* (1962) and Lothar-Günther Buchheim's *Das Boot Roman* (1973), both German-written perspectives that reflect a burdensome weight for postwar Germans that has carried through successive generations. Others such as Michael Tournier's *The Ogre* (1973) look into the event as a way to explore the continued impact of war on human beings. The genre of literary fiction continues to find the event fruitful, with Ian McEwan's *Atonement* (2003) and Michael Ondaatje's *The English Patient* (1993) being two among many.

Even more prolific, popular fiction encompasses a wide spectrum of styles, genres, and modes. Examples are Ken Follett's *Eye of the Needle* (1979) and *Jackdaws* (2002), as well as Jack Higgins's *The Eagle has Landed* (1975) and Alistair MacLean's *Where Eagles Dare* (1967), about aerial warfare. These sit alongside alternative histories, such as Robert Harris's *Fatherland* (1992) and Philip K. Dick's *The Man in the High Castle* (1962), examples of the blend between popular and serious fiction offered in today's complex publishing field.

Serious screened fiction, primarily in the form of cinema and documentary, addresses the war as a pivotal event in the twentieth century. Both have captured the most difficult of the war's subjects, with films that explore the Holocaust having increased in number since the 1990s, with *Schindler's List* (1993) being among the most popular and award-winning.[4] It and others cover complex topics, with an example being the adaptation of Bernhard Schlink's *The Reader* (1997), released in 2008 and directed by Stephen Daldry, which shows how war crimes become a constant form of painful remembrance after the event. These and others form an archive of demanding simtexts that are far outside the scope of most simgame players' immediate interests.

Such serious screened fictions have been produced alongside many popular films and series that focus on WWII. While some series emphasize the humorous, such as *Hogan's Heroes* (1970–1971) and *McHale's Navy* (1962–1966) for American television, many other series for global viewing markets have provided differing perspectives. Beyond the foundational screened simtexts foregrounded later in this study such as *Saving Private Ryan* and *Band of Brothers*, screened dramas have continued to prove popular. The German series *Das Boot* (2018) by Sky Network captures the specific experience of those involved in submarine warfare. Since the turn of the century alone, settings have included the massacre of Nanjing, the broader war in the Pacific, and the German experience on the Eastern Front.[5] Just as emblematic is the increase in Russian WWII films that mythologize the 'Patriotic War,' creating a reconfigured place of popular memory that is very much alive in the minds of contemporary Russians.[6]

The Pulitzer Prize winning novel *All the Light We Cannot See* (2014), by Anthony Doerr, exemplifies a curious but also appropriate example of how literary fiction represents WWII in an exploration far outside the immediate needs of simulated gameplay. Rather, it delves into simulation as a literary device, within a frame that foregrounds early technologies of the simulated imaginary, such as the novel and the radio. Doerr's novel may seem to be an odd choice for a key simtext in my analysis of the simgame–simtext dynamic as a literary fiction, but the novel foregrounds a type of simulation that is represented within the literary imaginary, moving historically from architecture and its sacred spaces to the visual arts, then on to literary texts that use fiction to prototype ideas that can be enacted in the real world. With the development of technologized modernity, more complex technological configurations have emerged both to construct new spaces (an example being VR) and to imagine new ways in which fiction can be created.

A clear analysis of the novel reveals that technological simulation speaks to the importance of this increasingly dominant mode of fictionalizing. Such a novel represents technology as a means of connection, as well as destruction; it asks the reader to see how the imagination, fantasy, and simulated environments work together to create a lived real-and-fantastic space within a major event such as WWII.

In Doerr's novel, these modern configurations of the simulated imaginary appear in the science fiction of Jules Verne and the technological space of his submarine, the *Nautilus*. But the author represents this literary mechanism of an imagined submarine existing within a literary frame as if it were already fading as a dominant mode. Radio features much more in the novel as a mechanism of the imagination situated at the time at which it is set. It is used to tell stories, as well as to wage war; the radio forms a bond between the two protagonists, German soldier Werner Pfennig and blind Marie-Laure LeBlanc. She reads aloud from a braille copy of Verne's *Twenty Thousand Leagues Under the Sea*, the story heard by Werner over the radio.

In the novel, Marie-Laure is displaced from her home in Paris to the seaside town of Saint-Malo, where her uncle has taken her for refuge. She finds there a large house with a radio that is used to send secret messages to the Resistance. Her story is juxtaposed with that of a young boy, Werner, who is naturally gifted in engineering and an expert at radio repair. As a child he heard a man talking in soothing tones on the radio about science and the natural world. He was soon caught up in the war, his gifts for radio repair turning him into a hunter of radio signals—and also enchanted by the voice of Marie-Laure and her reading of Verne.

Marie-Laure's uncle has crafted a miniature city of Paris for her to memorize so she can walk its streets, find her way to the Museum of Natural History, and return home. They must abandon this precious model when they retreat west ahead of the invading Germans, but he makes her another one that maps their new home. The simulated urban space is one she must enter through tactile memorization so she can better navigate the actual world. In a novel set during WWII, at the very beginning of the computer age but prior to the radical social change it brought about, the simulated imaginary is still very much a mental configuration of a material object, rather than being represented as digital simulation. She must remember, using her imagination, the miniature 3D map her uncle has made her, which her fingers touched.

In much the same way as a reader of Verne might remember the written description of the *Nautilus*, the simulated environment must be remembered and the literary imagination triggered to form representations of objects that have never been seen but only felt. At the heart of the story is a pinch of magical realism and an enchanted jewel that is clandestinely transported from the museum in Paris to Saint-Malo. The quest to find it, though, is minimal, its role being to hint at the fantastic in a story that is primarily about the magic of radio, of imagined spaces, and of survival. This novel, then, acts as a sort of internalized simtext, rather than one a player might read and directly relate to history or even to gameplay. Like the most demanding of professional scholarship, it is probably unread by most players, yet it still fits within the category of simtexts that frame the war far beyond what is offered by simgames—for those players intrepid enough to crack open its pages.

While simgames point to simtexts, complex written and screened fiction is probably the genre least penetrated by players. Approaching subtle fiction requires a different engagement than viewing or playing, as does serious historical analysis, even if many of the elements within fiction are utilized in those other modes. Yet the connection can be made, especially if the fiction is geared toward mass audiences. And while the trajectory is often from the simgame to a variety of ancillary simtexts, with the intention of illuminating the game through the reading material, this dynamic provides an involuntary form of approaching the war through through unlikely material such as Doer's novel.

## Technical Descriptions

Of primary importance for understanding the simgame–simtext dynamic is recognizing the postural shift from a literary to gameist mode; instead of focusing on characters in settings working through conflict, as we would in most novels or films, for example, simgames foreground the technologies of war as dominant elements. In a flight simulator, one would expect aircraft to be of singular importance; in a shooter, the weapons chosen are primary elements. In strategies, these mechanisms become abstracted, not into material technologies, but as tools all the same—from policies on how to wage war, to economic measures, to diplomacy as an arena of political pressure and brinkmanship.

In all these game modes, the technologies of war encountered by players require interpretation. This begins with grasping the engineered purpose of the machines/weapons within proper gameplay use for specific situations, such as high-altitude warfare or small infantry squad tactics. For many players, a simgame asks for nothing more than these immediate scenarios, and the interpretive demand ends there. In an FPS, players may be happy mastering particular small-arms weapons so that in multiplayer games they are successful—and nothing else.

But those interested in role-playing their virtual soldiers or pilots might be drawn to more complex forms of gameplay. This can occur in multiplayer servers that provide dynamic campaigns, and also in virtual squads that track details of gameplay successes and failures through after-action reports, which follow each mission and track details. It can also take place if players are less interested in the competitive side of multiplayer scenarios and focus more on single-player games, where you can not only follow the career of your virtual self, but also chart biographical detail, as well as adding your own historical flavor (see Chapters 3 and 4). But this level of historical integration, and its latent interpretation, is secondary to the prevalent and immediate engagement with the machines of war—through technical descriptions.

Along with materials that cover history, biography, and fiction, a wide range of simtexts dating back to before the war that detail the numerous weapons employed by the belligerent nations have been published. Inherent in these detailed technical descriptions are debates over the merits of different technologies—which were best, which had advantages or suffered disadvantages. The debates are often located within particular cultures and their national heritages, and their ways of remembrance.

As mentioned previously (and detailed in Chapter 4), the role of the Spitfire in the Battle of Britain is one example that has become cemented in the minds of the British (and others); it is hailed as a supreme hero that met the challenge of defending England against the attacking Germans and won against the ubiquitous high-flying Messerschmitt BF 109, a feared and effective predator. In military history, the 109 represents prowess of the Luftwaffe because of its production numbers and the number of kills achieved by its pilots. The 'Emil' variant's yellow nose is emblematic of the early machine and its dangerous abilities, even as the Allies developed machines that surpassed it. Alongside the 109 variants, the Focke-Wulf 'Butcher-Bird' 190 entered the war as a devastating blow to early Spitfires (such as the Mark V) that were developed to challenge the 109s. The 190s proved to be one of the most dominant planes of the early to mid-war and are often a favorite in WWII combat sims because of their advanced cockpit and hard-hitting dogfighting capabilities.

The range of texts published on these competing weapons cover all of the different branches of the military, from ground warfare to sea and air. To follow the previous example, the Soviets quickly adapted from being fully outclassed by the Luftwaffe in the early part of the war to producing planes as powerful as the German machines. At the beginning of the war, they produced a variety of solutions for low-level air warfare, such as the Polikarpov I-16 'Rata', a nimble fighter and one of the earliest fighter monoplanes of merit. This was the Eastern counterpart to the Spitfire, being a match for the 109 when piloted well at low altitude. This rivalry began in Spain and continued on the Eastern Front, with the Soviets proving just as formidable with their La-5 FN and later Yak-3; their ground attack solutions were also so effective that the IL-2 has become a symbol of rugged Soviet tenacity, recognized as the Spitfire is as a plane of nimble yet deadly grace.

The Americans also had several aircraft with the same level of symbolism thanks to numerous technical descriptions, from Lockheed's twin-engine P-38 Lightning and its distinctive forked tail and the large barrel-bodied 'Jug,' the P-47 Thunderbolt. Most symbolic is the P-51 Mustang, an iconic aircraft because of its late-war dominance. In the early part of the war in the Pacific, the superior Japanese Mitsubishi A6M2 'Zero' variants, along with the KI-43 series, proved to be a challenge for US pilots because of their speed and maneuverability over the outclassed early Navy aircraft. The simulation of 'Zero' fighters today is based more on anecdote than on meticulous reverse engineering of technical documents or research into actual aircraft owing to a lack of viable research material, another example of how the dynamic informs developers in the interpretation of data just as it does players. It should be noted that the developers of *IL2* over a twenty-year period have noted in a number of comments, interviews, and clips that they work from meticulous sources in detailing their aircraft. [7]

Technical descriptions of the weapons of war are readily available online, but also form the backbone of many published technical volumes. Pen and Sword Books is a UK publisher that focuses on military subjects, with a large catalog of technically focused publications on the same popular level as many online sources. One example directly relates to the arms race mentioned earlier: *Dogfight: The Supermarine Spitfire and the Messerschmitt 109* (Owen, 2015). This is written by an engineer, rather than a military historian, and foregrounds the two aircraft as the protagonists of a battle between two competing machines, especially over England, the Channel, and Normandy. Many books such as this have been published, revealing these aircraft as extraordinary flying machines, or as symbolic 'characters' in wartime aviation stories (for two Spitfire examples, see Price, 2012, and Dibbs and Holmes, 2016; for the 109, see Feist,

Harms, and Dario, 1978, and Watanabe and Grinsell, 1980). Such simtexts marry technical descriptions with dramatic tension, transforming machines into heroic symbols.

But rather than mining such works for their historical accuracy or insights, we see that technical descriptions act as a type of manual for simgame players, allowing them to understand the weapons within a game. And while the details of how these and similar aircraft developed during the arms race as engineering problems to be solved, dogfighting techniques translate from simtexts directly into a simgame such as *IL2*. The content works well enough that it correlates players' learned in-game techniques with those found in simtexts directly related to aviation combat maneuvers.

A seminal simtext that addresses this relationship is Robert L. Shaw's *Fighter Combat: Tactics and Maneuvers* (1985). While this simtext is written for modern military fighter combat, its chapter entitled 'Basic Fighter Maneuvers' points to early air combat simulated in *IL2*. Techniques such as high and low 'yo-yos,' flat and rolling scissors, and lead or lag pursuit are addressed, proving helpful for a simgame such as *IL2* that simulates dogfighting with complex flight modeling. Such a simtext demonstrates that these maneuvers work differently based on specific aircraft capabilities (the sort of information referenced in most engineering-based technical simtexts); the game allows players to take such knowledge and directly see results in game.

The description of combat maneuvers by actual pilots forms a direct link from real-world embodied action to the simulated space of simgames. Yet in a curious example of gameist irony, a transfer of knowledge has happened that even non-pilot players can become 'experts' (in sim flying). An example is *In Pursuit: A Pilot's Guide to Online Air Combat* (Kylander, 2006), the author of which has no combat credentials, not even a pilot's license. But what he does with skill is translate his countless hours of sim experience to guide a new virtual pilot along a path to competency in simulated air combat. He was granted an introduction written by an actual American WWII fighter pilot, Russell S. Kyler, a gracious comment by a veteran who flew fifty-seven missions during the war. Kyler even claims that the reading of *In Pursuit* taught him many things he wished he had known when flying during the war (Kylander, 2006: 5), a sure sign that some parts of air combat are simulated well enough that there is a correlation between the experiences of lived WWII pilots and their imagined reconfiguration. *In Pursuit*, then, is a type of purist manual for simgame pilots who want to master techniques each generation of simgames has refined, and now find powerful simulation in today's computing systems.

This dynamic, in its simplest configuration, can be thought of as playing-as-learning. A more complex approach sees these two aspects overlap, so that what emerges is an experience of the event in which a player is enmeshed in these assemblages of reimagined digital machines and texts. But even more critically, the player engages these historical simulated elements, replacing what was highly dangerous, deadly, and destructive with an appreciation of the past, often for the sake of honoring those who risked their lives, but just as much for the thrill of experiencing a hint of what they faced.

Engineering and technical books of the war function, then, as simtexts of the imagination, rather than simply as game aids. Yes, these texts aid gameplay, an expected use of outside sources when learning a simulation, but they also function in a similar manner to how fantasy literature maps imaginary worlds. Each provides the necessary scaffolding to frame a fictional world or gameplay. These technical books thus become a type of literature in the broadest sense. These popular simtexts, taken as an archive, thus offer a powerful form of knowing in a time of increasingly engineered spaces, moving beyond traditional 'book-learning' into more complex, enmeshed, embodied forms of analog-and-digital interaction.

## Scholarly Works

Following memoirs, literary and popular fiction, and technical descriptions, the most difficult simtexts a player might encounter are those produced by professional historians. Military specialists feature prominently here, but so do historians with a wider range who examine elements outside military operations, tactics, and strategies. The most informative of these merge the actions of militaries, their leaders, and the people affected, while also examining deep motivating factors. Selecting examples to illustrate this topic can only offer a brief dip into the serious historiography of this subject, which is far too extensive for comprehensive comment.

The most exhaustive and difficult yet illustrative simtext can be found in the *Germany and Second World War* series (1990–present) (Maier et al., 1991;

Schreiber, Stegemann, and Vogel, 1995; Kroener, Muller, and Umbreit, 2000, 2015; Boog, Krebs, and Vogel, 2006; Blank et al., 2008; Echternkamp, 2014; Boog et al., 2015; Deist et al., 2015; Frieser et al., 2017). This long-time project by German military historians has been widely reviewed and praised by professional historians as providing a factual analysis of the war in Europe based on deep archival research. It is detailed enough that it serves as a foundational text for a professional historian such as Stephen Fritz, one that has to be interpreted within his own thesis about the war in the East (see Chapter 5 and the introduction in Fritz, 2011). Such a challenging and broad historical account from postwar German scholars exceeds the interests of most sim players, and indeed their patience. Other challenging simtexts beyond the biographies mentioned earlier focus on detailed accounts of battles, primarily showing how the different military operations unfolded, along with their motivations and impacts. These have been published in every decade since the war, with an increase in their number since the Soviet Union opened its archives.

The number of historians writing in these fields is also far beyond the scope of this study. Historians writing in English such as Antony Beevor, Andrew Roberts, Max Hastings, James Holland, and Stephen E. Ambrose form a bridge from the professional to the popular sphere with their detailing of major battles that took place at Normandy, Arnhem, Stalingrad, Berlin, and so on. More academic, and often more difficult, simtexts fall outside this range and are less likely to influence gameplay; they often examine major battles beyond their strategic or tactical impact, with examples being Jochen Hellbeck's *Stalingrad: The City that Defeated the Third Reich* (2016) and its account of the experiences of Red Army soldiers, and the detailed and thorough account of Stalingrad, David Glantz's *To the Gates of Stalingrad: Soviet-German Combat Operations, April–August 1942* (2009).

Other simtexts in this range correct lacunae missing from gameplay rather than augmenting gameplay for most players. Such corrective simtexts offer avenues into the most harrowing of topics, such as issues in moral philosophy. Timothy Snyder's *Bloodlands: Europe between Hitler and Stalin* (2010) exemplifies this mandate with an account of the murder inflicted in Eastern Europe both by Germany and the Soviets. It is but one of many histories that work through difficult topics that are undersimulated in computer games (see Chapter 5). Those who find themselves led to explore such topics will leave the world of simgames for the unsettling realm of humanistic interpretation in which history confronts us with its weighted past. In most cases, though, the distance afforded to players by a mediated, digital experience shields them from uncomfortable investigations into the actualities of war. Still, in the simulation of aspects of the past, doorways are opened for those who are willing to venture through.

## Conclusion

This chapter has argued the centrality of simtexts for the simulated experience that is afforded to players through the simgame–simtext dynamic. It offers the reconfigured historical gameworld as a space where players engage a new mode of agency through their encounters with these texts. Such an engagement separates this new mode from earlier forms, such as those found in traditional literature and history, while still utilizing many of the older form's elements. We see this connection most clearly when recognizing how simgames are embedded in a massive archive of accompanying simtexts. This connection works through the professional sphere's publication of war histories, but even more so through forms of popular memory. The primary substrate for this dynamic is the digital, being the ground upon which simgames function, but how these simtexts are distributed and consumed is also key. This chapter has worked through various examples in order to foreground the primary types of simtexts—from personal memoirs, to histories of battles, to broad histories, to technical descriptions, and even to written and screened fiction.

# 3 Simgames: Shooters

This chapter locates in the FPS a middle ground between the highly simulated environments of simulators, with their cockpits and tank hulls, and GSGs, with their god-like perspectives high above the experiences of individual soldiers. FPS simgames focus on the immediacy of shooting a gun, often without the need for narrative or story to drive gameplay. The case studies in this chapter foreground particular aspects of infantry-based WWII combat, and also create gameworlds in which history can emerge in the background, readily available to be investigated by those interested.

An exhaustive study of first-and-third-person shooters that have been released since id Software's *Wolfenstein 3D* (1992) is far beyond the scope of this chapter. The number of FPS games is numerous, spanning a wide range of subgenres from challenging tactical shooters, such as *Counter Strike* (2000) and its recent 'hero-shooter' variants such as *Valorant* (2020), to survival shooters such as *Escape from Tarkov* (2017). More 'casual' shooters have emerged as well, such as *PUBG: Battlegrounds* (2017) and *Fortnite* (2017), the 'battle royal' mode being a new and popular form that allows players to engage in free-for-all or squad gameplay rather than team versus team focused play. Electronic Art's (EA) *Apex Legends* (2019) works in the same science fiction and fantasy-flavored hero genre as *Valorant* and *Fortnite*, its billion-dollar revenues demonstrating that it is proving more popular than EA's earlier and also successful *BF* series, a game that began as a WWII shooter.

With the first major WWII computer game being released by DreamWorks Interactive, *Medal of Honor* (1999) (*MoH*), WWII-focused FPS simgames developed through a remediation of cinema. Following the success of *Saving Private Ryan*, *MoH* was conceived by Steven Spielberg himself, and the later

*MoH: Allied Assault* (2002) began with players storming the beaches of Normandy, directly providing players with first-time iconic historical experiences lifted from the film. Other studios followed, such as EA's *BF: 1942* (2002), initiating its expansive series that has from the beginning allowed players to play as infantry, but also fly planes, drive tanks, and so on. Its combined-arms gameplay was a ground-breaking approach to comprehensively replicated warfare that ushered in team-based play simulating small-scale and large-scale combat.

Infinity Ward's *Call of Duty* (2003) (*CoD*) series followed in creating fast-paced FPS gameplay, along with Gearbox's *Brother in Arms: Road to Hill 30* (2005), which added a squad-control mechanic that has recently been adopted by Gaijin's *Enlisted* (2020) (*EN*). This tactics-oriented, infantry-based WWII game within their *War Thunder* (2013) (*WT*) engine was originally designed for tanks and aircraft but has followed the *BF* model of combined arms. Many other FPSs across a wide range of modes have been produced, with the *CoD: Warzone* (2020) series proving to be a popular entry, along with EA's return to WWII with the controversial *BFV* (2018).[1] *BFV* faced a backlash when it launched with what appeared to be a focus on race and gender diversity for player customization. This appeared to some players to move beyond historical accuracy. The trailer showed a female soldier with face paint and a prosthetic arm functioning in some critical infantry role. The developers responded via Twitter, explaining their explicit goal to achieve diversity by moving beyond a typical European white male audience. Others have focused on particular experiences, such as *Sniper Elite* (2005), a third-person shooter with its sniper mechanics and the more tactical *Red Orchestra: Ostfront 41–45* (2003–2004) and its Eastern Front focus, which foregrounded the often-neglected Soviet perspective (discussed later).

The period from 1939 to 1945 has drawn the most interest from developers and players, even though games with a Cold War setting and those that focus on Vietnam have also proven popular to American and European audiences. Yet beyond WWII, regional conflicts have also found traction. Games such as *CoD: Infinite Warfare* (2016) and the latest *BF 2042* (2021) are inspired by current events, being grounded more in regional conflicts than national interests as primary mechanisms of war. Games produced since 1989 and the fall of the USSR also prove interesting because of their simulation of particular warzones around the world that people find themselves in today, the life and death reality of their lived experiences being in stark contrast to the digitally mediated world in which one can only lose a virtual life. Rather than seeing the distance provided by literature and cinema, then, aspects of once-lived history are becoming playable even as people in the real world suffer the traumas of regional conflict (van den Heede, Ribbens, and Jansz, 2018).

This chapter is organized around a detailed examination of a few important concepts that clarify WWII FPS combat simgames. It begins with the importance of war-games as precursors to digital computer FPS games, many of which were analog. The move to computer-based games encouraged many developments, primarily in how time and space are simulated. This has not only factored into gameplay, but also into how the past is remembered through such simgames. This chapter approaches these key categories by asking what sort of interpretive process occurs when players seek answers both about how to play a game and also (in the context of WWII simgames) about what may have actually happened.

In this chapter, we see such agency-as-learning in approaches to virtual history, museum studies, and heritage sites, each of these engaged with the challenges of capturing the past meaningfully. Traditional interpretation as a written form that occurs when someone learns of the past through its description is less important in the context of this chapter than the foregrounding of shooter-inflected gameworlds. Although academic classrooms and their requisite teacher–student relationships remain valuable in our digital age of democratized knowledge developed in the popular sphere, the gameworlds afforded through simgames provide particular experiences. This chapter seeks, at the intersection of simgames with digital simulations, the particular nature of these new experiences for players, both in how they learn and how they play.

We see another precursor for this combination of entertainment and learning in reenactment societies, with these examples of embodied popular memory grounding understanding in the lived experiences of soldiers rather than in the broadest views of history curated by professional historians. The tension between approaching history via popular forms versus professional can be mitigated if both sides move toward an inclusive middle ground that draws understanding from both. The academic classroom, then, bolsters informal examinations into games as tools of learning history, while scholars turn their eyes (as I am doing) to simgames as tools of learning and playing, but also as a key category in which the past is reconfigured.

This chapter ends with a focused look at FPS categories that are found in the simgames chosen for this study, primarily *Hell Let Loose* (*HLL*) (2021), *Post Scriptum* (*PS*) (2018), and, to a lesser degree, *EN* (2020). The mechanism of space as created within simgame maps is a core category of analysis, one that provides highly detailed but curated simulated 'snapshots' for key events and battles that occurred during the war, and now in gameplay. These are often already represented in cinematic screened texts, with foundational films and series including *Saving Private Ryan* and *Band of Brothers* (see Allison, 2010, for the impact of cinema on WWII games). These maps also often reflect the dominance of European narratives of the Allied victory, especially the D-Day landings, the move down the Cotentin Peninsula (also called the Cherbourg Peninsula), and the challenges later faced during Operation Market Garden. The German counteroffensive in the Ardennes offers a continued focus on the challenges faced by the Western Allies in this theater.

Even so, this chapter acknowledges that the Eastern Front is increasingly being simulated within simgames, just as WWI is also finding its footing as a precursor war within the neglected mode of FPSs. Along with maps, equipment and character classes/roles are two other key categories that define player experiences within the game, as well as acting as historical foci for players. Taken together, these categories allow an entrance into more than just FPS simgame shooters; they point beyond the immediacy of what is simulated to other clarifying simtexts, which offer insights into both the game and the past.

## Education

The types of popular learning within the simgames examined in this chapter have often been seen as opposing traditional forms of education, such as those contained with regulated curricula. Using digital simgames within classrooms has proven to be a fruitful activity, though, with some examples from higher education opting for a hybrid classroom with a traditional teacher–student relationship, books to be read and analyzed, papers to be written, and, in some cases, games to be played (Sabin, 2012). Professional academics are increasingly teaching history at university level with games as a focus. One class, History in Video Games, exemplifies this shift toward examining the core categories of game mechanics, economics, and cultural bias, among others, to more complex concepts such as determinism and contingency. The effects of combat allow history to be taught through the counterfactual scenarios and theoretical discussion of games (Wainwright, 2014: 2019).

Within such a game-focused university course, two differing places of learning come together through the presentation of simgames: the traditional classroom with teachers or professors providing information, reading materials, quizzes, and tests intersects with communities of players and their broad ranges of gameist materials. There is synergy when academics are also players, and when players stumble across an informative simtext that is produced by a professional or independent historian. Serious simgames, then, can function as subtle teaching aids that cross these boundaries. A GSG publisher such as Paradox Interactive hires historians to work on their titles, as do many other game studios. The object of study (or play) becomes a new site of learning that involves agency alongside interpretation. In contrast to traditional classrooms and their scaffolding, such simgames present historical elements to players, often in the background, opening doorways to the past through any number of activities, from reading to viewing screened clips to study of historical materials, and to play.

Many of these learning elements, though, are ignored in casual FPSs, whose in-game goals are often much more immediate and specific—such as the frenetic desire to engage in a gun fight and earn a 'kill.' This narrow scope can be seen in typical fast-paced 'run-and-gun' shooters such as *CoD*, while at the other end of the continuum a serious simgame such as *PS* demands patience from players. Many teachable aspects are also lost in popular FPSs because of constraints on the map acreage that can be simulated given a computer system's resources. As this chapter demonstrates, a simgame shooter's dominant element is a constrained topological gamespace with soldiers on foot carrying equipment or riding in vehicles within a constrained space. These demarcated maps function as limiting factors but also as areas of control for gameplay, being subtle nods to history as containing specific places of remembrance.

Taking the key FPSs in this study, I traverse their maps, looking at the landmarks that are simulated and asking how they form a tapestry of historical mystery for someone with little understanding of these places or of WWII. Without reaching back to the first games such as *MoH* and the original *BF* and *CoD*, we can see in the current development of serious shooters trans-remediation beyond simple marketing to sell games or beyond the provision of brief introductions for gameplay. We may regard such simgames as playable memorials. These mediated elements point to key effects of the power of cinema, in foundational screened texts such as *Band of Brothers* and *Saving Private Ryan*, for example, with their focus on D-Day landings, the initial taking of Carentan, and the critical areas surrounding Caen (discussed later). We also find a focus within simgames on later moments in the Battle of the Bulge, both from Allied and German perspectives. With a new Eastern Front focus from *HLL*, we also gain the Stalingrad experience (typically ignored by both Western cinema and FPS games).

These transmedia connections function as paratexts that bracket the experience of gameplay; they demonstrate how the simgame–simtext dynamic presents a variety of elements to players that must be parsed as accurate or inaccurate historical elements (Genette and Macksey, 1997). Many of these present simplistic narratives of commemoration that reinforce the mythologies of heroes and deeds. Yet the more complex the game and the more agency afforded in players to alter expected gameplay, the more the dynamic creates a space for investigation into the past. When a player new to WWII simgames first realizes that he or she can play on the German side, something that is a recent phenomenon, a type of interpretive demand is made in parsing the differences (if any) that existed between German military organizations such as the Wehrmacht and the Waffen SS.

This type of learning is complex because the insights gained are uncurated by professional historians who might steer understanding along culturally accepted lines of interpretation. Pieter van den Heede argues that contemporary digital computer games that focus on WWII are "fundamentally transnational in nature, in contrast to many school curricula" (2020: 608); he focuses on marketing paratexts, those elements that sell the game to gamers, thereby expanding the range of elements involved from what is encountered during actual gameplay. He asks what themes emerge when this scope is broadened to marketing materials that frame and represent WWII as an event with a historical past that can be taught to students.[2]

This focus on mediating factors is helpful because it reminds us that we are embedded not only in the technologies we use, but also in relationships of mediation that act as a layer requiring interpretation. Van den Heede recognizes that such mediation situates players (responding to Adam Chapman's developer-historians) as content creators who are in powerful positions to frame particular representations, which then foreground particular thematic elements. "By formulating these themes and developer narratives, game creators partly transform their online community platforms into sites for historical and commemorative expression" (van den Heede, 2020: 610–11).

Expected narratives such as Western triumphalism or the USA's inevitable victory over the evils of National Socialism, among others, are expected in games that simplify WWII to heroes and villains for consumable gameplay that is based on certain cultural/national markets. Van den Heede's approach, though, reveals that across differing genres players gain a type of education into military technologies used during the war—beyond what is learned in traditional historical curricula that privilege a nation's own narrative. He presents this as a pedagogical opportunity to move beyond the particular technologies of arms races into more abstract, critical contexts that require players to reflect on the impact war has on individuals and society. What is expected in such games, these "'battle-centered' developer narratives" (van den Heede, 2020: 615), can give way to human-focused perspectives in which other areas of concern emerge, many of which require careful consideration. For example, within the study of philosophy and history, causality and contingency are key components in understanding war and its effects.

Rather than remaining rooted within a particular game narrative that provides a player with agency, for example by imagining his or her actions as critical in turning the tide of a battle or even winning the war (a simplistic notion of causality), learning of a wide field of human and non-human agents (contingencies) refocuses understanding about the event on many unrecorded or seemingly insignificant moments that may have played a larger role than expected. Players of complex simgames encounter these many contingencies once they follow the dynamic to simtexts, their in-game roles being unexpectedly clarified.

## Above and Beyond

Players of serious FPS simgames are primed for realism that moves beyond well-simulated objects such as machines or environments to more realistic experiences that embed players in the lived experiences of historical agents. This departure from tactics to reality signals a type of critical awareness of the past, presenting players with more challenging gameplay aspects; these are almost memorials to the loss and destruction within war, rather than just challenges within the game.

The sort of realism asked for by thinkers such as Galloway and McCall (discussed later) or even the critical remembrance sought by thinkers such as Ramsay (also mentioned later) have yet to be seen in popular WWII simgames, especially FPSs. While true gameplay simulations of the actualities of the war may continue to be outside the range of player interest or developer possibilities, a VR game such as *MoH: Above and Beyond* (2020) (*AaB*) provides an example of narrative-focused first-person gameplay that maintains many of the shooter-genre's expected elements, while foregrounding fictive elements over purely gameplay challenges. This is a game designed for VR that provides visceral experiences of key moments such as storming the beaches at Normandy. Because this is a VR game, visual fidelity has been decreased because of hardware limitations and the necessity to run the game with a pleasing resolution and a suitable number of frames per second. Still, it provides a different type of experience for players of typical FPSs.

The concept of immersion has been offered by media studies thinkers when they foreground the literary device we have seen in science-fiction stories of holodecks and cyberspace (Murray, 1998). More recently, the concept of presence has emerged as a key factor in situating a person within a believable and well-rendered environment. Regarding both immersion and presence in a simgame such as *AaB*, gun play is one major experience that is taken from shooters, while flying in a bomber and shooting at 109s finds its roots in simulators. There are espionage scenarios that suggest the stealth of earlier first-person games such as *Thief: The Dark Project* (1998) and its later series, where hiding in shadows and sneaking up on enemies replaces 'run-and-gun' techniques. There are also scenarios that require jumping out of planes and shooting from the back of moving trucks, the sorts of heroics seen in many action films.

*AaB*'s attempt at an immersive character-driven experience within its FPS frame is laudable—even if as it fails to address the most difficult of subjects. For *HLL* and *PS*, attention is paid to specific places, classes, and equipment, particular to the expected roles of an infantry soldier. *AaB* offers degrees of focus for these categories while foregrounding spectacular moments of narrative excitement beyond securing the beaches at Normandy, such as playing as a sniper, a bomber gunner, a tank commander, and a commando.

From a historical perspective, both combat- and narrative-focused FPS simgames emphasize machines, classes, equipment, and events. *AaB*, though, tries to capture a subjective experience rather than render a topological game-world, one that leans toward the cinematic. Its focused gaze allows a player to move close to spectacle without truly engaging with it historically or crossing troubling boundaries into the realities of war. *HLL* and *PS* foreground objects rendered as realistically as possible, both in how they appear and how they function. A combination of serious gameplay mechanics and powerful story lines within VR will hopefully go beyond the first steps taken by *AaB*. And if it does, both major approaches should be enhanced as they merge. What is most impressive in serious simgames (and in the attempt at immersive narrative in *AaB*) is the amount of detail added to the environments, a sense that each object has been handcrafted (even if it has not) and that each nook and cranny in the landscape could represent the environment as it actually was, even if limitations remain within expected frameworks.

This type of simulated remembrance is configured from popular memory, one often rooted in the mythology of good versus evil, and one that dominates a Western meta-narrative of heroic victory. This justification has also been part of the *MoH* series since the beginning, and can be seen in Spielberg's particular cinematic vision in which a small band of soldiers risk their lives for one of their number who has lost his brothers, and whose potential death would be seen as too great a sacrifice for the nation to ask of a mother (see *Saving Private Ryan*).

*AaB* attempts to recapture such a past as told by the victorious allied West, its gameplay experience of being in precarious but winnable situations taking precedence over a critical understanding of the past. Even so, thoughtful and innovative portions are unlocked as the player gains access to documentary footage, a technique that reaches back to the beginning of the series. *AaB* provides high-quality interviews with veterans who visited memorials and shared their stories, the developers even traveling to Europe with some of them. Respawn Entertainment also produced *Colette* (2020), a documentary by Anthony Giachinno that was nominated for an Academy Award for Best Documentary Short Subject.

These elements depart from tactics and combat to demonstrate how such simgames can move toward simulating the past in ways that approach careful remembrance by providing simtexts outside gameplay.

## Remediation and Propaganda

Viewing simgames as part of a long trajectory in how we reimagine the past, from our first attempts with oral poetry to tell stories of gods and humans, to more complex epics and romances, later to novels, then to film, and now to a variety of new digital media often in the form of popular games, we are faced with a constant remediation in which parsing what is distinct from what came before proves as difficult as it is ubiquitous. This remediation occurs in FPS simgames and helps to frame the key categories under examination in this chapter, primarily its use of battle maps; these remediate elements from other media, especially cinema, as a way to turn representation into simulation and gameplay into remembrance.

A basic tenet in media studies for understanding the reappearance of earlier forms of representation is that they work through remediation (Bolter and Grusin, 1999). If we accept this process of remediating as a type of reconfiguration, we can also accept it as applying to how computer-game players absorb curated history. This allows us to side-step the question whether they can understand the past with the same depth that is provided by studying the works of professional historians. In so doing, we can then investigate the massive archive of these different forms of remediation. For example, one such approach to the recent past is to view cinema as capturing the nostalgia for different earlier periods, WWII being a favorite (for recent examples, see Shull and Wilt, 1996; Suid, 2002; Brode, 2020a, 2020b). This reconfiguration of the past through elements from cinema that are remediated in gaming often tells us as much about the present as about the past, especially about the myth-making process.

Our understandings of these reconfigurations are limited by current gaming technology, rather than by the potential for simgames to engage with the past (with more advanced technologies, such as VR and haptics, the range of experiences will increase). FPS WWII games are combat focused beyond what we see even in the most action-packed cinema, especially those games that allow for easy spotting of enemies, easy firing and hitting of enemies, easy healing, and so on. These gameplay mechanisms reduce the amount of time spent waiting around or trying to find an enemy, or recovering when killed or wounded. However, newer serious simgames have increased the difficulty of gameplay, making enemies harder to find and spot, shooting much less accurate, and in-game death much quicker, thus increasing the time spent carefully navigating maps and forcing players to reduce their visibility to avoid being seen. A distinction, then, needs to be made between arcade-style FPS shooters such as the *CoD* series and even *BF* and more demanding games. For example, the 'Realistic' mode for *BF2* (2005) was a first step toward the sorts of demanding FPS that I examine here. It was developed to encourage squad play, careful tactics, situational awareness, and lethality. Combat is still the focus, but strategy and tactics now frame gameplay so that a more histori-cally accurate gameworld can be experienced—even if so much of the lived experiences of historical soldiers is not simulated.

Conversely, less serious arcade-like FPSs tend to focus on low-stakes, quick-reaction-time shooting within an easy-to-navigate digital space that is separate from the real world and its dangers. Such in-game elements as slowing down the 'time to kill' are popular in fast-paced arcade shooters, where getting shot and surviving with ubiquitous healing is the norm. Yet this reconfigura-tion of arcade versus serious gameplay reflects how contemporary warfare is becoming more mediated by technology; game and reality remediate in differing degrees with different effects. The issue remains how WWII shooters (casual or serious) reinforce contemporary military activity as digitally remedi-ated from cinema or novels, rather than simply as gameplay that engages the past as visceral action.

In combat-oriented serious shooters such as *HLL* or (even more so) *PS* in which the goal is to win a battle by claiming victory points over an enemy, the focus has shifted from fast-twitch gameplay and ease of survival to squad-play, in which patience and positioning often lead to a burst of activity that sometimes lasts only seconds, especially if a player's soldier is shot. Tanine Allison provides an argument in *Literature/Film and Quarterly* that arcade-style shooters such as *CoD* "better reflects contemporary warfare, providing a representation of the present disguised as the past" (2010: 184). Allison's article was written over a decade ago, quite a long time in computer-game development. Since then, the types of shooters that have appeared have become much more complex. However, what often happens in such popular games as *CoD* and *BF* is remediation grounded in popular cinema that exists for entertainment purposes, rather than being a serious attempt to capture the past; this lack of historical credibility is remedied to some degree in a specific type of programmed framing of the past in serious FPSs, as analyzed later.

Media studies clarifies the effectiveness of media movement across forms or 'convergence' (in this case into a new form, the simgame). The impact of cinema as inspiration for transmedial content into digital computer games is extensive and far beyond the scope of this study. Examples in other genres beyond WWII can be seen in the influence of *Blade Runner* (1982) on cyberpunk-influenced games such as a tabletop version of *Cyberpunk* (1998) and its transmedia, digital interpretation by CD Projekt Red in *Cyberpunk 2077* (2020). We also see this in films such as *Top Gun* (1986) emerging in games such as the *Ace Combat* (1995) series, or in any number of spy games influenced by James Bond films. Outside video game adaptations of films, such as the many *Star Wars* examples that attempt to recreate George Lucas's imaginary world or present its characters, cinematic moments often act as driving forces within digital computer games, promising to capture a touch of the experience witnessed in film. Such overt attempts to capture cinematic drama within a game can be seen when beginning with a film such as the *Scarface* (1983) remake, which gave rise to *Grand Theft Auto* (1997) or even in games such as *Dead Space* (2008), with its abandoned spaceship and horrors from the dark that capture Ridley Scott's xenomorph from *Alien* (1979). More recently, the open-world Western *Red Dead Redemption* (2010), with its harsh brutality, evokes Cormac McCarthy's difficult *Blood Meridian* (1985) in ways that exemplify how transmedia moves from the cinema to gameplay.[3]

The simulation of serious WWII FPSs thus provides a vast canvas of potential understanding and gameplay for players, which suggests rather than demands that they parse the past by analyzing simtexts in the present. While WWII video games have a long history of remediating cinema, the explosion of events being simulated in digital computer games finds its roots in two touchstone screened texts within serious cinema that came long after the beginning of computer gaming, the film *Saving Private Ryan* and the TV series *Band of Brothers*. These provide specific moments enacted in gameplay, especially key battles such as storming the Normandy beaches.

The predominance of narratives of the Allied D-Day landings and invasion has been part of digital video games of WWII since *MoH: Frontline* (2002) first captured the terrifying twenty-minute opening scene of *Saving Private Ryan* and the Normandy beach landings; see also *MoH: Allied Assault* (2002), *CoD 2* (2005), and *CoD: WWII* (2017). The cinematic impact of Spielberg's opening sequence on simgaming cannot be overstated. Rather than providing expansive historical context that covers the detailed differences between the given beaches, or even the differences between the American experiences at Utah and Omaha (the two most Western beaches) and those of the British and Canadians along the other beaches (Gold, Juno, Sword), Spielberg's harrowing representation condenses the hours and numerous lived experiences involving the water crossing, the dangerous landing in which men drowned, the advancing along the beaches into enemy gun fire, into the critical moment for those soldiers who faced continued gun fire from German emplacements that survived naval and aerial bombardment.

Those first FPS attempts at the beach landings were limited by the technology of the time, their visual representations being far inferior to the fidelity and detail in today's simgames. But, just as important as these initial steps toward simulating the visceral experience of capturing Utah and Omaha beaches (i.e., the favorites for simgames), the attention to the historical rendering gamespace of the more recent attempts has redefined these visual advancements. *HLL*'s Utah map simulates a few sectors that were critical during the invasion of Normandy, each offering a very different experience for players who are moving through a landscape that simulates the challenges of navigation and endurance that were faced by real soldiers who fought beyond the beaches. The beachhead, though, remains an iconic space of remembrance, as does the rural area in which the fighting continued.

Along with this spatial game-focused remediation, another way to approach simgames is to view them as a type of sophisticated propaganda, or even a type of marketing for the military-industrial complex, inculcating players with an acceptance of war. Applying such an approach to WWII simgames, for example, one might view Hitler and Nazism not just as the myths and symbols of a political system that drove Europe into war, but as sophisticated examples of the destructive power of marketing when applied to the political sphere. Nazism as propaganda can be considered "as the ultimate, because [it was] the biggest and most historically significant, political marketing and propaganda campaign in history" (O'Shaughnessy, 2017: xi).

Without arguing for the core causes that created a leader in Germany such as Hitler or a politics such as National Socialism, or even what led to the war itself, whether logistics or winning battles, or maybe even a willingness to submit to authority, or, in the worst instances, a culturally embedded anti-Semitism, using the language of marketing proves apposite when we think of swastikas and the SS death's head (*totenkopf*) skull and crossbones as brands, or as Hitler selling to the German people a 'product' comprising myths, symbols, and rhetoric (O'Shaughnessy, 2016). But how helpful is this approach when we recognize that computer games are not just marketed commodities themselves but tools that simulate imagined and configured historical spaces that can be transformed by players through modding? Determining what can be simulated is first a technical issue, but within these developer constraints, players alter the product beyond its original use.

Embedding such simulations and their marketing strategies within a wider matrix of forces related to past military tactics and strategies, or even real-world military practices in the present, shows where a possible contentious overlap occurs. In the most pessimistic case, players are brainwashed into accepting (and embracing) a continued technologized militaristic conflict through the mediated space of screens (Huntemann and Payne, 2009). This grooms players to accept the idea that such a world of war and conflict must exist. A less pessimistic view, though, provides players some agency in resisting such forces, especially when marketed games of war can be modded to resist dominant meta-narratives even as they retain core combat-focused aspects. To take one example, the trajectory that began with *BF2* (2005), then to its realistic mod, 'Project Reality,' then to the *Arma* series (2011), and eventually to *Squad* (2015), demonstrates how players can retool what has been marketed to them into something marketers can actually study for its effectiveness in meeting the demands of a particular player demographic.

What we have is a continuation of theorizing that foregrounds key categories such as ideology, propaganda, discourse, and narrative, coupled with warfare, in a world where products are sold and marketed. Just what is being sold and how much determinacy versus agency is involved is a philosophical issue. At the heart of this is the role of warfare technology in these new media and their effects that go beyond written or screened communication. As detailed later, agential mechanisms exist that afford players not only ways to influence gameplay, but also place them in positions of curated control when they approach the past, even if constraints must exist. The key, though, is in working through the sort of environment that is created and how accurate it is, especially in configurations of the past.

Eugene Pfister argues that a weighty but problematic reconfiguration of these missing historical elements used by Hitler to sell and implement his ideology often occur as a science-fiction reimagining in FPSs, similar to how alternative history works in literature. In the *Wolfenstein* series of games, they developed from the earliest *Doom*-like killing of Nazis in *Wolfenstein 3D* (1992) to more story-driven games such as *Wolfenstein: The New Order* (2004) and the *New Colossus* (2017), with overt imagery that evokes the horror of concentration camps (Pfister, 2020).

Pfister argues for the importance in challenging the whitewashing of the war's most egregious aspects, something that was once 'marketed' to devastating effect. "If we want to remember the Holocaust as a warning for our and future generations, we have to keep this memory alive in our every-day culture, and not only in museums" (Pfister, 2020: 280). To insist that these gameplay lacunae be filled, avoiding the effects of depoliticization, sanitization, and outright erasure, means we open simgames to the worst parts of the twentieth century. In doing so, player agency is provided that goes beyond the already violent actions of militaries killing each other (and often civilians) into areas of genocide. How can gameplay lacunae be addressed without providing this level of repugnant agency? In essence, how can this be done responsibly?

Game developers could focus on the lived experiences of those who suffered trauma, simulating their stories across all nations in the conflict. This would mean, of course, simulating atrocity to some degree. The seriousness of this mandate means that gameplay needs to be rethought as being closer to the experience of literature or cinema, in which one encounters a text that evokes an emotional or intellectual response and should elicit understanding (rather than simply entertainment).

At this point, we are no longer playing a game, but encountering ideas outside the game, among other types of texts, that provide context. The frame has shifted. Developers will somehow need to determine which in-game agency is acceptable for simulated atrocity; justifiable playable agency, then, will allow players to move through spaces that evoke the past in a way that fosters awareness, even in some cases difficult awareness.

It should be noted that *CoD: World War II* (2017) adds a portion of gameplay in which the characters enter a POW camp. I find this attempt by *CoD* as a first step toward engaging with such difficult material, a point I make with *MoH: AaB*. This ending of the game channels cinema, rather than agential gameplay in which a player can truly explore (or somehow attempt to have fun) in a WWII prisoner of war, concentration, or death camp (be it German, Russian, Japanese, or even Allied). It occurs as an epilogue of cutscenes in which the player has minimal control but can look around and even make some critical choices. Just as the entire game channels cinema through keystone films addressed in this book, the final scene parallels *Band of Brothers*, Episode 9, 'Why we Fight.' However, rather than engage with the Holocaust as history, *CoD: World War II* moves through its cinematics quickly in these final scenes. While this attempt offers more than the overt erasure of most WWII games, its cursory nature might as well be full erasure.

This, then, moves us closer to digital memorials than to playable games, even if the two share mechanics. Still, caution is required.

## Maps, Equipment, and Classes

When looking at FPSs as a popular form of WWII (and increasingly WWI) computer gaming, and when looking at serious forms, rather than arcade-focused versions, we see a few major developer choices that frame how players engage with the past. Primarily this occurs with consistent and critical elements, such as battle maps, along with combat-role classes of playable soldiers and their usable equipment (discussed later). The more serious the simgame, the more these elements demand that strategy and tactics become a consideration, but regardless of the combatant (Allies versus Axis), these function across both so that tactics used by the Allies work if one plays as the Axis, even as these are tailored to specifics based on historical weaponry or manpower.

Moreover, these simgames are highly constrained by mechanics inherent in playing games with a computer screen and peripherals. For example, even in the most tactical shooters, key aspects of war beyond the obvious of putting oneself in physical danger cannot be simulated. Even as squad-based communication has increased with sophisticated apps such as Teamspeak, Discord, or in-game systems, non-verbal communication that takes place in tight-knit teams, such as those by special-forces operators who often communicate with minimal speaking, does not occur because players separated via distributed networks cannot engage with these critical non-verbal forms of communication. In many ways, popular WWII combat FPSs are an entry into a historically focused experience for players that is highly constrained rather than a training simulation for real-world combat; by their very nature, as an action-focused experience, FPS simgames have a much more limited scope than simulators or strategy games.

Rather than being single-player narratives of cohesive stories with cut-scenes that dramatize interludes between playable moments, both simgame shooters and simulators in this study center on playable maps of varying sizes with detailed historically simulated equipment and classes. For FPSs, compared with simulators, these maps tend to be smaller because players are on foot or in vehicles and can move along streets and up close to objects. This proximity means that players are able to see their textures, so these objects must be rendered with enough detail to convince. Flight simulators tend to focus less on these 'ground' objects, since much of the time is spent above them. This elevated scope also allows developers to provide much larger maps.

A closer examination of these FPS simgames reveals the importance of such maps as boundaries for both gameplay and as gateways for curated historical awareness, rather than comprehensive understanding. In providing this framed scope, these offer snapshots of history with particulars of key moments or battles rather than a general, abstract understanding of the broader war. Instead of an FPS presenting a player with a map of Europe that highlights where the Battle of the Bulge occurred, then providing dates, key commanders, outcomes, and so on, the simgame case studies in this chapter place a player within a map in a small part of the location for a curated but virtual combat experience, albeit one constrained by the narrow confines of a 2D screen, a computer, its peripherals, and, increasingly, a VR headset.

This important concept of the cartographic snapshot is similar to how an analog map might reveal the coastline of Normandy with the names of the beaches and their areas, in order to foreground the specific landing sites of the coordinated Allied attack (discussed later). These refracted elements become historical markers that successfully represent the importance of particular moments, while simultaneously suggesting that outside their immediate range the war's impact fades. Of course, this is untrue. In-game maps provide this sort of blinkered but manageable refractive quality; they provide limits to a playable area that encapsulates the action and, in doing so, wrongly suggests the war only occurred there.

When one examines how key battles such as the D-Day invasion and the later Operation Market Garden are simulated within FPS simgames, one encounters not only classes of soldiers with properly kitted equipment, but also reimagined and configured landmarks, some of which are taken from cinema rather than documentary photos or film footage, and done so with a layering technique that uses mostly accurate maps, along with their roads, rivers, railways, hills, town centers, and so forth.

With often high degrees of fidelity, these can be overlaid on aerial maps from the time with impressive accuracy. Yet the exact placement of buildings can vary, which allows transmedia to influence such historical simulations. What is being simulated, though, is a virtual gameworld that registers the particulars of once lived places as background elements for an overall effect; this is done to ensure a convincing engagement with gameplay that allows for tactics and strategy, and the thrill of executing one's goals and surviving. This imagined and configured gameworld is entangled with historical resonances that extend from the simgame outward to other media and texts. Accuracy here is wedded to the simulated imaginary to provide a gameplay experience, rather than directly correlate all of its elements with an accurate rendition of the past.

The simulation of well-equipped classes of soldiers moving through developed topologies of game maps, confronting the elements within them, becomes a defining factor in how a player encounters the past. While the maps in a flight simulator are far more expansive in terms of acreage than those of an FPS, covering a variety of different horizontal and vertical configurations for aerial or ground games, or combined arms and so on, the FPS focus on room-scale objects means a higher demand is made on the player's computer, as well as the game servers, in tracking and rendering these objects.

We see these constraints in each of the maps within *HLL* and *PS*, the amount of detail provided to players being enough that the gameworld map-space takes many hours to fully survey, much less learn for tactical supremacy. When a player enters an empty server, he or she has the opportunity to avoid the expected conflict of enemies with guns, and to move through the empty map as an observer (discussed later). This provides a different type of gameplay, one no longer framed by the immediacy of winning or surviving. It allows the ability to learn maps as historical and gameplay spaces, and, if one chooses, experience them as playable digital heritage sites.

Both a historical map that delineates a battle and an in-game map that provides an environment for play shrink the focus for gameplay, whose purpose focuses on combat tactics and strategies of individual soldiers. Such movements of scale are necessary. The narrowing of scope here is similar to techniques used in literature that range across varying points-of-view. The psychological depth achieved in a Dostoevsky novel sees movement from the broadest omniscient understanding to the narrow POV of individual characters. The maps of a combat-driven FPS limit player scope through topological demarcation rather than by highlighting the subjective experience of a character in a story, unlike story-driven experiences such as those of *MoH: AaB*. Playability there is often focused on representing complex characters, human drama, and the past. Yet moving through maps in *HLL* or *PS* is given a new inflection. They become subtle monuments to the conflict, ambiguous and open for investigation, even as they limit historical awareness to particular places.

A simgame such as *EN* sits on the borders between the pure arcade experience of *CoD* and more serious tactical WWII shooters such as *HLL* and *PS*. *EN* is published by the same company that first developed *WT* as a tank and flight simulator after earlier experience with other simulators, such as *IL2: Birds of Prey* (2009). They originally opted for a combined-arms approach, similar to the one *BF* made popular but without the infantry. With *EN*, Gaijin's developers, Latvian company Darkflow Software, offer FPS infantry maps designed for frenetic gameplay where the 'time to kill' is very quick, meaning that when you engage your enemy (and are engaged) you will most likely succeed if you accurately shoot first. Each of its maps are pleated into a wider fabric that evokes the broader picture, but does so through railroaded mini-maps that focus combat and move players progressively through combat areas; they thus hyperconstrain players rather than simulate the more open-world approaches of *HLL* and *PS*, these more demanding simgames providing snapshots of larger areas where historically important battles occurred.

*EN* utilizes many of the same interface elements as *WT*, such as hit boxes on tanks that reveal X-ray-like areas of damage. It also adopts a similar approach with its free-to-play progression system for squads and equipment, its focus on squad advancements based on success in campaigns, and the application of upgrades to their capabilities and equipment. No single-player mode exists. Casual players, at the time of writing this chapter in the winter of 2022, are dropped into the roles of US, British German, Italian, or Soviet soldiers. The maps are limited to Moscow, Normandy, Tunisia, Stalingrad, and Berlin, and the focus is on fast action. These historical gameplay elements work in the background rather than as elements in need of clarification, although curious newcomers to WWII simgames will find differences, for example, in the rapid fire of a German MG-42 compared with its slower American counterpart, the Browning M-1919, and may seek answers regarding the effects of such differences. The MG42 was well regarded and feared by the militaries that faced Germany, some even claiming it to be the best infantry weapon of the war. Military historians often refer to it as a feared weapon. One such quote reflects its effectiveness: "American infantry weapons equaled or outclassed the weapons of their foes with the exception of the German light machine gun, the MG42" (Murray and Millett, 2009).

A defining characteristic of this simgame that separates it from the others in this study is the fact it is a 'massively multiplayer online game' (an MMO) that provides free content; this requires incrementally more time spent in game achieving points, so that increasingly more difficult but more powerful elements can be unlocked. While it focuses on fast-paced gameplay, it demonstrates one area of historical depth beyond the more serious simgames and their focus on creating demanding environments for players. The multiplayer experience of Gaijin's approach in both *WT* and *EN* is one in which players are confronted by detailed 'tech trees' of equipment, initially of airplanes and tanks in *WT*, then later helicopters and ships, and now, in *EN*, infantry-based equipment that can be upgraded and customized. Each nation has its own tech tree, with the machinery divided by tiers and links to detailed information for each weapon. This is an introduction for new players into the history of these weapons, and Gaijin's approach provides depth at no cost to the player, other than time spent 'grinding,' or playing with a mind to advance.

This historical arms-race focus emerges as a secondary aspect of gameplay, overshadowed by the demanding process of upgrading these weapons. Gaijin's original approach in *WT* offered extensive data on the different capabilities of, say, the armament of a BF 109 through its life cycle in which different versions offered different selections, such as the addition of a nose-mounted 20 mm in the 109 F-2, or later versions with a 30 mm cannon. The options for tanks are just as granular, with the different thickness in frontal and side armor of an early Sherman tank versus that of a Tiger 2, for example, reflecting the vastly different protection. Such accurate characteristics can be completely ignored as historical elements in a free game such as *WT*, with its arcade mode—and even in its realistic and simulator modes. The inclusive simgame is designed for quick multiplayer matches that allow you to jump into a plane or tank and find immediate action, regardless of your knowledge of the machines, their histories, and how to use them. And now, with *EN*, you can jump into an infantry squad and take the FPS perspective of an individual soldier on the ground.

The player's experience, though, of a game such as *EN* is much closer to the gameplay of other popular WWII FPSs such as *BFV* or *CoD:WaW*, although it does add a mechanic taken from the *Brothers in Arms* (2005) series in which a player can control a squad. This, in effect, increases the number of combatants on a map, also increasing how quickly one enters a firefight, earns a kill, or is killed. These gameplay elements represent effective examples of playability over the creation of more demanding challenges, which often accompany a sense of greater historical accuracy. The latter demand becomes a critical component of serious simgames, although expectations about how much realism or authentic gameplay mechanics they provide falls short when confronted with how games shield players from the reality and horror of war.

Along with game maps, a focus on classes and equipment is key for simgame FPSs. An entry-level simgame such as *EN* exemplifies how choices by the developers allow players to easily engage opponents within specific combat classes, thereby increasing clarity of roles and, for most casual gamers, enjoyment in playing to specific strengths and weaknesses. As mentioned earlier, *EN* opts for immediate action and continual combat over slower types of gameplay, where squad-based tactics demand careful consideration (e.g., especially, *PS*).

Accepting that simgame FPSs do not replicate in any significant way the actualities of physical violence, they do present certain accurate historical elements through limited simulation. The degree to which they offer this historical ground in an FPS often corresponds to how much care is taken in constructing gameplay elements, such as maps, equipment, and classes. The numerous WWII arcade-like games that can be found on mobile, console, and PC platforms fail to give players a deeper connection with historical contexts for a variety of reasons, primarily that if gratifying and immediate gameplay success requires little understanding of the historical elements in the game, then the past (including its historiography and topography) is less important.

Unlike the granularity of equipment, which can be upgraded to certain degrees, the classes or roles chosen in these serious simgame FPS are much more limited in scope. In *PS* we see the most restrictive approach, with players offered key representative roles within a WWII land-based infantry group, such as a platoon (or squad) of soldiers led by a squad leader who communicates with a commander. These are two critical roles that separate the serious from more arcade-like games, many of which do not make any requirements on players to work as a team. In *PS*, you must be in a squad, and if you lead that squad you must have a mic to communicate with the commander (also with a mic) and your squad.

Other important roles such as a medic, rifleman, machine gunner, radioman, sniper, and engineer can be seen across the simgames, with varying names, but the roles remain very similar. The rifleman engages in tactics to simulate a mid-range type of gun engagement (which allows for medium to longer distances over the close combat of a sub-machine gun). Support often comes from the suppressive fire of a heavy machine gunner. Engineers typically construct elements that allow some advantage, from defensive structures to sapping to artillery placement. Snipers, of course, handle longer-distance shooting and reconnaissance, while medics are often kept in the rear of the squad to heal or revive anyone wounded or dying. Antitank personnel are equipped to destroy tanks. Along with these exist roles such as tank commander and crew, or even mortar and artillery teams.

These roles are generic, but in *HLL* and *EN* you can see the soldiers in each squad as individuals with personalized faces, clothing, and weaponry, another nod that brings narrative toward gameplay so players care more about the lives of their virtual soldiers. These can be upgraded as you advance, the actual members of squad aging through the weight of years of combat stress as a player progresses. *EN* also provides names for individual soldiers. This approach is different from simply focusing on mechanics that allow you to upgrade your classes and roles as you advance, or to upgrade in game by finding weapons caches with no thought about how this relates to a virtual soldier with a name and history.

## Historical Game Space

One key reconfiguration of (war/combat) simgames is how time and space are translated into a player's simulated experience of the past. The assumption is that free-form movement across sprawling maps is expected in an FPS, even those that contain environments that 'rail-road' players along certain paths. The turn-based mechanic that dominated analog war games up until the first computer game *Spacewar* (1961) introduced a continuous flow of action within a constrained environment is still prevalent in many strategy simgames, yet shooters and simulators bracket out real time in manageable periods, usually over map-spaces that capture particular places and events. An important issue here is how such maps and their delimiting of space encourage or discourage accurate awareness of the past through constraining elements that reduce the past to a few key battles or places. While this narrowing of focus exists, such maps and how players move through them provide contexts that highlight specific experiences (discussed later).

Debra Ramsay presents the evocative idea of 'smearing,' in which time and space in simgames, such as *BF1* (2016), act as a liminal process that transforms these core categories for players and performs a helpful type of reconfigured remembrance (Ramsay, 2020). She focuses on *BF1*'s use of single-player content, which is extensive for a typical multiplayer game. This narrative focus is in marked contrast to the lack of single-player content in this chapter's case studies. Thus, in-game single-player narrative and its reliance on time and space as key categories point to how shooters in this study are less about storytelling and the framing of characters and their conflicts, and more about experiences afforded to players that reconfigure the past.

Ramsay notes that the issue of trauma is a concern because digital computer games ignore this unmistakable, and ultimately horrific, aspect of war. Yet she sees in *BF1* ways in which its narrative does represent trauma. I agree with her assessment that in representing trauma itself a process of liminal transformation occurs, at best distantly painful for those who would remember, at worst a mechanism for more trauma.

I can see in future FPS-oriented simgames with narrative focuses a space for such traumatic simulations and how they might reconfigure aspects of war that current simgames avoid, even if today multiplayer experiences have yet to simulate trauma in any meaningful gameplay way. In *HLL* and *PS*, for example, when you are shot, your screen greys or shutters into a blurry mess to replicate suppression fire. If you are wounded, it reddens, and you hear your virtual avatar's ragged breathing. If you are too wounded, with a quick tap of a key you can retrieve bandages and heal yourself, or call for a medic who can aid you. Such unrealistic elements are an abstracted, time-saving gameplay mechanic that reduces trauma to a few seconds of recovery, rather than weeks or months, or even a lifetime. Simulated trauma in these instances is truncated to a few brief moments of digital simulation.

Where Ramsay's analysis helps is in demonstrating how narrative and its ability to represent (or simulate) dramatic moments and choices offered to players provides this space for 'smearing.' I find her metaphor poignant because it evokes trauma if one thinks in terms of the bloody results of violence, and also the unexpected and sometimes pleasing configurations from creativity that comes when elements move across each other in unexpected ways.

She even applies the term to how emotional states are smeared between gameplay and actual war—for example, in the thrill of hitting a target, as attested by actual individuals who fought in WWI, with the thrill of hitting a virtual target in a game. This speaks directly to the idea that players of simgames are afforded experiences both rooted in the imaginary and the historical. They provide gameplay fun, along with accurate contexts that encourage awareness. These sometimes smeared spaces thus also provide another important way to conceptualize how imagined but reconfigured simgames function by making interpretative demands on players. The dynamic between game and text acts as a ground for awareness because of the increasing movement between the two, especially in historical simgames where the historiography of an event such as WWII is so massive.

As I argue throughout this book, the framing of simgames within historical gameworlds located in a technologized twenty-first century accepts that a variety of simtext forms exists, many of them digital alongside analog. And rather than use traditional critical methods, such as found in the study of cinema or literature, the dynamic between simgames and simtexts asks us to answer how it creates experiences of the past, with differing degrees of accuracy. In essence, it places a technologized phenomenological subject-player within a gameworld. In such a place, the dynamic works for such players, especially when viewed in full relief, and becomes its own sort of medium, one that reconfigures history through several primary abstract categories—that is, time, space, agency. The FPS as a simgame form, then, refracts these abstractions even more, especially in its focus on classes of soldiers with specific equipment traversing maps of important battlefields.

Space functions as a controlling idea for FPSs, even though it works for each of the three types of simgames analyzed in this study and even though the virtual, imaginary, simulated gameworlds in each have different scopes. In a flight or tank simulator, you are literally stuck in your cockpit or hull (except for a few seconds when you may have to bail out and hang precariously from a parachute or try to exit a burning tank), while in strategy games you primarily exist outside traversable space and, instead, look down on an abstracted map of the entire gameworld. This is complicated in games that mix the broad perspective of GSGs, such as the *Total War* (2000) series, with the ability to focus on the perspective of troops on the ground. The scope here shifts from the broad to the narrow.

In an FPS, this spatial awareness begins by peering beyond your nose to explore the environment as if on foot. You can enter buildings, vehicles, and trenches, for example, seeing rendered objects full of details. The effect is immediate, especially compared with a strategy game where you are positioned outside these spatial constraints so that you can better grasp the organizational elements needed for play. In this sense of player positioning, the size of a map is less important than the level of detail experienced. In a flight simulator the spatial map for gameplay can be huge, much larger than a typical FPS map, because when you are flying at 430 kph indicated airspeed at 10 km altitude you need much less detail rendered on the ground than if you are walking along a path, looking for ways to navigate through rubble. (The visual fidelity of a game such as *HLL* means every blade of grass or texture on a wall can be scrutinized, and must be rendered. These will not be seen even 1 km from the air.)

This player positioning within rendered space proves to be fertile ground as a controlling idea problematized by thinkers interested in agents and their goals. These player-agents function within gameworlds alongside constraining elements that allow for strategies and choices that arise from within them (McCall, 2020). This combination of agents positioned within rendered game space, then, is helpful in differentiating the primary simgame types in this book, even as I shift the focus to the sort of experience that emerges from this positioning for players for each type. For example, Jeremiah McCall details the different types of agents that we see in historical games, foregrounding the non-historical agent. These, like those found in the *Assassin's Creed* (2007) series, are represented as historical within the game even though they never existed. A player takes a third-person perspective as he or she guides the playable protagonist Enzo through the game story. The simgame FPSs under examination in this chapter present the player with scenarios devoid of historical agents; just as much, the experience of being an anonymous agent in an FPS simgame situates the player in the central role, not as a protagonist within a story, but as an abstracted role within a combat scenario. One becomes a sniper in an elite Wehrmacht unit, a machine gunner, a recon soldier, a medic, and so on.

In FPS simgames such as *HLL* and *PS*, a player's character is not even given a name. *EN* (2021) is a rare exception. It does provide you with names of the individuals within your squad, all of whom you can play. This is one step closer to integrating narrative elements that create continuity for players who may feel more connected to their in-game agents. Other players see you by your virtual soldier's username. You are, in this sense, closer to the idea of what McCall labels an archetypal 'player agent' (2020), even if you are still anonymous. The very classes assigned to such players are standard types, be they squad leaders, machine gunners, recon snipers, or medics.

This is important for simulators and FPSs whose players fill roles, while McCall's idea of a 'collective agent' describes strategy games because it separates the individual experience from that of how a collective works in which a nation must marshal its resources often directed by governments. Individual experience is less important in strategies; the player controls abstracted forces, such as economic groups or military logistics, broader processes than those of the lived experience of an individual soldier.

Of importance is how simgames construct game spaces that provide some form of accurate historical understanding. Formalistic accounts such as McCall's and others are helpful in abstracted categorization of key elements such as agents, roles, goals, resources, and so on, as well as in a refocusing of historical games away from asking if they reflect actual history and, instead, ask "how does the overall historical problem space, including genre conventions, shape how this component functions and, accordingly, presents historical content" (2020).

In resisting looking to simgames for a direct correlation with historical fact, McCall's approach recognizes the limitations of these virtual game spaces, as he calls them. But I would widen the scope beyond what is simulated for player-agents directly within a simgame's virtual, playable historical space; that is, beyond the game itself and outside to other spaces. These spaces beyond the game are often in the form of materials that require interpretation, such as books, videos, and films, simtexts that add to the experience in a wide variety of ways, from providing in-game information to clarifying aspects of the war itself.

Yet developer-curated boundaries disappear with the dynamic, which allows for new ways of understanding once a player leaves a gamespace to widen the gameworld with simtexts. For example, a player in a serious FPS may have no idea what the different historical infantry roles entail until placed in a squadron and told to be a medic. You may not have binoculars or an automatic weapon; if you are in a US squad you may be offered a semi-automatic M1 Garand rather than a single-bolt action M1903 Springfield; you may not have any medical supplies or you may have a kit. These specifications become evident within gameplay as historical once the key categories are understood through a bit of study.

Another important question that players of serious simgames discuss is how the developers can do a better job in adding accurate historical elements. This drive for more 'realisticness' (2006: 72), as Galloway writes, can be seen within simgames across all three major genres, especially in the settings that provide such granular realism from the developers, as well as from the modding communities. We see this with *PS* most clearly, itself based on *Squad* (2015), which was a reworking of an earlier realistic 'Project Reality' mod from *BF2*. In contrast, *HLL* was built from the beginning to be a more serious game experience than earlier WWII shooters such as the *MoH* series. Complex tactical elements are designed to increase challenge and to directly reflect a historical awareness of the difficulties involved in wartime combat. Its realisticness is focused on this type of gameplay experience.

## WWI and The Eastern Front

A close look at core categories in FPS combat simgames reveals a few commonalities that reflect an attempt at curated historical authenticity and are framed by public memory of both world wars. These have been undersimulated in games of WWI, as well as the Eastern Front of the German-Soviet War of WWII—both being corrected across a number of simgames. Many of these simgame commonalties find their roots in the military history of these two world wars, rather than other conflicts. Yet Andrew Wackerfuss notes in *Playing with the Past* (2013) that "there is no Battlefield 1916" (2013: 233), a clear indicator that at the time of his article, WWI was still highly underrepresented in the genres of FPS and third-person shooters. I would add that the Eastern Front had also been mostly overlooked. However, this has been corrected, much more so for the Eastern Front than WWI.

Representing WWI has proven difficult from a gameplay perspective; a challenge exists for developers when balancing authentic experiences with those that are also fun (and possible) to play. We see this attempt at balancing in a game that answers Wackerfuss's challenge that no real *BF* FPS exists for WWI; that is, *BF1* (2016). As mentioned earlier, Ramsay analyzed it in relation to how it used its single-player mode to approach trauma as represented in gameplay, but it can also be looked at as an early example of a simgame that provides a particular gameworld for players, especially when compared with more serious WWI simgames.

*BF1* is a recent simgame set during WWI, but one that makes many concessions to gameplay over authenticity, while *Beyond the Wire* (2020) (*BtW*) is an indie WWI simgame created in the same engine as the modern-combat shooter *Squad* (2015) (with an engine also used by *PS*). The more popular *BF1* was developed long after the *BF* series began, with several other iterations located in Vietnam to modern and near-future science fiction-based conflicts, examples including *Battlefield Vietnam* (2004) and *Battlefield 2142* (2006). As Wackerfuss notes, within the limited scope of aviation simulators and their tendency to reduce the war to what happened in the sky, FPSs have their own constraints, many of which (as *BF1* does) fall on a spectrum between 'run-and-gun'-style arcade shooters and more tactical variants that require slower movement and action (an example being the earlier *BF2* realistic mod, 'Project Reality').

Balancing narrative cohesion with historical authenticity is difficult, but is attempted when games introduce complex single-player story lines that must be engaging. As Ramsay also notes, *BF1* provides this narrative focus, even though it still centers its player experience on a robust multiplayer mode with its maps, classes, and equipment, this central form of gameplay extending back to *BF 1942* (2002). The difficulty in such a delicate balancing act can be seen when looking at those core categories such as classes and equipment and how well they balance gameplay and history. In this sense, *BF1* has been criticized as fun but unrealistic because there are too many varieties of guns, together with ubiquitous automatic weapons and fast-moving tanks, although it certainly achieves some degrees of accuracy. It offers a type of narrative drama by broadening the war to its global scale to tell untold stories, rather than just rehashing expected locations at Verdun and Somme for a white, European audience.

Its single-player episodes highlight this balancing attempt by the developers to capture some of the elements usually lost in historical FPSs, such as a too narrow scope that only looks at the experiences of one individual or group (usually the Americans as representative of the Allies). To counter this, *BF1* uses an anthology approach to these episodes that spreads unconnected stories of soldiers across the war, most of which are tragic. In the very first episode, called 'War Stories,' you are told you are not expected to survive even as you are commanded to hold several positions, each one overrun, and each time the player dying and learning the name of the fallen soldier. The horror and loss of the event works as a thematic element, one that resists the tendency for FPSs to simply be about shooting guns at enemies.

An important monograph within historical game studies, Chris Kempshall's *The First World War and Computer Games* (2015), demonstrates how cultural memory of a traumatic event such as WWI is both fragmented and contradictory, and that, as in other forms of popular culture, games have their own inflections. Kempshall is helpful in a number of ways. He echoes the understanding that most popular war games, influenced as they were by foundational screened texts, such as *Saving Private Ryan* or *Band of Brothers*, often replicate a simplistic view of morality within the war:

> In the same way that Second World War films can explore both the hellish nature of warfare whilst set against the justifiable necessity of stopping Nazi Germany, the games that are then inspired by them also reproduce this environment. It is a world of very pure and defined boundaries between right and wrong. (Kempshall, 2015: 21)

Kempshall details many 'indie' games that resist the pressures demanded by triple-A games designed for a broad market, while I have chosen WWII games that have a shared ambiguous tenor in their presentation of moral winners and losers. In each simgame that I have chosen, a designed neutrality (some might consider this to be an overt ambiguity) allows players to choose sides separately from moral convictions over the right and wrongs of the war's belligerent nations, ideologies, and commanders. We see this not only with WWII simgames, but also with those that have been and are now being developed for WWI.

Since *Wolfenstein 3D* (1992) first inaugurated the celebratory shooting of 3D Nazis, the Germans have often been posed as unplayable enemies. Even as recently as *AaB*, this perspective has continued because of the narrative that most WWII games employ, with (primarily Allied) good triumphing over Nazi evil. But more serious simgames allow for the Wehrmacht or Luftwaffe to be playable, rather than the most criminal of organizations such as the SS. The encounter (or lack thereof) with the swastika and National Socialism's most nefarious groups is often a first moment of interpretive demand, even more so when it is erased or replaced rather than actually used (which is rare).

To take one curious possibility, when the swastika is seen on the side of a Finnish Air Force Brewster Buffalo as a hook-cross, this might cause confusion and instigate investigation. The player is then pointed outside the game for clarity. It had been used as an ancient symbol in the form of a blue swastika on a white background since the force's inception in 1918, long before Hitler's unfortunate appropriation. A quick Google search reveals a curious historiography: it was dropped after the war but used in some instances, then finally removed for good in 2020. Yet Finland had its own form of National Socialism and aligned with German National Socialism under Hitler's rule. This sort of historical context requires clarity for any player who is interested in understanding why the Finns used a different colored swastika.

As Kempshall and others have noted, problematic gaming elements related to the war's most egregious crimes (e.g., the Holocaust, fire bombings, use of the nuclear bomb, and a wide range of horrific war crimes) are absent in popular computer games, as are other aspects of war, from needless slaughter of civilians to deprivations and traumas suffered through prolonged exposure to conflict (see Chapter 5). The particular FPS case study simgames I have chosen also do not simulate such difficulties, their scopes being too focused on combat tactics and strategy to directly address them, but their erasures are also owing to legal issues such as the banning of Nazi imagery, as well as development choices about which segments of the conflict should be simulated with workable gameplay and which should not. Germany lifted its ban on Nazi imagery in 2018. An argument can be made that a strategy simgame such as *HOI4* consciously erases horrific aspects of the war, such as the Holocaust, even though it claims to represent the major political and military forces that nations employed in their broadest strategies and tactics (see Chapter 5). And even in the shooters and simulators, Nazi imagery is absent along with any references to their politics.

Kempshall recognizes that, unlike the complex moral ambiguities that the cultural memory of WWI raises, everyone believes in most WWII games that the Nazis are the 'bad guys.' While this is true for the bulk of WWII games, in recent 'serious' games you are often faced with fighting the Wehrmacht or Luftwaffe, rather than Nazis. This erasure of National Socialism can be seen when SS units, if seen at all, are often underrepresented or simulated without their symbols.

In FPS simgames, this removal of politically motivated units locates the conflict at the level of the individual soldier, who is anonymous in most cases—even though some games such as *EN* give them fictional names. This myopic scope reflects a desire to tell the stories of soldiers rather than those at the level of villainous world leaders and their ideological-driven crimes. We are asked to imagine such history as a lived experience by individuals, rather than as a battle of political ideologies forged by supposedly 'great' men and their destructive ambitions. Strategy, then, becomes a way for simgames to differentiate themselves with genres of simgames, but also as a way to remove the difficulties of politics from the game. Rather than cultural or ideological strategy, strategic thinking becomes one of either map control (in shooters and simulators) or military planning, execution, and logistics (in strategy games).

Like Kempshall, game historian Adam Chapman asks an important question related to Erik Champion's concern over games being meaningful (discussed later) and Ramsay's interest in war games and trauma. Chapman is concerned with popular history, erasure, and computer games of the world wars, arguing that because of limitations within such games, as well as the sensitive nature of the events, they do not fully engage with traumatic memory as a form of historical representation. When his article was written in 2016, the indie tactical WWI FPS *BtW* had not been released. Chapman focused on a variety of earlier computer games, and with the use of Goffman's frame analysis worked through fifty-eight WWI games to see what sort of collective memory emerges and, therefore, what sort of cultural memory appears within popular history (as seen in his extensive list of games).

Chapman's readings of WWI historians, along with his own understanding of the event as a context within a wider ranging historical discourse, presents certain aspects of how the war is told as critical to how we understand it. Trenches come to mind. They represent a dominant element in the narrative of WWI that forms a powerful image of suffering in mud and gore. This sort of recurring symbol finds itself embedded within a larger spatial field, this other dominant element being the devastated no-man's-land of artillery-blasted landscapes between trenches and their combatants. This can be seen dramatized in the recent Netflix version of *Im Westen nichts Neues* (*All Quiet on the Western Front*) (2022). It represents with the power of cinema the blasted landscapes of no-man's-land and the mud-covered soldiers living in sodden trenches.

Since this binary of trenches and no-man's-land, punctuated by the suffering of the soldiers who lived within them, constructs the prominent collective memory of the war, Chapman's analysis seeks such elements within computer games to demonstrate their historical facility in representing them.

> Those WWI games that visually represent the experience of frontline infantry soldiers, so central to the popular memory of WWI and to which the other important imagery (no-man's land, trenches, barbed wire, gas, mud, rats, remains etc.) is inextricably tied, have been categorised as engaging this memory. (Chapman, 2016: para. 6)

Since Chapman's article was written, a few developments in FPS simgames have occurred, notably the increased 'seriousness' of computer war games analyzed later, such as *HLL* and *PS*, and just as recently *BtW*. *BtW* is notable as the first tactical WWI game that provides large maps with servers that can handle up to one hundred players at a time. While the game is in early access at the time of this writing in the winter of 2022, it follows the type of game-play associated with the modern tactical shooter *Squad* (2015) (built from the same game engine as *PS*) and, critically, demonstrates a much more granular simulation of Chapman's two requirements for cultural memory in computer games: some sort of effective approach to trench warfare and a replication of the dangerous space of no-man's-land.

Playable factions, so far, are the French, Canadian, German, and Americans, with no good versus evil thematic framing. Unlike in *BF*'s recent attempt at WWI combat, *BF1*, *BtW* provides realistic weapons and tools, limiting a player's ability just to pick up an automatic weapon (which would not have been readily available) and begin mowing down enemies. This is a game where the brutality of the event is attempted in its particular simulation elements, where even melee has its own mechanics beyond those often found in a typical FPS. It also does not shy away from the use of chemical weapons, even offering chlorine. The landscape is crisscrossed with complex trench systems, smoky and blasted wastelands, and command centers deep in enemy or friendly territory.

While it attempts to capture details of trench warfare and the dangers of entering no-man's-land, the game both addresses aspects of our collective cultural memory and minimizes certain difficulties in favor of gameplay. For example, the idea that a player would be happy to join a group on a suicidal attempt to leave a trench and rush 'over the top' into no-man's-land only to be mowed down has not been lost on the developers. Such challenges, while historically accurate and a salient part of our popular memory of what most marks the timbre of WWI warfare, do not lend themselves to entertaining gameplay beyond an attempt or two. As is noted several times in this study, so much of actual war is not simulated, from the extreme boredom of long moments of inaction, to the true terror and trauma of real violence that is associated with massive explosions or constant gunfire, and to the long recovery times often required after injury.

These games, though, have varying approaches to wounding and death, and most have some sort of recovery. In arcade shooters, such as the original *Doom* (1993) or *Quake* (1996), you simply ran through an icon that gave health. In more recent games such as *BFV* (2018) and *CoD:WWII* (2017), a number of quick healing techniques allow a player to return to the fight with little difficulty. In *HLL* and *PS*, you can be killed outright with no chance of revival from a single well-placed shot. Both games, though, provide some form of bandaging; but the process is simply that of taking a wound, bandaging oneself, and then returning to battle, sometimes with full health, sometimes with half, sometimes with some sort of negative penalty to shooting or moving. All the actual trauma and terror is excised. For an important anthology on cultural memory, see Erll and Nünning (2005); Olick, Vinitzky-Seroussi, and Levy (2011) is also useful.

As with WWI in general, the environments of the Eastern Front in WWII have often been underrepresented in computer games, a phenomenon that has been brought about by marketing pressure over the last three decades, in which appeal to Western audiences has been regarded as central. The Western Allies have had the most told stories, which has resulted in these becoming games, and then being sold into a primed market that is ready for tales of Allied victory.

This dominant inflection has shifted in the last decade as Eastern European and Russian developers have pursued the Eastern Front as a place in which the war was won and lost. The *Red Orchestra* (2006) (*RO*) series of FPSs was a rare example by an American company, Tripwire Interactive, that resisted the dominant trend. It was first released for *Unreal Tournament 2003* as *RO: Combined Arms* (2003–2004). Its *Ostfront 41–45* version came a few years later in 2006, with *Heroes of Stalingrad* in 2011. It added an expansion, *Rising Storm*, in 2013. This latest version was released over a decade-ago, leaving players interested in the region with little in the way of Soviet-focused gameplay. Public memory has shaped what has been simulated in FPSs, as well as what has been ignored. And this is changing.

Since the early days of *RO*, no popular FPS simgame was released with any real impact that offered FPS tactics in the Eastern Front until the makers of *WT*, Gaijin, released *EN* in early 2021. It offered a 'Battle of Moscow' map, focusing on the more-rural outskirts rather than the city and centering on environs around a monastery with rolling hills and wooded areas. This was a curious choice as an initial map, one that forewent the hoped-for blasted destruction of Stalingrad; however, this missing FPS Stalingrad experience has been addressed in *HLL*.[4]

With the release of *HLL*'s update 10 in 2021, the indie simgame moved from three years of 'pre-released' game versions that saw nine earlier updates consistently add new maps, features, and elements. With the simgame moving from this testing phase into its official version, it added the often-neglected Eastern Front and a focus on Stalingrad and Kursk. This demonstrated how the range and inflections of public memory in digital war-gaming is shifting away from a Western-dominated narrative that typically only focused on the USA and its allies invading North Africa, Italy, and Normandy and the key events that followed for what has been often overlooked or even downplayed: the crucial role the Soviets played in the east and their costly resistance to Germany's invasion, in particular how Stalingrad proved to be a pivotal moment that saw Germany's first major and (possibly) most impactful land defeat (see Chapter 5).

The challenge for FPS simgames that hope to capture these underrepresented environments is how to best simulate such iconic battle space; they require detailed maps of pivotal locations whose scope (and, therefore, perceived historical impact) must also be limited owing to the number of rendered objects required to fill the space. A focus on the urban warfare of burned-out buildings that characterized the ruins of Stalingrad was chosen for *HLL* (along with another Eastern Front map that captures the open areas required for tank battles in Kursk), and recognized as a major challenge because of how many objects had to be rendered, even if constrained.

*HLL*'s Stalingrad map contains a detailed and textured but limited portion of the city, rather than its entirety, which can be seen from the air in a simulator such as *IL2*. This truncated map in *HLL* centers on a train depot and intersection but provides some key historical places, such as Pavlov's house, a symbol of resistance that sat in the center of the city with a Soviet garrison maintaining it for several key weeks. There is also a nearby brewery, along with what is called the 'L-shaped' building, while others such as the important grain elevator are missing. The experience here for players combines navigating the verticality of blasted buildings with their open windows or missing wall sections with the wide streets of the city and its detritus that provides cover for both sides, rather than a full recreation of the city and all its landmarks.[5]

Kursk, on the other hand, offers another map that represents a historical place of remembrance embedded in the resistance of the German invasion. It is an archetype for one of the largest battles in the war, and one that exemplifies mechanized warfare in which tanks proved crucial. Rather than the burned-out urban environments of Stalingrad, open fields and ridges allow for more range and visibility, while still offering plenty of trench systems and their fortifications for infantry to attack. A key moment in the Soviet defense during the German-Soviet War, after others such as Leningrad, Moscow, and Stalingrad, centered on this area, especially the 'salient' or bulge that pushed west through Kursk. Southeast is Prokhorovka, another key place of armored conflict in the larger battle for Kursk, where the Germans had a chance to encircle the armored Soviet divisions in the north.

What we see in both maps is a limited portion of the particular topographies, with care taken in capturing an overall feel of the general environment. Rather than directly recreating landmarks as direct memorials to specific moments or places, these maps hint at what could be achieved if a wider landscape was rendered. Yet, even so, they point to how such spaces function, especially when care is taken in recreating, as much as possible within game constraints, remediated snapshots that work in a wider scope of virtual heritage.

## Virtual Heritage and Reenactments

One accepted approach to understanding how we reconfigure the past is through these elements of digital history and virtual heritage. It asks, in essence, how we use computerized forms of history such as reconstructed sites to understand the past. This focus on virtual history and heritage, along with simulation, augments gameplay as a source of entertainment or diversion into a direct confrontation with historical artifacts that references the past for an educational purpose.

The link between a narrative simgame such as *AaB* and the experience of a virtualized museum tour comes to mind, where the analog and digital combine to form a unique experience of the past.[6] Historical awareness through these digitally and materially mediated encounters remains an important technique to approach the past. When adding games, we see a concern by game formalist Erik Champion that "we do learn from games, but we don't necessarily learn meaningfully" (2015: 154), an assertion that gameplay provides too many constraints on players' engagement with the past to matter.

I am sympathetic with a critical approach to virtual history that raises consciousness across a variety of disciplines, history being only one, or even foregrounds current social and cultural issues. Yet I see meaningful learning occurring in computer simgames over, say, what happened during the Battle of Britain or at Stalingrad or in the Ardennes. If at all, learning occurs obliquely, but it does happen. My approach is focused on the phenomenological experience of the player, rather than on degrees of vetted physical and mental training; this experience that teaches unexpectedly is interesting because it is grounded in a particular curated gameworld that refracts aspects of the war, while inadvertently pointing players toward spaces of clarification. We see this in how gameplay works within a larger field of heritage studies and digital memorials, and the mythologies they encourage.

To take one example that informs shooters, simulators, and strategies, and is used throughout this book, learning about how the RAF resisted the Luftwaffe in 1940–1941 forms a powerful narrative of resistance that has emerged across a variety of media, infusing British culture with notions of heroism and perseverance. One encounters symbols such as the nimble but mighty Spitfire and the overlooked but effective Hurricane, about key decisions such as the formation of the 'Big Wing,' or construction of the seminal radar defense network. These elements are often assembled into a foundational story, one that forms a mythology that requires interpretation and can be tied into key texts, such as Churchill's speech to the House of Commons on August 20, 1940, in which he claimed that "never in the history of mankind has so much been owed by so many to so few."[7]

Stalingrad, as well, forms a core mythology for contemporary Russia as the singular moment of their 'patriotic' war in which so many millions of Soviets were killed. These sorts of claims and perspectives are culturally located, with public memory often at odds depending on whose story is being told. The increasing use of WWII within Russia as an event of remembrance, which memorializes the actions of individuals in the past, may be internalized quite differently for players in the Baltic region or Ukraine than for a player in Moscow. Attempts have been made recently to see beyond the rhetoric of political remembrance to learn about such a battle from the perspective of the Soviet infantry soldier, a task that proves difficult because accessing primary materials is sparse. See Hellbeck (2016) for first-hand Red Army accounts by those who experienced the battle's front lines.

Issues of interpretation still arise when we encounter less critical questions than how different cultures perceive a war, such as what happens in game when a player masters a particular weapon within certain combat scenarios or the battle tactics that were used by the Wehrmacht versus Soviet infantry on the Eastern Front. Rather than make a critical demand that seeks how meaningful this learning is or whether it encourages rigorous interrogation of the past, an encounter with the past occurs through simgames, often accompanied by tertiary simtexts. This is internalized in some way that enhances gameplay either through in-game techniques or simply through a greater appreciation of the historical context. The past is reconfigured, then, along a multiplicity of pathways, some critical, some less so. This variety of learning is expected because history is now so often approached from outside the confines of the professional academy, and learning has been democratized far beyond the control of gatekeepers.

When a historical game theorist such as Champion writes, "we must also work out ways to make them [games] more meaningful" (2015: 154), 'serious games' that do more than entertain are foregrounded as games that should become socially responsible in terms of the past and the present. A focus on player experience rather than this admirable but difficult mandate, though, reveals a wide range of potential inflections or reconfigurations of the past that push up against the 'meaningful' without fully embracing it in the same degree as, say, our most serious histories, fictions, or philosophies.

For example, while a WWII simgame might have a playable German MG-42 machine gun or an 88 mm 'FlaK' artillery cannon, a player learns in an FPS such as *HLL* or *PS* the historical operational differences of these weapons in varying degrees through simulated experiences along a broad spectrum of historical accuracy. Even as a particular experience might illuminate the workings of a single weapon, these differences are embedded within the wider context of their actual use during the past, and therefore may point (for those players curious enough to look) towards an understanding of the lived experiences of actual soldiers—and much that is not simulated within the game.

The meaningful learning that occurs from the experience of operating a weapon such as a machine gun or artillery piece demonstrates how the process of interpretation continues beyond the immediate gameworld experience into more traditional methods, such as the reading and viewing of simtexts. And instead of demanding that such an experience and its potential investigation be framed within a 'serious' game with a critical focus on historical heritage or meaningfulness, it can be focused on gameplay in the form of combat simulation, strategic management of resources, squad-based tactics, and so on, rather than a critical encounter with the past. The past, though, creeps in unexpectedly.

Within the discourse of historical game studies, we also see a concern that popular war-related 'mil-sim' games such as *CoD* or *BF* not only lack meaningful learning, but also dangerously misrepresent the war (and war in general) and its effects, through programmed game elements. These developer choices instill a hyperfocus on combat through constrained level design that relegates conflict to a limited number of places and events, thereby distorting the war. Add to this the marketing of the war for gameplay 'fun' mentioned earlier, which means that arcade simgames have been highly successful as entertainment even as they reinforce problematic aspects of public memory such as the previously noted furthering of Western triumphalism or the encouragement of weapon fetishism. Casual arcade-like games have been the worst offenders in this, but serious simgames suffer from a blinkered view of the war in its entirety because they limit their scope by the very nature of game design. This limiting factor has been seen in other forms of popular memory, with digital simgames just being the most recent version.[8]

Simgames as a form of playable public memory that attempts some form of meaningful awareness have a precursor in reenactment societies. One important point of distinction between reenactments and simgames, though, is the idea that with reenactment there is a focus on embodied action rather than digitized agency. One carries a physical musket, maybe even at the actual place of battle, such as Gettysburg; one wears a uniform of a seventeenth-century hussar; or one can even drive a tank or mock-fire artillery. A simgame, though, is mediated by both the digital world within a 2D screen or, even more expansively, with increasingly powerful VR headsets and their haptic peripherals (see Chapter 4). These provide degrees of material mediation, especially in an FPS, and should be no surprise because the past is also digitally remediated, even if through the consumption of various materials from casual memoirs to serious academic study, through films designed to entertain, or through documentaries designed to elicit understanding.

Even more so, heritage experiences such as museums or walking tours are mediated by the objects and spaces constructed to replicate the past or by the locations that allow one to stand at the exact places where the events occurred, such as memorials spread throughout the major conflict zones. As I detail later, this translates within simgames to a traversable digital map that acts as a snapshot of a particular battle and thus refracts the war to these particular local places and moments.

Reenactment studies provide an approach to the past as an embodied form of learning and performance with their costumes and props, and their focuses on degrees of authenticity through role-playing that acts as a precursor for the digital experience of simgames. The serious shooters and simulators examined in this study obliquely fall into this category, one that Josh Smicker considers to be central to the major genres of historical war games, in which "re-enactment games try to recreate and reproduce, as accurately as possible, specific wars, battles, armies, and equipment" (2009: 111–12). Smicker writes in the context of near-future games, which he calls 'proleptic,' for their ability to predict potential outcomes of armed conflict. And while he has a second category called 'revisionist,' he provides examples that allow for the replaying of defeats as a way to know the past rather than as an example of counter-factual gameplay. As I see it, with Smicker such defeats provide tactical and strategic awareness that may have direct educational purposes for military history, while counterfactuals for most players allow for a reimagined recon-figuration of the past simply for entertainment.

Reenactment, though, has a much wider scope of analysis for thinkers such as Smicker than my use as a way to illuminate aspects of simgames.

It encompasses several key activities beyond capturing the past, such as religious ritual that establishes the sacred as an act of remembrance in the present; for example, the performing of the Christian Passion Play during Easter or the often once-in-a-lifetime pilgrimage to Mecca for Muslims, the Hajj. Reenactment also finds different inflections in different disciplines from forensics, ethnography, archeology to theater and musical performance. For more on reenactment, see Agnew, Lamb, and Tomann (2019), especially in how it argues a momentum away from history as the primary discipline or with battle recreation as its most important form.

War reenactment has often been seen by the public and the academy to be the domain of odd men in costumes playing at war, primarily the Civil War in the USA, or the world wars or Napoleonic Wars in Europe, with a heavy dose of medievalist performance from RPGs to Renaissance fairs. It has also found a digital form in serious simgames along with a fantasy inflection, live-action role-playing (LARPing), with its own rules and adjudication process. For a full investigation into LARPing as a fantasy form, see Stenros and Montola, 2010. Still, it is often viewed as strange, if not suspect.

Whereas serious professional history has typically overlooked reenactment societies and their interests in local and lived histories, rooted as they are in popular history, within digital computer war-gaming, simgames provide a meeting ground between the two with their own version of authenticity. This is now a foundational concept in historical game studies, fertile as a field to be analyzed in its investigation into digital reenactment simgames, especially as players sit at computers and don VR headsets. We can thus accept the fact that a simgame fails to simulate a full range of activities central to the experience of war, while still seeing how curated developer elements work toward degrees of accuracy and authenticity beyond those of less serious, more arcade-like games. This attempt finds common ground with earlier types of war reenactment societies and their focus on crafting workable examples of the lived experiences of soldiers (Daugbjerg, 2019).

An issue of contention still remains within the broader discourse of history, as a foundational discipline within the humanities, and the more recent reenactment studies, over the scale that such performances should be placed in. The totalizing, meta-narratives that would view an event such as WWII from its widest perspective of battling ideologies or nations at war, wielding all the mechanisms available from the economic to the military, conflict with a narrower approach foregrounding the lived experiences of individuals outside such monolithic control structures. Simgame shooters and simulators tend toward the narrow scope, while strategies utilize the wider forces and their requisite scale. What is understood about the event/events from gameplay, outside game mechanics, is constrained by these views (for more on this tension, see Agnew, Lamb, and Tomann, 2019).

In such ways, then, even FPS simgames function as digital and playable memorials created by popular memory, but with a more immediate inflection; that is, simulated configurations of that past that do more than entertain. They encourage investigation into the past, functioning in a similar manner to reenactments at heritage sites. Yet rather than the creation of a digital museum experience in VR, say, of Pearl Harbor that may allow one to walk along the piers where the battleships were at anchor when attacked, simgames simulate similar environments for particular forms of play.[9]

A narrative-FPS game such as *AaB* adds story elements that hint at the power of, for example, a future simgame that recreates the attack on Pearl Harbor so a player might engage in the attack or defense, or spectate the conflict as if walking through a living diorama. Such experiences will become more prevalent as VR continues to move on. The close-subjective perspective of shooters and simulators will provide the scope. Games such as *AaB* will add personal narrative and drama from the close first-person perspective, especially poignant for such an event as WWII.

## FPS Case Studies: Beaches and Bocage

I have argued that a curated awareness of the past with degrees of accuracy emerges in serious simgames through three primary mechanisms: 1) players' use of equipment and machines assigned to specific roles within those spaces; 2) the classes the players choose in which to play; and 3) maps and their reconfiguration of historical space. When we examine these categories together through a detailed analysis of specific maps, we see how history emerges as constrained, but also provides a curious experience of the past. The FPSs in this case study solve the problem of narrow scale and numerous objects by utilizing their rendering engines to provide a focus on fully equipped infantry soldiers with feet on the ground, while also allowing players to jump into vehicles, both experiences limited to the immediate vicinity of the infantry. We see a shift from arcade-focus gameplay and experiences when we start looking beyond arcade FPSs to *HLL* and *PS*, especially when centered on the locations provided for gameplay.

Serious tactical FPS simgames provide more historically located and detailed maps than most popular WWII shooters that are designed for a wider audience. As I will show, these channel popular memory toward areas of expected conflict in recognizable snapshots, such as major battle locations, into a gameplay space that is manageable by being constrained, but also channel the past for players interested in looking outside the game for research and learning. The places of chosen conflict become digitized memorials that players encounter in a similar manner to heritage sites, yet such inductions into an awareness of the past are performed subtly as an oblique, secondary phenomenon. These may reinforce common meta-narratives of the war, even as they push toward less known and sometimes overlooked events.

At the time of this writing in the winter of 2022, working through the maps of *HLL* beyond the recent Eastern Front additions, we see a common prevalence for American and British operations and topographies, such as the Normandy landings (only at Utah and Omaha), the Allies' capturing of key towns, villages, and roads in the Cotentin Peninsula, such as Sainte-Mère-Église and Sainte-Marie-Du-Mont, as well as the move down Purple Heart Lane, a highway leading south into Carentan. These maps exemplify historical snapshots of the early part of the Allied invasion, while the others, such as Foy, Hürtgen Forest and Hill 400, occur much farther away than the initial landings and objectives. These also occur later, closer to the war's end, when Allied forces pushed deep into the Ardennes, during the Battle of the Bulge, and the last-ditch German counter-offensive. The Allies encountered stiff resistance by the Germans at this point, which has been documented and dramatized in a number of key simtexts. The *Band of Brothers* episode 'Bastogne' represents the troubles of Easy Company during the winter of 1944. Such plights of the American forces have dominated this narrative, especially in WWII simgames.

For both *HLL* and *PS*'s simulations of the D-Day landings, rather than attempting to recreate the exact placement of bunkers and pillboxes at Omaha and Utah beaches, the connecting trench lines or footpaths and so on, the developers used landscape features from aerial photography to replicate the area to a certain degree of accuracy. *HLL*'s Omaha Beach map and *PS*'s Utah Beach map both simulate these critical areas of conflict. The historical awareness for players at the level of infantry soldiers slogging through the sand and up banks to emplacements with firing enemies has less to do with simulating the exact historical space and more with creating an impression, one located within the cinematic touchstone *Saving Private Ryan*, especially in its initial scene when Tom Hanks as Captain John Miller has to survive the landing and clear out the first bunker.

The developers simulate the beach as a kill zone, often dramatized in film as a moment of horror when the Higgins Boats' front bow ramps dropped into the water, presenting the exiting soldiers as targets for primed German rapid-firing MG-42 machine gun emplacements. The challenge of the beach landings in these simgames means avoiding enemy fire, but also mines, artillery, and obstacles. Players encounter log ramps and metal hedgehogs, razor wire, sea walls, dunes, and so on. All of these impediments have to be traversed to arrive at a shingle where players can hunker down and attempt to take higher ground. This is a common gameplay challenge from the earliest examples, all the way up to the most recent in *HLL* and *PS*. But the Omaha and Utah maps also provide much acreage behind the initial bunkers along the top of the sand bank, which *Saving Private Ryan* and *Band of Brothers* also dramatize as the Germans flee to secure areas behind their front lines, both combatants fighting in open fields and farmhouses, outbuildings, hedges, flooded areas, dirt roads, streams, and vineyards. They do so among dead livestock, burned-out defenses, artillery craters, and stone field walls. The map's scenery thus changes from the body-strewn beaches to rural Normandy.

Beyond the beachheads with their machine-guns and bunkers, the flooded lowlands behind them form another dangerous sector filled with retreating but resisting Germans. The *bocage* of the Normandy countryside, its woodlands and farm areas, open fields, streams, and rivers, dot the landscape of these late-war maps as a marred bucolic countryside that is peppered with destruction. Behind the beachheads there are also the paths that lead deeper into Normandy, where the invading soldiers eventually arrived at key towns and roadways. These maps provide a few notable landmarks, such as the area behind Utah beach and the village of Le Madeleine, while the overall effect creates the overcast, oppressive atmosphere of that 1944 summer.

For players, the immediacy of the beach landings and the taking of the emplacements at Omaha and Utah is frenetic and difficult. A player experiences these spaces, though, differently outside a full multiplayer server. Without enemies, a player can move through the maps and consider what the landings must have been like when they were full of real combatants who died on the beaches and in the bunkers. Nothing in the game intentionally forces this awareness upon players. Rather, the empty spaces suggest a past that operates as a subtle force. The entire map space when emptied thus becomes a type of memorial, especially when considered outside gameplay. Whether this latent awareness occurs or not is up to the sensitivity (and interest) of the player, many of whom may wander through empty servers only to better identify tactical locations, such as the different exits from the beaches, but others may gain a growing sense that the simgame only touches on the barest truth of such lived realities, then look elsewhere for clarification.

## Gamespace: Battle Snapshots

An examination of maps as historical spaces provided by serious simgame case studies reveals them to be curated snapshots rather than comprehensive recreations of the past. *HLL* features three key towns beyond the D-Day landing beaches that demonstrate the degrees to which these simgames simulate accurate historical gameworlds: Sainte-Mère-Église, Sainte-Marie-du-Mont, and Carentan. Each of these bears examination because of the detail they employ.

The US Airborne dropped on June 5, 1944, the night before D-Day, to secure the Cotentin Peninsula so that the Allies could establish a foothold in northern France. Sainte-Mère-Église was the first town to be liberated by the Allies. The town (and game map) is dominated by a church in its center, where US paratrooper John Steele would find himself hanging by his chute and pretending to be dead. This dramatic element is often detailed as a key moment in the town's history, but in a tactically driven FPS such as *HLL* such human-oriented storytelling is ignored. Here, in-game cinematic transmediation is muted, while the church itself as a historical space is foregrounded.[10] Rather than focusing on stories such as Steele's, *HLL* provides a gameworld in which historical elements can be found but hide in the background.

The Sainte-Mere-Du-Mont map also simulates critical first victories in the environs of a small town located near the southern portion of Utah beach, and one the Airborne needed to take in order to clear a path inland for the beach-landing infantry. Like Sainte-Mère-Église, the Du-Mont map includes a church with a bell-tower that acted as a central area of conflict and control during the invasion. It is a place toward which players naturally gravitate. Along with the church, the map offers interesting landscape features such as a cemetery and downed aircraft. These aircraft evoke the scene in *Saving Private Ryan* when men from Easy Company are looking for the rest of their company and find a downed glider with the grisly remains of a dead pilot inside. In such a simgame, the cockpits of the downed gliders are empty rather than containing the dead bodies of crew and passengers, a reminder that these maps are memorials rather than grisly documentary footage, cinematic spectacles, or unedited photographic records. The bodies of the dead are largely absent from these maps (other than set in key places, such as the beach landings); avatars killed in game disappear after a short time, leaving no trace.

An example of how transmedia emerges in *HLL* can be found with Brécourt Manor, another place that features as a key historical event in the taking of the area. *Band of Brothers* dramatizes this moment in the episode 'Day of Days' when Lieutenant Richard Winters and Easy Company found refuge after their assault on the Brécourt artillery firing on Utah beach, a mission now used to teach tactics to small infantry elements taking a position and one that earned the Allies control of artillery positions on the peninsula. But in game, it can be overlooked or never even encountered by squads who may navigate past it for other tactical locations. Investigation on an empty server allows interested players the ability to casually stroll through the area, as if at a memorial site.

These two maps together with Purple Heart Lane simulate the push south down the peninsula that saw Allied forces encountering stiff but crumbling resistance by the Germans. *HLL*'s Purple Heart Lane simulates the place where a dramatic historical event occurred when Airborne commander Robert G. Cole charged German positions along Highway N13 north of Carentan, another story often told of American heroism. Cole was tasked with capturing four guarded bridges. He and his battalion charged rather than remain static and be eliminated by artillery; the successful charge took heavy casualties. None of this is simulated.

Instead, this map evokes danger, even empty of combatants. It is an overcast, rainy environment, with flooded fields to either side of the main causeway that has to be crossed. Any record of the heroism of Cole and his men, though, is absent, this erasure a sign of how a tactical FPS functions as a combat gameworld rather than as a story-driven simgame with a first- or third-person perspective, or even as a direct memorial with aids for key points. It provides particular gameplay challenges for players who must move along the causeways, without any hint of the real life and death moments experienced in the past.[11] Here, the developers offer players the difficulties of rivers and streams and bridges, dangerous choke-points that create interesting and challenging game-play but also simulate the dangerous historical elements that soldiers faced (without direct reference to them).

Purple Heart Lane is a map that connects the other two, with the key objective found in Carentan, a map exemplifying a digitized simgame-memorial gameworld that allows interested players a space to explore a topography that only become understood with outside study. Like all of these maps, it is also devoid of the human carnage of war even as it reconstructs an environment in which war occurred.[12] What we notice with such maps in current, serious tactical FPSs (shooters) is the simulation of playable memorial spaces, but also of chance encounters with historical landmarks that find immediacy beyond those in simulators and strategy games. This configuration of a chance encounter with recognizable historical places, though, is often subtle, as it remediates dramatic moments of these historical places for players.

The Carentan episode in *Band of Brothers* has been represented as a key moment in the war for the US 101st Airborne Division's 506th Parachute Regiment and its Easy Company following the writing of Stephen A. Ambrose's monograph on the subject (1992). Along with *HLL* and *PS*'s highly detailed Carentan maps, popular games such as *CoD2* (2005), as well as the more recent *CoD:WWII* (2017) all have Carentan maps. Deciphering how well such simgames accurately simulate cartographic details of Carentan at the time of the war is difficult, even though a quick YouTube search reveals interest by players, and aerial photography does exist that can be overlaid with game maps.[13] This literal grounding of the area frames it as playable history, thereby granting the location importance because it is being simulated to certain degrees.

Carentan sits inland within the Cotentin peninsula, situated southwest from Utah and Omaha beaches, near where the 82nd and 101st Airborne landed. The town proved critical because it allowed the Allied troops on the two beachheads to combine in their push south. A key landmark dramatized in the *Band of Brothers* episode 'Carentan' is the road southwest of the small town where Lieutenant Richard Winters and Easy Company came under fire on June 12. In the HBO series, he and his men are shown moving toward the village from the southwest when a German machine gunner in a building at the end of the road opens fire.

In this scene Winters crosses the street, bullets flying through the air and pinging off the ground, Winters demanding that his men advance. In *HLL*, a fan-made short movie was constructed within the game engine that recreates the action, while using audio from the series. As of the time this chapter was written, the real-world building at the end of the street is occupied on the first floor by the Bar du Stade, while in the series we see that the first floor contains the fictional Café du Normandie. The series was based on the book by Ambrose, whose account does not explicitly state such details that become important in a screened text designed for drama.[14]

Such a touchstone moment of heroism in *Band of Brothers*, like the beach landings on D-Day or the taking of Carentan itself, find remediated simulation in simgames but only through the landmarks that remain in the background rather than as full replications of the actions of individuals. While the actual drama of a commander braving gunfire to force his men to follow orders is not typically part of games such as *HLL* and *PS*, the map as a historical place contains these framing elements that act as hidden historical memorials of past heroics. In *HLL*, another landmark, the Hotel du Normandie is in a different place than its fictional location in the HBO series, much closer to the town center and at a railroad crossing. It is also facing west rather than south. When a player encounters such a landmark, they might follow a curious trail and learn about their representations in the film series, even questioning if they existed at all.

Again, the place as an area of transmedial history is the focus, not the persons or deeds. A foundational written simtext such as Ambrose's monograph *Band of Brothers* (1992) reveals that the particular building housing the German machine gunner represented in the series when Winter's company comes under fire may not have existed at all. Instead, when Winters told his men to 'move out' along the road they encountered a different scene: "The German machine-gun opened fire, straight down the road. It was in a perfect position, at the perfect time, to wipe out the company" (Ambrose, 1992: 95). Ambrose's account simply says they arrived at an intersection wherein they took fire from up the road. Winters' account in his memoir, though, places the machine gun "in a building at the foot of the hill" (Winters, 2008: 103). Another landmark seen in the series is the Restaurant Desire Ingouf; it is placed on the same block as the fictional Café du Normandie, as seen in the series but not mentioned by Ambrose or seen in photos taken by the 101st Airborne Division. In *HLL* it sits farther into town toward the railroad tracks.

Such historical and cinematic landmarks are obviously not designed by the developers as would the caretakers of a heritage site carefully replicating the past as best as they can, often scaffolding it with teaching aids that use pertinent information. Instead, these maps provide a gameist environment that evokes the past through specific locales as examples of playable transmedia. Moving through these spaces, especially when they are empty, reinforces the fact that these are simulated gameworlds located in a reimagined past, reconfigured for play.

Even so, these examples of playable transmedia foreground specific moments from the war that only become knowable through additional research or media consumption. A danger for players who take a casual interest and look outside a simgame for clarification is that the war becomes only these places, but in the process of seeking clarification about what happened in these game spaces, a player engages the past through a process of gameplay-inspired interpretation. This may clarify how a mystery fits within the game, but may also point to more expansive research, and even critical interrogation of the past.

These initial Normandy maps therefore provide a few iconic snapshots, as one would expect, each with a similar aesthetic that reflects the French countryside of the region and the particular challenges they impose. The other maps in *HLL* depart from this bucolic but war-torn environment. The snow-covered fields of Foy and the wooded hills of the Hürtgen Forest and Hill 400 maps each offer a different look and feel, as well as gameplay tactics and strategy.

The Battle of the Hürtgen Forest occurred on the Belgian–German border during the fall and early winter of 1944. Field Marshal Walter Model commanded this region at a crucial time in the German defense, and it describes one of Germany's most critical moments in the late war. The Germans fought to stop the final push by the Western Allies, with Hill 400 being one of the last critical capture points. Like the town of Sainte-Mère-Église at the beginning of the Normandy invasion, Aachen became the first major city to be retaken by the Allies in this campaign. The game space provided here departs from the Cotentin maps quite significantly.

Some unique features, such as the 'dragon's teeth' fortifications of the Siegfried Line can be found in game as historical markers, but the atmosphere itself provides a compelling simulation of the past evocative of several years of war. The map captures the desolation and destruction wrought by both sides on the environment. It is a map of mud and barbed wire, with trenches, guardhouses, and hidden pillboxes littered throughout a forest full of shadows. The color is ruddy brown, with gray mist and gray stone. The leaves of fall have turned rust-colored. The villages in the lower portion of the map also appear burned out and desolate, players experiencing a plodding march up onto the hill as an increasingly darker trek into danger, while those defending hide in gulches and crevices, waiting for the first sign of movement. The blasted tree stumps, the crevices and crannies, the ridges and bedrock outcrops provide cover for lurking enemies on both sides. The effect evokes the anxiety and misery of what occurred in such a historic place, the hill itself a curious snapshot of conflict and suffering that only becomes clear with explanation outside the game.

Foy for *HLL* is another historical transmedial gameworld evoked in a map that finds inspiration in cinema and one that is drastically different. The combat that occurred at Foy is also represented as a major dramatic moment screened in *Band of Brothers* during the initial part of the Battle of the Bulge, deep in the Belgian Ardennes Forest. Foy is a small village a few kilometers north of Bastogne. In the winter of 1944–1945, Captain Winters has been tasked with taking control of the snowy woods around the village. In Episode 6, 'Bastogne,' we see the traumatic effects of German artillery barrages in which trees in the Bois Jacques woods explode after being hit and men are forced into fox holes for safety. Later, on January 13, after taking control of snow-filled, wooded areas around Foy, Winters orders his men to assault German positions closer to the village. Unlike in the series, in which Winters' command post is directly behind his attacking platoons, where we see him urging them on, Easy Company was situated in woods further west.

In the series, Winters witnesses his men in a field being pinned down by German artillery, which is dramatized in Episode 7, 'The Breaking Point.' He also sees that his first lieutenant (Norman Dike) leading the assault is ineffective (in the series Dike cowers behind cover rather than taking charge). Winters bravely prepares to rush into fire, but his commander demands he stay back. He immediately tells Lieutenant Ronald Speirs of Dog Company to relieve Lieutenant Dike of command and to eliminate the German 88 mm firing on them. The scene demonstrates the power of cinema, as we follow Speirs on his brave but suicidal run across the field to relieve Dike. Continuing with the daring, Speirs then runs directly into close German fire to take out the artillery—and then runs back, earning the dumbfounded respect of Easy Company (Ambrose, 1992).

This sort of dramatic reimagining of heroics, which condenses an eighteen-hour attack into a few scenes, reveals the differences in mode between cinema and simgames, the latter receptive to dramatic moments such as those in *AaB*, but whose primary effect in tactical FPSs relies more on a tapestry of gameplay elements designed for tactics and strategy than in providing the stories of individuals. For example, rather than replicate such a cinematic scene as Speirs running across a field again and again for players who might want to try such a heroic mission, *HLL* provides a map of Foy with its snow-covered fields and large hay bales, any of its sectors ripe for conflict. The open areas south of the village mean cover is sparse once one leaves the forests, the Germans already reinforced behind structures with cover and areas of fire supremacy pocketed with buildings.

A simgame such as *AaB* rather than *HLL*, though, replicates heroics over spaces from a personal perspective because of its narrative-based story line, while *HLL* only hints at the personal history that occurred in such a contested site. Instead of directly translating screened drama to gamespace, serious simgame shooters thus provide historical context in the background. The past is literally beneath a player's feet, the objects around which a player passes only becoming known through outside investigation.

## Conclusion

This chapter has examined a few tactical FPS simgames to show how they reconfigure WWII combat into playable reconfigurations of the past. It looks to war games as a precursor to the FPS, even as the specific form of the shooter presents time and space to players as new experiences. Such categories also present remembrance in novel ways, redefining how we experience the past beyond traditional forms. It is to this digitized historical gamespace that this study ultimately looks, seeing in the FPS a first step toward providing challenging experiences for players who seek gameplay, but also may seek understanding. A connection exists with earlier forms of popular memory, such as reenactments, the focus here on the lived experience of soldiers juxtaposed with broad history. This speaks to how the past can be learned both through traditional classroom techniques, with its teachers and students, and also playable means.

The subgenres that use aspects of the FPS demonstrate this potential, such as those in the narrative VR simgame *AaB*, while the tactical shooter remains constrained in how it presents history. Even so, the maps they offer function as digital memorials. They are often embedded in transmedial relationships with other games and with cinema. In particular, foundational screened texts such as *Saving Private Ryan* and *Band of Brothers* inspire much WWII-based computer gaming. Yet the more serious simgames approach them not as films to be replicated in games but as representations of experiences, some of which can be simulated in game.

The Normandy D-Day landings, the securing of the peninsula, and the push into Germany provide the focused moments of the war, condensed into specific snapshot areas of conflict that become playable maps. The most prevalent subject matter of WWII FPSs has focused on the Western Allies and their victories. I argue that, along with WWI, the Eastern Front is becoming increasingly more important, an example of a shift in meta-narratives and one explored in depth in Chapter 5. I try to show that these new foci work through consistent categories in the FPS, along with maps and their configurations, classes, and equipment. These latter two provide historical details in the roles of infantry soldiers, along with their weaponry. The maps, though, feature as the central place where all unfolds in the curious gameworlds of serious simgame shooters.

# 4 Simgames: Simulators

Chapter 3 on shooters and this chapter on simulators share a common subjective experience from a first-person perspective. Within the video game industry, distinctions are made between games in which you look through a character's eyes, often seeing your hands resting in front of you (first person) and those where the camera floats behind your fully rendered character (third person). This creates a psychological or subjective correlation between the player and the virtual character that translates into an intensity of experience. The effect of widening from first to third person distances a player from the closest type of subjective POV similar to what is seen in fiction, and closer to a third-person POV in which a character is described by an objective narrator.

But this slight distancing step from first- to third-person perspective in a simgame is far less impactful compared to the immediacy of moving in the opposite direction from a 2D screen to VR. This intensity is compounded when we move from FPSs in VR to simulators in VR, in which you sit within a virtualized machine that you operate with available controls in the form of computer peripherals. While VR FPSs have the same sense of narrow scope as simulators, current limitations in room-scale movement or the need to control walking or running with a button removes the player, if only slightly, from the degrees of connectedness within simulators. This is a subtle but important difference. The direct link, though, between these two chapters is that an experience is offered with particular effects in both shooters and simulators, those that for this study are situated within constructed space designed to simulate particular aspects of the past.

This book argues that a sophisticated, reworked interpretation of the past emerges for those players interested in looking beyond immediate gameplay, an insight seen most clearly in this chapter's focus on simulators, primarily military aviation during WWII. It foregrounds demanding in-game elements associated with lived historical practices that often meant success and survival or failure and death for pilots. This chapter shows that simulators such as *IL2:GB* and *DCS* offer degrees of accuracy and authenticity in learning the management of combat aircraft, and through this process a player not only understands how to master particular machines, but also how they functioned in the past as elements within a larger history.

This chapter examines how degrees of technical focus separate serious aviation simgames from more casual flight simulators. Technical knowledge acts as a foundation for approaching the basic historical understanding of differing aircraft, complexity increasing for tasks such as proper landing, take-off, navigation, and dogfighting. With technical details a concern for players, they can perform a simple Google search for gameplay information to clarify how to perform a quick test flight, or they can study more detailed technical descriptions that describe the history of engineering for specific aircraft and the arms race among the competing nations during the war. In the popular sphere, these helpful introductory sim(game/history)texts continue to proliferate through the interests of popular memory. They become a foundation for a reconfiguration of the past that often points to more complex and wide-ranging simtexts that open the war beyond its machines.

A detailed analysis of the case studies in this chapter reveals sophisticated simulators of WWII planes and tanks far beyond the arcade simulators of the past. And while these primarily offer a curated experience of a fighter or bomber pilot or tank gunner or commander, largely devoid of the political world that dictated overall war aims, the requirements to learn how to operate these machines point players toward simtexts that do more than provide technical details. They act as gateways into history, for the newcomer first steps that reveal a complex historiography of the event, and for the amateur historian a way to engage directly with digital artifacts that sometimes leads to embodied experiences with actual machines. I have noted concerns regarding the training of individuals through computer games for the real-world use of weapons. VR games do have study-level gameplay that involves small-arms weaponry that can be used for training in the present. Many examples exist, reflecting how VR is increasingly being used.

This chapter is organized around the core idea that the aircraft and armored vehicles used by the major nations act as symbols as much as weapons. These form mythologies that are related to how the war is remembered, especially in popular memory. Serious simulators utilize these powerful symbols as the machines in their simgames, without foregrounding the ideological differences that dominated the opposing worldviews of Western liberal democracy, fascist National Socialism, and Marxist-Leninist communism. Instead, this chapter focuses on how the stories found in key simtexts such as aviator memoirs are translated into playable gameworlds; rather than individual stories of pilots and their exploits, simulators such as *IL2* and *DCS* create gameworlds in which players experience aspects of WWII combat aviation, and only those. (The bulk of *DCS* content is modern aircraft.)

This chapter includes an examination of the common idea that pilots dueling in the air were somehow different from infantry struggling on the ground in a brutal war. The idea that chivalry existed among aviators is another prevalent theme in memoirs that, to some degree, informs simulators. Rather than seeing chivalrous aviators as knights in the sky, this chapter looks to how the experiences of virtual pilots are mediated through digital and analog devices and through the simgame–simtext dynamic. This process frames players of those virtual pilots differently from virtual pilots who are training for real-world scenarios; it looks to how immediacy, immersion, and presence are provided in a reconfiguration and reimagining of the past. Simulator pilots gain a particular type of simulated experience rather than learning to fly aircraft in real-world combat. With this in mind, it looks to how VR is becoming more popular in simgames such as *IL2* and *DCS*, providing more intense experiences that more deeply immerse players.

The chapter closes with case studies of *IL2* and *DCS*, working through their single-player campaigns and multiplayer modes to reveal the differences between the two. The single-player campaigns provide scripted scenarios similar to specific location snapshots in the maps of shooters. These campaigns capture particular aspects of the air war with historical accuracy in mind. The multiplayer experience, though, proves to be where the most demanding gameplay occurs, as well as attempting to replicate the difficulties and, on some servers, the seriousness of surviving and not losing one's virtual pilot. It works through some of the more demanding multiplayer servers, such as the Tactical Air War, to show how such simulators require not just gameplay knowledge but also true mastery of the aircraft and their roles, demanding outside study and practice.

## Serious Simulators

While WWII provides the context for the most serious of early military aviation simulators, the developers of the most recent *IL2:GB*, 1C Games, also offer an expansion simulation of WWI aircraft, *IL2: Flying Circus* (*FC*), with a single map on the Western Front. These early aircraft hark back to the beginning of computer simulation gaming and its WWI games. The basic biplanes and triplanes, along with simplified mechanics and flight modeling, allowed developers to render these slow-moving aircraft with early computer technology and to progress toward simulating WWI and WWII air combat. Released first as Volume 1 in 2019, *FC* moves far beyond these initial examples to offer the same attention to detail as the more advanced WWII aircraft found in the *IL2:GB* series, but with a focus on the tight-turning and in-close dogfighting of such nimble craft as the early Spads, Sopwiths, and Fockers.[1]

When looking at combat simulators of the two world wars, then, we find a series of simgame precursors with roots at the beginning of the home-computer revolution when arcades still housed massive stand-alone machines. Atari's *Red Baron* (1980) offered WWI aviation as a coin-operated arcade experience, later to be reimagined as a PC game by Dynamic in 1990. In addition, the early version of *Microsoft Flight Simulator* (1982) (*MFS*), which focused on general aviation, offered a dogfighting mode in a WWI plane. Thinkers have since argued that the success of *MFS* (1982) within PC games drove a directive for authenticity that influenced not only aviation simulators, but also war games in general. Wackerfuss, in particular, argues that such flight simulators "risk imparting a warped view of the war" (2013: 234). He asks why such dogfighting games garnered the largest part of the WWI game catalog, concluding that such early games reflected the way the first combat aviators presented their air war to the public, one in which brave, winged knights fought valiantly in the air, while brutality and horror occupied the trenches and their suffering occupants below (the scope of FPSs). These early iterations inspired many later flight simulators, from the first with their simple biplanes up to the most recent and advanced, with modern jet simulators becoming a favorite.

As computer systems grew more capable, flight simulators began to increase their learning curves, with some developers such as the *Jane's Combat Simulations* (1996) series being notorious for providing in-depth (and substantial) manuals for their aircraft. While a focused look at the release history of WWII simgames is beyond the scope of this chapter, a few notable precursors to the case studies presented here are *B17 Flying Fortress* (1992), *European Air War* (1998), *Jane's WWII Fighters* (1998), and *Rise of Flight* (2009), just a few examples of those that directly influenced and inspired the drive toward demanding combat flight simgames from WWI up to the twenty-first century.

The *IL2* series examined in this chapter has a complex, two-decade history of different developers, different game engines, different play styles, and even different focuses for aircraft. It is a product primarily of Russian game development, first in 2001 as the creation of Oleg Maddox and his company Maddox Games, along with the support of the larger 1C Games. Under the direction of 1C, the simgame was developed into several different versions. *IL2: 1946* (2006) combined a number of different releases into a long-running version that is the most expansive with the largest plane-set, covering global fronts from Europe to the Pacific. *1946* was followed with a new development approach by Gaijin Entertainment's *IL2: Birds of Prey* (2009), which allowed for more arcade-like play, while still offering a huge selection of aircraft. The later console version, *Birds of Steel* (2012), influenced Gaijin to release its own free-to-play and very popular WWII air combat MMO, *War Thunder*, which then added tanks, but now also has helicopters and ships, as well as modern versions of its vehicles.

While the earlier *IL2* games often provided a huge tapestry of locations, along with the ability to fly vastly different planes, *IL2: Cliffs of Dover* (2011) (*CloD*) focused the action and plane-set on the early war over southern England, the Channel, northern France, and Belgium. As with the extensive modding of *1946* that has kept the game being played with updated graphics, *CloD* was updated by a group of modders who formed Team Fusion to release the Blitz edition of the game (2017), and later a North African expansion, *IL2: Desert Wings – Tobruk* (2020). These exemplify a trend to focus the map and plane sets into more refined classes and locations, rather than providing the widest selection possible.

The most recent iteration of *IL2* is the *GB* series; it released as *IL2: Battle of Stalingrad* in 2013. Its maps, like those of the FPS case studies, provide a curated tapestry that frames the war along very specific lines. *GB* maintains the similar limited focus that is found in *CloD*, but started on the Eastern Front with a mid-war plane-set and a detailed Stalingrad map covering over 300 × 200 km. The choice to begin this version of the series at a midpoint of the war, rather than chronologically and with an earlier period, as seen in their subsequent *GB* release, *IL2: Battle of Moscow* (2016), foregrounds Stalingrad as a critical moment, one in which the Soviets saw a momentous victory, the Germans a crushing defeat. *IL2: Battle of Kuban* (2018) and its mid-war planes simulates the Eastern Front at the Crimea with a solid range of advanced and powerful planes for both sides. More recent releases of the *IL2: Battle of Bodenplatte* (2019) and the forthcoming *IL2: Battle of Normandy* return the conflict west and to the final stages of the war, with its most advanced aircraft.

Along with *IL2*, this chapter examines *DCS*'s WWII simulation modules, in particular those of its Normandy and Channel maps, along with its limited but in depth near study-level aircraft, such as the Spitfire Mk IX. In terms of serious attention to detail, *DCS* provides this focus beyond *IL2* with clickable cockpits, a more demanding flight model, and aircraft management for its limited aircraft. Where *DCS* separates itself, offering itself as an exemplary simgame for analysis, is in its detailed aircraft, especially when we look at them within its single-player content.

## VR instead of 2D

This chapter examines *IL2:GB*, rather than the earlier *1946* or *CloD* versions, because of its exceptional VR support, even if the game engine has limitations in how many objects can be rendered without overloading a server.[2] *1946* is an older game, offering hundreds of planes with less fidelity but the ability to render more of them; it has no in-game VR support and lacks the overall visual finish of *GB*, even if it has an active modding community that has upgraded its graphics for 2D screens. The number of variations and aircraft across the differing nations is extensive and, along with *WT*, *1946* provides the most comprehensive WWII collection for a player.

*CloD*, though, takes the opposite approach, limiting its aircraft to early-war British and German, and the *Tobruk* (2020) expansion enhances this with a

North African campaign and a number of aircraft specific to that setting. *GB* sits in a middle space between these two extremes, yet distinguishes itself with a robust VR implementation for small-scale squadron-based air combat in 4k that offers a unique, historically located experience for players. VR technology has an interesting history that is beyond the scope of this chapter, but a brief comment on its current capabilities clarifies why the *GB* version of *IL2* is the primary point for this case study, along with *DCS*'s single-player campaigns.

VR for the consumer market had emerged (and failed) as a hopeful entertainment technology several times before Palmer Lucky and Oculus began a Kickstarter project that released its first developer's kit, the Rift, in 2013. At the time, these were impressive in capturing computer gaming with high-quality LCD screens, each eye looking through lenses at 1280 x 800 pixels to create stereoscopic gameworlds. A second developer's kit was released a year later, switching to OLED screens and their richer colors, as well as increasing the vertical resolution of the lenses to 1080p. Many other technical problems had to be solved to make such a device work, such as reducing latency, increasing the amount of frames-per-second displayed, and comfort.

By the time John Carmack, formerly of id Software (and its influential *Doom*, 1993, and *Quake*, 1996, series of games), joined as chief technology officer, Oculus had solved the challenge of delivering headsets into the hands of consumer gamers. By 2016, Sony had entered the picture with its PSVR that worked with the PS4. HTC also released its Vive headset, a device developed in close conjunction with the game-distribution company Valve to work seamlessly with PC games developed for VR. Microsoft also released a number of Windows Mixed Reality (WMR) devices (which are actually VR headsets, with rudimentary pass-through cameras), the Samsung Odyssey and its OLED screens an early standout that increased resolution. Valve released its own headset, the Index, in 2019, along with an eagerly awaited sequel to the *Half Life* (1998) series, *Half Life: Alyx*. This title was released only for VR and demonstrated what a fully optimized game in VR can look like.

The technology race for providing better comfort, increasing resolution, decreasing latency, widening field of view (FOV), more complex lenses, dynamic foveated rendering[3], true HDR brightness, and so on has continued, with several companies such as Meta Platforms and Apple now focusing on VR. Today, though, the most advanced version of WMR, the HP Reverb G2, only offers lenses with a resolution of 2160 x 2160 pixels. In headsets designed for gaming, rather than commercial use such as the Varjo XR3, this is bested today by the HTC Vive Pro 2 (VP2) with 2,448 vertical pixels and an FOV wider than the G2. At the time of revising this chapter in the late winter of 2022/2023, there are a variety of headsets now such as the standalone Pico 4. Others can be purchased like the Pimax 8KX with a larger FOV, but with some distortion issues and a requirement that the headset be run in a parallel projection mode, with its performance cost, for software that has not adjusted itself to Pimax's canted displays. Other high-fidelity headsets are promised, with many new advances from eye tracking to multiple lenses that will further the fidelity of simgames. The jump from the first Oculus developer's kit to the VP2 is a huge increase in visual quality to the point you cannot see a 'screen door effect,' or a pattern of pixels on the screens, even though your eyes are only a few inches away. Recently, with Facebook's (now Meta) acquisition of Oculus, the Quest line of stand-alone-headsets provides players with a mode to use VR without being tethered to a computer.

As computer simulation hardware has increased in fidelity, the power to generate enough frames per second to avoid causing VR sickness has also increased, especially in optimized games. The current 4000 series of Nvidia graphical processor units (GPUs) and the latest AMD GPUs can now easily manage at least forty-five frames-per-second and often ninety or higher. The new Nvidia 4000 series is expected to provide a major leap in GPU processing power, which will further increase the fidelity of VR. With software solutions that add extra frames by 'reprojecting' single frames to double the total, even less robust systems can provide a working solution for combat flight simulations to run smoothly on home computers.

This foregrounding of VR in my analysis is not to denigrate the power of 2D as a part of the simgame–simtext dynamic. More players than not still choose accessible 2D over VR. Some have multiscreen displays at their disposal, and even expensive TVs and projectors, all of these forms of mediation being suitable to effectively construct an immersive past within a high-quality 2D frame. The move toward VR, though, in this example of vehicle simulation (as we saw in Chapter 3 with a story-driven FPS such as *MoH: AaB*), offers fully rendered 3D environments that lend themselves to the argument that simgames in VR provide an intensified experience.

This valorization of VR may seem to dismiss the many 2D games as no longer appropriate or relevant. On the contrary, this intensification trend in simulators has adopted VR rapidly while working alongside continued 2D popularity. However, VR is becoming more prevalent. Even the latest version of *MFS 2020* (2020) backtracked on its initial launch with no VR to quickly implement it, while the bulk of its development remains for 2D. The auto-racing simulator industry has also adopted VR, with major titles such as *Project Cars 2* (2017) and *iRacing* (2008), along with others such as *Automobilista 2* (2020) and *Assetto Corsa* (2014), with no stop in the development of 2D. You can also race rallies in VR and even drive eighteen-wheeled trucks. With these cockpit-focused vehicle simgames, the experience of sitting at controls and looking through windows at your environment lends itself to the improving resolution offered with current VR technologies that already provide enough details to see gauges and dials, and much progress in resolution for distant objects.

A focused analysis of this VR-mediated simgame experience and how it encourages a secondary interest in simtexts that clarify the game (or the past) begins with the interiors of these machines. The key FPS categories of maps, classes, and equipment still applies to WWII combat simulators, but rather than focus on them, another category of the cockpit offers a unique way to examine this particular type of simgame simulator. 'Simpit' is a popular term for the physical space a player creates that houses his or her simulator peripherals that mediate what happens in the virtual in-game cockpit. A player sits with a VR headset strapped to his or her face or in front of one or more 2D displays, with joystick in one hand and often a throttle in the other (together called HOTAS, for hands on throttle and stick), maybe even with rudder pedals at his or her feet. Players are thus embedded in a playable analog-and-digital configuration within this physical and virtual simspace.

Even with a rendered game environment that visually simulates events from the past in a high-fidelity 3D view, this reachable hardware-oriented space appears to have very little direct relation to the lived experiences of WWII pilots. Most of these devices such as joysticks are for modern aircraft, especially the entry-level ones designed for any type of flight simulator (be they for modern aircraft or science-fiction spacecraft). Moreover, their shafts are short, creating a much more sensitive and twitchy correlation between degrees of movement by the player and what is translated in game.

Along with this limitation to capturing the proper feel of using an actual flight stick, most available joysticks have no force feedback, the judders and jitters of a moving plane no longer being translated up the shaft to the pilot's hands (much less through the seat into the body). Peripherals can be used that attach to chairs and vibrate, simulating engine revs and guns firing. More specific types of peripherals can be used that closely mimic real flight, say a flight stick of a historic BF 109, or at least feel closer to the actual historical machined parts. The modding community has even created a do-it-yourself process in which a player can 3D print the major components of a Spitfire cockpit, wire them through the guidance of helpful guides, mount them to a frame, and (when using VR) thus reach out to feel material components rendered digitally in VR.[4] This is one step closer toward a realized historical configuration that more closely corresponds to the past, but without g-force haptics.

This chapter's focused interest in these analog-and-digital devices concerns how they are able to create a unique experience (with degrees of accuracy), something that is similar to how imaginary (and historical) worlds are encountered in other media, especially literature and cinema with their imaginary and screened subjectivities. But rather than believing oneself to be in a real Spitfire cockpit, a player sees with high-visual fidelity a convincing-rendered space all around and can (in a variety of ways) manipulate it. As stated earlier, this interfacing begins with peripherals connected to a computer, some of which are expensive HOTAS setups that provide a sense of presence and direct control without the full reality of a WWII aircraft moving at high speed through crosswinds, weather, and turbulence.

A mediated connectedness then extends from these devices to how a player interacts with the virtual cockpit and its views, sometimes digitally rendered hands and fingers being able to manipulate clickable elements. Along with more sophisticated haptics, these sorts of interfacing technologies will eventually allow a player to reach out and feel the components, such as when a pilot reaches up with a left hand to drop flaps on a Spitfire or reaches down to turn the stabilizer wheel on a 109. And, even more surprisingly, at-home motion simulators are being built to provide degrees of movement that suggest, rather than truly mimic, strong g-forces. These will increase both the presence, immediacy, and immersion of the experience afforded to players, with the past becoming more knowable.

This simulator environment has such an impact because when one is flying a simulated airplane or driving a simulated tank, one is sitting at analogues for the actual controls. In a flight simulator, the peripherals are constructed in a tight space like a cockpit that closely mimics the space of an actual pilot or driver. Auto-racing games have proven very popular in VR for this reason. For most players, they will not experience any g-forces (unless they have a system built on hydraulics that mimics gravity without actually imposing the same pressure) or temperature and pressure changes, but in a VR headset they can achieve a visual acuity for nearby objects that exceeds the immersion of looking at a 2D screen. And with new advances in blending VR with the actual world, often called mixed reality (MR), analog cockpits can be built that can be 'seen' with passthrough technology and a virtual world around it.[5]

## Immersion, Presence, and Immediacy

Analysis of the virtualized experience provided by simulators, often called 'immersion' in media studies, finds continuity beyond reading novels and watching films as primary ways of engaging with imaginary worlds, and increasingly the past. As we encounter complex digitally constructed reconfigurations of the past through computer systems, some historical, some purely fantastic, we have at our fingertips hardware that now provides more than a 2D-screened interface. It adds what I call immediacy and presence, two concepts that augment the broader idea of immersion with that which is reachable and right in front of you (immediacy) and that which appears to be real and full-bodied (presence).

The concept of immersion in the fantastic, as detailed by thinkers such as Janet Murray, remains a continued interest for anyone who has used a VR headset to walk through the forests of Skyrim, or even just sit in an X-Wing, or experience any of the fantastic environments offered in VR computer games— see *Star Wars: Squadrons* (2020). One important theoretical discussion has been over the problematic binary real versus unreal (or imaginary) and our supposed potential inability to parse the two as these immersive imaginary worlds increase in fidelity. This disconnect has been described as the 'immersion fallacy,' similar to earlier fallacies from literary criticism that, for example, suggest the idea that one can know (or should look for) the intention of an author in his or her work (the intentional fallacy) (Zimmerman and Salen, 2003).

The fear that we will not be able to determine reality from fantasy continues to be a concern for the future use of VR-like systems. This fear can be seen in the near-future film *Strange Days* (1995), in which people can deploy a device to fully experience virtual worlds to the point one's mind cannot escape the rendered world. This extreme is science fiction. Digital computer games remain 'half real,' and, as Jesper Juul argues, incoherent, because they provide only partial aspects of any virtual gameworld (2011). This incoherence, or perceived incongruity, also encourages an awareness that the experience is mediated, providing a type of safety, an ironic distance that allows for the use of dangerous machines, such as warplanes, within the context of a historical event that only becomes 'real' through play and study.

While the future may present truly confusing hardware and software configurations for a user, players remain fully aware today that their immersion occurs within gameworlds cushioned by game rules and their components. With advances in neural links between human brains and computer systems, we may see the potential for a true liminal space that causes confusion. Valve, the primary digital PC game distributor, and also the developer of the VR headset Index, is currently working on a neural interface for future VR technology.[6] Today, though, players still control what they see with material peripherals and the movement of their head and body. In the most immersive of this chapter's case studies, the cockpit and interior of a plane or tank, players remain aware they are playing a simgame even when using VR, safe in a chair without any moments of sustained delusion that real weapons will be fired at them.

While the case study simulators in this chapter have 2D modes that are used by most players, those of *IL2* and *DCS* both provide sophisticated VR gameplay that radically changes the experience. Analysis of them is limited to VR in this study because of the potential for a more immersive experience, rather than 2D, which often provides more competitive play at the cost of immersion. For example, in a WWII dogfight flight simulator in which planes fly slower than the speed of sound, rarely use rockets, and often engage each other at between 100 and 300 m, the 'low six' enemy is the most dangerous situation for any pilot and one that is particularly difficult for a VR user to spot. A typical scenario of an unwary pilot would see him or her flying along in a straight path with an enemy who has an altitude advantage. That enemy circles behind the lower aircraft, then in a split-S maneuver rapidly dives behind and below, slowly rising in a hidden spot (the low six) that the unwary craft can't see.

Players with a 2D screen, with a mouse for viewing and with a flick of a wrist, can 'check six' to see behind them, maybe even spotting a diving plane before it is in position. Other 2D technologies exist, including a 'Track-IR' infrared camera that reads the position of a reflector mounted on a player's headset. This allows players to turn their heads just a few degrees to have the in-game view rotate up to 180 degrees, swiveling the virtual pilot's head (and view) like an owl's. For the same advantage, a VR player must physically move his or her head or try to mod their headset to accept snap views, which can be disorienting in VR.

Applying this understanding of the limitations and capabilities of current computer hardware and peripherals to a historical context foregrounds an important distinction. Players engaging in historical simgames recognize they are virtual players in virtual worlds, but parsing the virtual configurations as one moves from 2D to VR becomes more engaging with the increased immediacy and presence of virtual space. Immersion, then, not only adds to the enjoyment of gameplay, but also adds to a sense of increased realism or historical accuracy, but never to the point of confusing the actual world with the virtual. Rather than immersion being a controlling idea for how to think of the potential dangers of increased realism, complex interpretation of these often-intense virtual experiences as a secondary process drives the dynamic between players, simgames, and simtexts.

In a serious WWII combat simgame, just sitting in a highly rendered cockpit with 4k textures of historical aircraft acts as a starting point that inspires clarification for a player. A new pilot is faced with the need to move through the areas of the cockpit to learn what the different gauges represent, the different dials, levers, and buttons. A player will need to learn these elements for in-game success, but will also learn their historic contexts. Approaching this interpretive demand from within historical game studies, and adding the past as a context to these game elements, provides a third experiential axis that is predicated on the other two. This mixture of understanding gameplay elements combined with an interpretation of virtual elements of the past situates the player experience as historically reconfigured.

While Juul might describe the experience of a player sitting in a virtual cockpit as incoherent, not in that it fails to make sense, but that it fails to make full sense of, say, flying an actual Spitfire, it succeeds in what its developers attempt in harnessing an imagined configuration: to provide some sense of flying such a machine, with increasing degrees of realism, along with increased difficulty the more serious the simulator. All this immersion is fully contingent on an acceptance that core aspects of sitting in a virtual cockpit and flying a Spitfire in combat are unsimulated.

Placing such a critique as Juul's incoherence insight alongside my ironic buffer of the imagined simulation into a virtualized historical reconfiguration, it may be suggested that the player experience fails to emerge as a full picture of the lived experiences of historical pilots while still simulating some aspects, reconfigured for the virtual gameworld. I agree, but still see degrees of simulated accuracy pointing to historical awareness. Others are concerned with this potential for incoherence between the actual and the virtual, often asking important questions regarding the realism of such a simgame, in particular the fact that these simgames are mediated by devices such as controllers with buttons that need to be pushed, which distances us from what is occurring on screen (Welsh, 2016: 131). This artificiality may blind us in a war game to the horrors of such realities. I would argue that no war game ever approaches the actualities of combat, real-world violence, or its effects. Rather, what is approached is a virtual experience of the past that points outward to clarifying simtexts, rather than toward the unimaginable horrors of real warfare.

Currently, most simgames are played on consoles or PCs, the former providing easy access to games within a reliable hardware architecture. The PlayStation and Xbox facilitate an arcade-like experience, as do many PC games, but PCs offer much more flexibility in terms of modding and therefore open up the hardware to serious simulators. The critical insight that the simulated past is mediated by distancing digital devices reinforces the idea that players are separated from the imaginary and reconfigured past, and thus insulated (for better or worse). This is reasonable, even though an increase in the potency of these devices is occurring that inches us closer to a space where we can, at least temporarily, be immersed enough to distract us from a mundane present, while ultimately remaining aware of the great divide between the simulation and reality.

But believing a delusion is only one potential future danger as virtualized realities increase in fidelity. The past can be sanitized or erased within such reconfigured spaces. What such a WWII simgame as *IL2* does, in the context of fears that computer games create a distance that removes players from understanding the real dangers and horrors of war, is to provide a gameworld that keenly reminds players (especially those using VR) of how deadly WWII aviation could be (without suffering any harrowing experience). In this sense, it draws a clear line between the actual and the virtual, while also simulating the extreme danger of such activity, and one not to be taken lightly outside the simulated gamespace.

This key point of discussing ironic distance in simulators between the player and the virtual world is critical because in FPSs most players today still play on 2D screens, highly artificial experiences in which one 'kills' a digital avatar of a player or even just a 'bot' that may only be several inches tall, on a screen resting on a desk a foot or two away from a player. Even though the visual representations within such simulations look increasingly realistic with today's modern CPU and GPU hardware, there is a direct link from the unreality of Pacman chomping on ghosts to shooting an enemy in *CoD* within a framed desktop display.

Of course, today, that enemy within a multiplayer game is often another person with the intelligence of a human being, but players are distanced from a digital avatar's fate and can remain in the game, or simply quit. The problem this distance creates for some thinkers is that such 'killing' may reinforce in players a casualness to the actual killing done in modern war, much real war also being mediated by distancing technologies such as remote-controlled and weaponized drones (Huntemann and Payne, 2009). This nuanced concern is convincing, even as VR-oriented gaming experiences seek to remove the perception of this mediation layer through increased visual and haptic fidelity and intensity that immerse the player in the presence of gameplay.

Another interesting approach to the disregard with which players treat an in-game death of an infantry soldier or pilot frames such lack of concern as an example of simgames simulating new, technologized virtual ontologies distanced from real-world consequences. Thinkers such as Colin Milburn (2018) see in the overt entanglement of human subjectivity with machines an analogue to how life emerges as a complex biological process, but now with organisms and machines bound in cyborg-like relationships that complicate the real/unreal divide. As this entanglement increases in complexity, awareness of our place within it may diminish, thus embedding us in a relationship in which we are primed for virtual violence.

Milburn examines the process in computer games of in-game death and instant restarts, or 'respawning,' as a way to rethink this entangled mechanistic/organistic phenomenon. He foregrounds respawning because of its prevalence and the ease with which it allows for other non-consequential processes such as reloading, resetting, and relaunching, all of which factor into games as safe-zones that mediate what a player experiences from any understanding of, say, violence in the real world or the past. The prevalence of hit-points or health bars in popular computer games can also be found, to differing degrees, in serious simgames, even if these often demand players pay much higher prices for taking damage or dying. All occur with no real impact on the player. Respawning as a mechanic, then, and the ease with which some computer games allow players to heal and return a virtual avatar, is a dividing line that separates the casual arcade-experience from the more serious encounter. Milburn finds in this process a unconscious effect in which the latent energy of constant respawning creates in players "respawn energy" (2018: 11) that points them outside the game into a variety of activities, many of which are generative, but some destructive.

I would add interpretive energy to this list. A study such as Milburn's acknowledges how such practices reinforce potentially dangerous links between video games and real-world training, especially when war is a theme. Even if one plays WWII games with the hope of only learning tactics and strategy, and even if those aspects still apply to combat, the bulk of the experience reconfigures the past more than it prepares a player to transfer in-game knowledge into the present, as do other war games set in more contemporary settings. Granted, with advanced computing simulation technology, elements from WWII can be used within real-world scenarios, for better or worse. Yet we see these translations in shooters more than in flight simulators. Simulators, though, offer the contained cockpit as a more immersive experience that more closely mirrors the reality being simulated, even though FPSs are not far off with their infantry moving through difficult terrain.

Milburn would call for hacking to balance how developers frame war for players as more than a political posture but a type of agential activism, one indebted to computer game modding, but also one that can bring about serious change in the actual world. This line of thinking reveals how other genres in computer gaming, such as science fiction, provide analogues, cyberpunk and its modding and hacking ethos being one clear example. But directly linking the cyberpunk genre within literature, cinema, and gaming to the critique of the globalization of war is a cultural critique of fictive genres, rather than an example of how to transfer to simgames a strong causality that one (hacking) leads to the other (positive change). Science fiction as a highly imagined genre allows for such imaginings as a challenge to global capital through various 'punks,' or forms of resistance, thus imbuing the genre with a constantly renewing ethos outside the constraints of a particular historical context.

More problematic issues arise with simulation outside its use as real-world training. We see this with the erasure of difficult aspects of remembering the war, especially in the whitewashing of Nazi or Soviet war crimes, or the decisions that led to wide-scale bombing of Germany by the USA and Britain and, of course, the use of nuclear weapons by the USA (see Chapter 5). Other aspects are glossed or ignored, such as the treatment of Allied prisoners by the Japanese or other less well-known war crimes such as those of the Ustaše in Croatia.

Rather than denying the importance of a historical cultural critique that would create awareness of these numerous, awful events, digital simgames offer degrees of simulated experience constrained by the limitations of the game environment, even as VR increases the fidelity of gameworlds. And rather than arguing that training replaces erasure as a relevant concern, simgames offer a way to approach the past in their afforded experiences. We see this when focusing on a type of post-phenomenological experience that works within a digital mediated space that creates a type of reimagined gameworld, yet one grounded in a reconfigured past with direct analogues that can be understood and practiced.

## Symbolism

Of central importance to the dynamic that emerges with simgames in this study is the idea of simgames as built artifacts and objects that act as arenas of interpretation rather than just as neutral objects. This corresponds to ideas within technology studies that view our technologies as extensions of our minds.[7] Thus, for a player of a simgame simulator, aircraft or tanks function as digital extensions of a player sitting in front of a computer. This entanglement of the digital and analog becomes a space that encourages examination into a reconfigurable past and its place in our present as mechanisms of experiencing history through such gameplay.

Yet they are not simply simulated machines; they are also historical symbols that can be both earnest memorials or odd fetishes. Thus, for example, the arms-race between German Messerschmitt BF 109s and Focke-Wulf 190s versus the British Hawker Hurricanes and Supermarine Spitfires becomes a site of interpretive play historically located in a contested past. Today, we see this contest without the rancor of a political past that pitted the RAF against the Luftwaffe or even the cost in human lives for pilots who actually wielded these machines to kill. Even so, these reconfigured contests are loaded with memory politics, and this sometimes still has damaging effects in the world.

The earlier concern of simulation as training, then, does not apply in this case of WWII flight simulators as it does for later aircraft. No one plays a WWII flight simulator to train to kill other pilots in the present with prop-based aircraft. In today's world of fifth- and (soon to be) sixth-generation fighter aircraft, most early pre-jet fighter aircraft are now relegated to airshows, even if combat prop aircraft are still used in some applications, including the Brazilian Embraer's Super Tucano, a propeller-driven light-attack aircraft that can provide close ground support over challenging environments. While many of the principles found in WWII simgames would directly transfer to someone learning to fly a Tucano, a pilot would need specific training to succeed in such a powerful, newer prop airplane.

A simgame such as *IL2* avoids the dangers of 'milsims' as training grounds for potential armed conflict because of its use of antiquated aircraft. Instead, it presents its playable gameworld as a site in which the symbols of the past are reconfigured in the present. In the worst case, this can lead to fetishizing historical weapons of war along national or political grounds, even today. Yet in most instances, across most of its servers and communities, WWII simulators are an example of how the unfortunate historical reality of war between nations and persons is replaced within game by an openness of players from once embattled countries.

Outside these contexts, a simgame for the general public such as *IL2* or *DCS* is inspired by a deep appreciation of the historical contexts, as well as an appreciation for the machines themselves. In many ways, this is an anti-humanistic impulse that removes the human cost from the picture, but it does so to offer an engaging gamespace for players devoid of human suffering, thus continuing a type of 'safe' adventure that one experiences in reading a novel or watching a film, which allows a reader or viewer to approach material through a mediating zone—this one of play.

When considering novels, cinema, and games as mediating spaces or mechanisms to engage the past, analogues exist from professional scholarship and criticism that show us how to theorize simgames as arenas of interpretation. Within flight and combat simgames, we find earlier thinking from the eighteenth century and the Romantics' foregrounding of the poetic symbol still relevant, in particular when we look at historical aircraft functioning as key agents of gameplay as well as symbols of aviation virtues. Looking at them as a type of poetic symbol, often ambiguous, especially to new players unfamiliar with their histories, rather than as purveyors of political ideology (for which they certainly could be used), encourages the experience of flying them in the simulations over their historiographies as military machines.

A dominant site of tension in WWII simulators, then, is the simulation of historical conflicts that emerged between the air forces of the primary belligerent nations. As mentioned several times in this study, the early German 109s are historically understood to have been advanced fighters at the end of the 1930s, enough to have dominated during the Spanish Civil War, the invasion of Poland, and the initial push into the Soviet Union during Barbarossa. These were highly automated planes, with governors for the propeller pitch as well as mechanisms to regulate the radiators, among other innovations such as a canopy that could open at speed through a controlled explosion. In game, a 109 is considered an 'easy' machine to fly, especially the 'Gustav' 2 variant with its ability to limit manifold pressure, thus avoiding a blown engine by a careless pilot (or new player). This degree of ease attracts many newcomers to a simgame such as *IL2* who do not have to worry about the real-world dangers of taking off and landing a 109 (two very dangerous historical aspects of its use). Yet it also reflects the virtue of German mechanical engineering as advanced and sophisticated, a cultural claim bordering on cliché that exists even today but emerges as a common understanding among players.

Likewise, in the classic narrative of machines as cultural symbols, the British Vickers Supermarine Spitfire found itself in the air in the early 'Phony War,' as well as over Dunkirk and during the evacuation of the British expeditionary force, to be an equal of the 109s. In aviation history, RAF Fighter Command and its squadrons of Spitfires take center stage (as do, it should be stated, Hurricanes) as they tangled in the Battle of Britain against the 109s, 110s, and other aircraft. While these aircraft are detailed in numerous historical simtexts, for many players they are known through other media. The early Mark I Spitfire and the 109 'Emil' are key symbols of resistance in the film *The Battle of Britain* (1969), as well as recently in Christopher Nolan's *Dunkirk* (2017), while the slower Hurricane features in a recent film of the same name about the triumph of Polish aviators fighting for the RAF.[8] Most of these aircraft are highlighted within tense dogfighting scenarios.

In a clip from *Dunkirk*, we see Tom Hardy's character, Farrier, leading his Fortis 1 squadron as they are engaged by a pouncing 109. This scene represents the tension and energy that a simgame such as *IL2* tries to capture. It even represents tactics, such as attacking out of the sun, coordinating with a wingman, or luring a 109 into a turn fight with the more agile Spitfire. The Spitfire as seen in such films has become a national symbol of resistance and survival in the UK, while in game it is recognized as a maneuverable and deadly artist of the sky, an equal for the early 109s in certain combat situations, if not in many cases its better. This type of narrative has become common in viewing RAF pilots as the saviors of Britain, a mythology that Churchill encouraged. Aviator memoirs and other simtexts have reinforced this grand narrative of human heroics, especially when they reveal the dangers and loss of life.

Such latent symbolizing emerges as gameplay elements among players for most of the major nations of the war. In *IL2*, American aircraft can be found early in the simgame, with the P-40 Warhawk and P-39 Airacobra, lend-lease machines sold to the Russian VVS, who refitted them for their own needs (in essence making the planes their own). The playable P-40 in *IL2* is a sturdy and durable plane, but one that is outclassed, reflecting a sense that the early American offerings were sub-par and reflective of a less than fully mobilized nation. In a later release, based on the Battle of Bodenplatte, a late-war, last-ditch effort by the Luftwaffe to stop a now-prepared Allied advance toward Berlin, *IL2* offers players the ability to fly a variety of high-powered American planes on an equal footing with their German enemies, such as the P-51 Mustang (B and D) and P-38 Lightning. The North American examples maintain symbolic weight as reflective of the reputation of its planes, those most popular in simgames often known for requiring tactics that rely on speed rather than maneuverability. They are sturdy, like the P-47 Thunderbolt, reproducible, and numerous.

Such symbolic in-game elements, along with the experience provided by a simgame such as *IL2*, then, become a site of analysis and curiosity for players. In this way we see that simulators refract a wide range of phenomena (heroic and daring, but just as often horrific and deadly) of WWII aviation into a safe game space that romanticizes the experience, but also reveals the dangers faced in the past by real pilots.

For *IL2*, such a discourse of the historically located, reconfigured imaginary frames the simgame in a way that elevates a sense of adventure, tactics, and strategy while removing the actual physical threats of real dogfighting, bombing, taking-off, landing, navigating bad-weather, flying, life and death on front-line airfields, disease, privation, and so on. This reality distortion is necessary because of the inherent fact of constrained, virtualized gameplay, but also because the games' intentions are to capture a touch of the romance and seriousness associated with the activity, along with providing an arena that encourages rewards for engaging steep learning curves.

## Aviator Memoirs and Chivalry

For simulators in particular, a key type of simtext beyond technical descriptions of the planes and tanks is the memoir (as mentioned in Chapter 2). One worthwhile attribute of a simgame such as *IL2*, and how it is played within its multiplayer servers, is that the game experience has mostly moved beyond the political ideologies that emerged during the war, be they fascist, communist, or those of liberal democracy. A simgame such as *IL2* is about WWII aviation and its appreciation, along with an understanding of aspects that defined a pilot's experience during the war. But as simgames point to the simtexts, so do they reveal the messy facts of history and their requisite interpretations. Memoirs reveal these difficulties in sharp contrast because personal perspectives often fit into a larger tapestry of narrative construction by the differing nations.

This problem becomes apparent when we look at how players use such simtexts, even within the context of an appreciation of WWII aviation. As a common form of written popular history, the memoir suffers from the same problems as any autobiography, especially if we look to examples as historical documents rather than as literary documents. A memoir is exemplary as a simtext, though, when we see how it presents specific types of personal experiences, especially those that influence the constructed mythologies embedded in simgames. Even more so, memoirs reveal in detail the many lived experiences of actual pilots that simulations attempt to capture but, just as much, fail to address.

The UK has produced by far the most impactful aviation memoirs in English, along with the USA. These often describe the stories of young RAF pilots who survived the Battle of Britain. Geoffrey Wellum's *First Light* (2002) is an example of such a simtext that has proven popular for the general reading public interested in the war, and is one that a WWII combat-simulator player interested in Spitfires might encounter. It details Wellum's challenge in joining the RAF as a young man, fighting in the Battle of Britain, ending up at Malta. It provides a close, subjective POV, yet does more than what is expected from such a narrative when viewed through the frame of asking what can be simulated from such experiences rather than simply noting its merits as a historical document.

For example, initially Wellum experienced a common problem with learning to fly 'tail-draggers' such as the Tiger Moth. On take-off, managing to keep such an airplane straight is difficult, causing all sorts of unnecessary swerving (Wellum, 2002: 12), also a common problem for first-time simulator pilots attempting to take off. We see how he is taught navigation and the difficulties involved, a core element in online servers that provide no GPS and require virtual pilots to fly by waypoints, time in the air, and so on. This reflection on the actual challenges of real pilots, problems with take-off and landing as well as navigation, finds parallels in simulators as important elements players must master. Again, the historicity of these texts works at an oblique level, secondary to a playable experience.

Such a memoir also acts as a game guide in how to fly key aircraft like the Spitfire, along with providing personal tips from experience on dogfighting tactics. In one of his first encounters with the enemy, Wellum describes tactics for an early Spitfire that directly translate to simulated games such as *IL2*. Remembering his thoughts as if a novelist, he speaks to himself: "Keep turning, Geoff, throw her about, don't fly straight for a second" (Wellum, 2002: 149), echoing a best practice by many WWII fighter pilots to never flight in a straight line once in a combat zone. Later he states plainly another maxim: "The Hun [German] that is going to get me is the one I won't see" (Wellum, 2002: 165). These interior monologues are common in fiction as well as auto-biography, where the reader understands that impressions are being translated into an account scaffolded with fictive techniques, yet that point to the sorts of truths gleaned from literature rather than history. This is a kind of wisdom translated into simgame techniques, rather than bare knowledge. In game, Wellum's advice translates as whoever sees his enemy first has the advantage.

Such a memoir can also reflect what is not simulated in current simgames, such as the pressure to pass ground examinations—that one might fail, and then receive a drubbing as Wellum did in dramatic fashion: "You must start to think about growing up, Wellum. The RAF wants men, not boys" (Wellum, 2002: 43). This sort of criticism by a superior, and the psychological and emotional effects it might create, are glossed in simgames, a major part of the experience that remains outside the experience of gameplay.

More dire consequences are also unsimulated. One is the spatial disorientation that can occur when a pilot accidentally enters adverse weather conditions, such as the time Wellum believed his left wing was dipping low while his instruments said it was level. He writes: "It takes willpower to ignore the feeling" (2002: 233); this critical and life-saving ability continues to challenge contemporary pilots operating with visual flight rules who have unwittingly entered inclement meteorological conditions. These lack of visual clues because of weather may cause navigation and even flight problems for players within game, but prove innocuous when one is sitting still in front of a computer, and have no adverse effects on a player's inner ear. Curious players, then, confront this obvious awareness that aspects of crucial lived history are ignored within the simulator, and even that the memoirs they read are often more literature than history. Certainly, the pain and horror of crashing (and most likely dying) is outside the scope of a simulator, but such simtexts open a player to a process of interpretation that may create more questions than expected, as well as a sense of empathy for those involved.

A grand narrative of aviator heroics is also evident when reading memories or biographies of Luftwaffe pilots, their perspectives situating a player in the middle of the discourse over how culpable ordinary Germans were, or how involved (or knowledgeable) the Wehrmacht were in war crimes, or (in this case) how ideologically driven Luftwaffe pilots were. This discourse often argues that by the end of the war German pilots were fighting to save their country from Western carpet bombing, rather than as ardent supporters of the war.[9] Historical understanding becomes a process of continued interpretation and a teasing out of such mythologies, especially when critical readers become aware of how German generals (along with many of the writers of German-perspective memoirs) wrote after the war to distance themselves from National Socialism, Hitler, and thus war crimes. Many memoir simtexts present the Luftwaffe as a superior fighting force in WWII, as do the numerous points of reference in broader works on the war. Its culpability, along with that of the Wehrmacht, remains an important topic even if many of the memoirs written about it foreground pilots as heroic defenders of Germany.[10]

Three of the more widely known written biographies concern three Luftwaffe aces: Adolf Galland, Hans Ulrich Rudel, and Erich Hartmann. Each of their accounts demand the same sort of interpretation required to parse claims made by surviving soldiers and pilots that they were something other than avid supporters of the egregious policies of Hitler, Himmler, and Goebbels. As an example, Galland was a leading commander in the Luftwaffe, whose battles over strategy and tactics with Reichsmarschall Herman Göring earned him a reputation as a troublemaker. His memoir recounts the war in such a way that conveniently categorizes him as an airman doing his duty rather than an ideologue (Galland, 1954). Questions remained until the end of his life over his sympathies for National Socialism, but he has also been represented as a chivalrous aviator who could recognize and respect the enemy as honorable and worthy (see the account of the RAF pilot Douglas Bader later in this chapter) rather than as a murderous National Socialist. Still, Galland was considered a Nazi sympathizer throughout the rest of his life, the difficulties in parsing his German nationalism from the sins of National Socialism being a mark that never left him, even as he attempted to remove it when working around the world in postwar aviation.

Rudel, though, continued to be an unabashed supporter of Hitler and National Socialism, "a notorious Nazi acolyte" (Smelser and Davies, 2008: 203). His memoir is a clear example of a postwar Nazi survivor attempting to justify himself. He rationalizes his belief that he was fighting for a just cause, a common refrain among wartime Nazi propaganda being that Germany and its Führer were protecting the West from Asiatic Bolsheviks and their new world order of communism. Rudel represents Stalin's army at Stalingrad as full of "religious fanaticism," claiming Stalin was like a god to those he ruled over and that communism was adhered to by "disciples of a new gospel. And so Stalingrad is to become the Bethlehem of our century. But a Bethlehem of war and hatred, annihilation, and destruction." And later after having a medal pinned on him by Hitler, he recalls hearing Hitler speak about defeating Bolshevism, "otherwise the world will be plunged into an appalling chaos from which there is no way out" (2012: 84). This is the rhetoric that attempts to justify all the criminality associated with National Socialism.

These transparent passages emerge in the best cases as blinkered delusion and in the worst cases as unacknowledged culpability. They stand as key points in Rudel's account, which details the particulars of his missions, mostly in the dive-bomber Junkers 87 Stuka. What we see is how a contemporary WWII flight simulation such as *IL2* attempts to capture the nuances of tactics and strategy performed by someone such as Rudel, while ignoring ideology and its political effects on individuals.

For example, Rudel details a difficult mission in 1941 in which he was tasked with destroying two Soviet battleships in Kronstadt harbor. The *Marat* and the *October Revolution* were the targets, as well as a number of smaller cruisers. A description of this encounter reads like a list of tips for players interested in learning how to dive bomb in a complex WWII combat simulator.

The Stuka formations fly at roughly 10,000 ft and use dive breaks when diving, only pulling out at low level, so that their speed is maximized as they retreat (Rudel, 2012: 31).

On another mission, he details how he would fly past a target, turn around, and only bomb after his vector was heading home, again to achieve the maximum amount of speed toward home without the need to bleed energy in turns (Rudel, 2012: 174). Rudel also writes how they chose to attack out of the sun and destroy flak batteries first before attempting to disable tanks. Of critical importance, we learn, was avoiding the blast from your own bombs, an element programmed into *IL2* (Rudel, 2012: 178). This sort of tactics-focused writing emerges in simtexts as areas of practice for players who may have no interest in the ideologies of the pilots, especially in how they are translated by developers and players into in-game tactics. What we don't see is that while Rudel was never convicted of war crimes, his association with Nazism never left him after he fought for its victory. Indeed, photos of his funeral show some individuals making the Nazi salute.

Hartmann, though, avoided the postwar stigma of latent National Socialism having been taken prisoner by the Soviets, and he is best known as the highest scoring fighter pilot in history. Hartmann's biography, *The Blond Knight of Germany* (Toliver and Constable, 1970), is an example of a popular simtext among WWII combat simulation players because it captures the tactics employed by the war's leading ace. These correspond to tactics that can emerge in gameplay, such as a technique perfected by Hartmann when approaching an enemy target: "See – Decide – Attack – Coffee Break" (Toliver and Constable, 1970: 46). Such a series of steps directly correspond to scenarios simulated within simgames.

Many novice players who spot an enemy in WWII flight simgames immediately dive in for an attack, usually unaware of who else might be in the area. As tunnel vision forces them to focus on the target, they are 'jumped' by an unseen opponent and shot down. Hartmann's 'See' and 'Decide' are critical initial steps before engaging: He is taking time to make sure he has situational awareness and is in a dominant position, which means he has an altitude or energy advantage before 'Attack.' 'Coffee Break' suggests that he must regroup and reassess his situation before beginning the process again.

Hartmann also used surprise tactics that his mentor, Edmund Rossman, taught him, and he had an instinct for "point blank firing" (Toliver and Constable,

1970: 49). This extremely close engagement range is another critical technique that demands discipline in a simgame such as *IL2*. Most beginners will fire when they are too far away, the tracers warning their target, who can then roll or dive away. Hartmann's technique of surprise and closing the distance proves very effective for players who have the ability to resist until the right time.

Hartmann was not only successful as an attacker, but also in escaping deadly situations, one of his techniques being usable within *IL2*'s flight model. His biographers write:

> Erich developed only one rule for breaking away as a last-ditch maneuver, and that was to execute a movement where possible with negative G's. An attacking pilot expects his quarry to turn tighter and try to out-turn him— the classic dogfight. The attacking pilot must turn even tighter in order to pull firing lead on his quarry. As a result, his quarry disappears under the nose of the attacker. At that moment the quarry can escape by shoving forward on the stick and kicking bottom rudder. The forces on his aircraft change from plus five G's to minus one or minus one-and-a-half G's. This escape maneuver is almost impossible for the attacker to sec or follow until it is too late. Erich made good use of this escape tactic, which threw the attacker instantly from advantage to complex disadvantage. (Toliver and Constable, 1970: 86)

Such specific simtexts as this passage describe complex techniques that the flight and damage models of a simgame such as *IL2* simulates, creating curated experiences that are rooted in history but translated through digital games.

Others, though, would argue that viewing Hartmann as a hero means taking on "ideological ballast" that includes "the racial tenets of the Nazis" (Smelser and Davies, 2008: 172). While his biography's use of 'blond' and 'knight' in its title signals, as the authors note, the racial superiority beliefs of the Nazis, simgame players who may have heard the name Hartmann but not read his biography encounter talk of him within simulators as a German ace without any racial ideology. Players will earn his name as a descriptor if they tend to fly very high, avoiding dangerous low encounters, just because they want to increase their kill count. This reference is devoid of any hint of political ballast or any suggestion that such high-flying 'Hartmanns' have any sympathy for National Socialism.

Such a critique that would link Hartmann and politics, though, also details how earlier publications about him and others fed into the myth of the German militaries as admirable and honorable, while today (in our mostly post-Cold-War societies) WWII simtexts reveal new (and sometimes problematic) meanings directly related to what is ignored in particular simgames. Hartman is still a symbol, but of a new relationship of player to past where gameplay outreaches ideology. The fact he fought over the Eastern Front where so many war crimes occurred beneath him is completely erased in a simgame such as *IL2*.

An important quote exemplifies how historians make demands beyond the interests of most simgame players:

> One wants to take nothing away from Hartmann in terms of his skill and daring as a fighter pilot. However, to divorce his exploits from the regime, which he loyally served and from whose leader he accepted its second highest decoration, renders no service. Nor does placing him not in the historical context of a war of racial conquest and annihilation, but rather in a romanticized feudal joust between knights for the hand of fair a lady. (Smelser and Davies, 2008: 173)

Many memoir simtexts broaden the scope from the personal memoir to narratives of battles and events between dueling knights, full of chivalry and daring, rather than address the uncomfortable truths of the war. These typically construct heroes of fighter pilots such as Hartmann, while others mythologize heroic stories of daring such as the Doolittle Raid (Okerstrom, 2015). Questions tend to arise, though. For example, if pilots such as Hartmann were chivalrous, players are led behind the confines of curated simgames, and outwards to uncomfortable answers.

Dan Hampton's *Lords of the Sky: Fighter Pilots and Air Combat, from the Red Baron to the F-16* (2015) details aviation from WWI to the present, and is exemplary in how he represents air combat as distinct from other branches. In it, he recounts major battles from WWI to WWII, such as the Battle of Britain and the air war in North Africa, up to the present. He recounts the exploits of fighter pilots from the perspective of a modern aviator, the same experience that flight combat simgames try to capture. These accounts of the lives of pilots work in a similar fashion as memoirs because they often use personal perspectives as their primary sources. Yet they further the fictionalization of these personal moments into heroics of virtuous aviators.

To understand how these insights are translated into games as an arena of chivalrous combatants, we should look again at literature and its power to create subjectivities with which readers identify. This relationship between writer and reader generates a type of purely imagined experience, one that in a simgame is simulated through digital space and its material peripherals. These accounts of the heroics of pilots are numerous, working within a long myth-making tradition of representing pilots as dueling heroes, distinct from the infantry grunts with their boots in the mud. Such a sentiment is directly reflected in a simgame such as *IL2* that presents all combatant sides as honorable.

One such account written for the popular sphere is that of Franz Stigler, featured in the book *A Higher Call: An Incredible True Story of Combat and Chivalry in the War-Torn Skies of World War II* (Makos and Alexander, 2012). Its subtitle places it within the tradition that tells the story of honorable avia-tors (in this case, German) as modern knights of the sky (such as Hartmann). It details a documented encounter between an American B-17 bomber and a BF 109 fighter. The bomber had made a bombing run over Germany and was badly damaged. On returning west in the hope of crossing the Channel and landing in the south of Britain, Stigler in a 109 found it—and escorted it to the Channel.

Stigler's life is detailed in the account, a project by an American (Adam Makos) who claims that in researching the book he had to overcome his ingrained instinct to think of all WWII Germans as Nazis. In it, he recounts how he learned about Stigler and his refusal to shoot down the bomber—what would be, according to Stigler, an act of murder. This account highlights a point of contention that is taken for granted by many non-Germans—the assumption that all persons who fought for Germany were also eager members of the National Socialist party. Stigler was a Catholic represented by Makos as having a staunch moral compass, who found himself in the unenviable position of defending his country, and the people in it, from increasingly dangerous and overwhelming bombing raids by the British and the Americans.

Verifying such accounts is beyond the scope of my project, other than recog-nizing them as published examples of how complex human stories emerge within reconfigured historical contexts, rather than as driving factors within simgames or as actual history. What does directly relate to my theme, though, is how interpretation also emerges as a secondary process for players who are searching for information on tactics and, curiously, perhaps clarity on what is not simulated (i.e., asking, if the story is true, what drove Stigler to save the bomber).

In *A Higher Call*, the American flying the bomber, a young second lieutenant named Charlie Brown, finds himself in a barely flyable aircraft. A description of what airmen experienced as they battled enemy fighters and struggled to survive goes beyond anything simulated in current WWII combat simulators. The description of what happened to the crew after 20 mm cannon shells ripped through the aircraft relies on literary sophistication for its emotional effects: "A cold breeze blew from one side to the other. Only direct hits from several cannon shells could have done this. Blackie turned Ecky by the shoulder then reeled back in fright. Ecky's head had been nearly severed and dangled onto his chest. His guns pointed silently earthward" (Makos and Alexander, 2012: 187).

Such harrowing moments are best described in detail or represented cinematically rather than simulated in combat simgames—which would change the experience from a simulation of flying to the personal impact felt by the destruction of war. This leads to weighty questions about the human experience. A player interested in Stigler's moral actions might see the war from his perspective; that as the war continued and veteran Luftwaffe pilots died or were captured, those who remained were forced to fly to the point of exhaustion. "Pilots began to fly drunk. In Fighter Wing 26, a squadron leader even shot himself in his cockpit with a handgun" (Makos and Alexander, 2012: 262). Again, one might imagine such scenarios in narrative-based VR experiences to highlight the extreme and unique circumstances pilots endured, telling a story rather than simulating curated combat. These would begin to function as consciousness-raising texts rather than games, simulated memorials to the human cost and the tragedy of war, rather than expressing the thrill of combat.

Memoirs such as these and other personal accounts allow us to understand history differently than we would by carefully analyzing primary sources. In doing so, memoir-framed simgames interpret and reinforce public memory of an event such as WWII for players with the potentially skewed view that the cockpit was the most important space for those fighting the war. Dogfighting simulators have proven successful because the constrained POV of a cockpit acts as a convincing simulation space for someone sitting at a computer screen. This mediating environment of players, their peripherals, and the simgame has always been integral given computer hardware requirements and gameplay mechanics, and such a relationship hints that the ranges of simulated experiences will expand.

Stories of chivalry among pilots reach back to the years just following the war's end, demonstrating marked stylistic choices that present their characters and events in an idealized fashion. One such novelized biographical simtext, Paul Brickhill's *Reach for the Sky* (1954), recounts the life of the flying ace Douglas Bader; it was made into a film in 1956, directed by Lewis Gilbert. The book details how he was captured, but lived to survive the war. He is represented as a dauntless, rough and tumble, adventurous troublemaker, who happened to be good at fighting Germans—and one who didn't believe in the chivalrous argument that honor above all else existed among dueling pilots. In this narrative-driven fictionalized simtext, we are asked to see these events through Bader's perspective, a type of close and subjective POV that attempts to simplify his experiences, rather than complicate them. When considered within the simgame–simtext dynamic, a player realizes this novelized account of Bader's life is less concerned with tactics and technical details than expected, but as in Wellum's account they still emerge as salient elements in the text.

We learn that when Bader first flies one of the early model Spitfires he is thrilled to discover he has eight machine guns in his wings (Brickhill, 1954: 115). Within the context of a simgame such as *IL2*, these sorts of personal emotional experiences resonate less than the technical details of why eight machine guns might be thrilling or not. Simgame players of *WT*, *IL2*, *CloD*, and so on become aware that the early Mk 1a Spitfire had eight Browning machine guns, yet had no heavy cannons as did the 'Emil' version of the 109 (which they faced in the Battle of Britain).[11] Tactics and weaponry in such simtexts are colored through the personal perspective of a real pilot who lived through these experiences, rather than just being a stat-sheet for a player wondering who has the better guns.

When Bader eventually fires his weapons, he hears a "shocking noise" (Brickhill, 1954: 129), and the passage details his experience of having an enemy fighter fill his windscreen, and of white and then flame engulfing the fighter, "flaring like a blow-torch" (Brickhill, 1954: 129). These horrific moments have impact within a literary context as they describe the human condition of a pilot under enemy fire, yet they are less dramatic within a simulation that removes the player from any danger besides falling out of a chair. A curious understanding emerges from reading a simtext such as Bader's life story and then playing a simgame such as *IL2* with its carefully simulated damage models in which aircraft are engulfed in digital flame or come apart in the air. As a player, you can even involuntarily flinch, especially in VR after shooting at an enemy plane when one of its ailerons comes off and nearly hits your propeller. But the simgame fails to provide depth for the emotional experiences one might feel if viewing (or even experiencing) this destruction in actuality.

A novelization such as Brickhill's book hints through fictionalized representation rather than a deep dive into these areas, as opposed to a complex literary representation such as Grossman's *Life and Fate* (1959). But *IL2* does provide windows into a number of areas that step closer to framing virtual pilots as simulations for lived pilots. For example, *IL2* provides a complex single-player career mode in which you can follow your virtual pilot through a series of sorties in which the pilot survives and moves up the ranks, gaining awards (discussed later). But we don't actually see the early morning rising that pilots faced, such as the RAF squadron at Hornchurch who had daily patrols at 3.15 a.m. (Brickhill, 1954: 130). We also don't see the relationship between pilot and crew, the demands of tired pilots who can't stay awake in the cockpit, or any other number of difficulties faced by pilots on the ground, such as interpersonal conflicts.

Bader, for example, was always challenging his superior officers in Fighter Command, especially their conservative formation tactics such as the three-plane 'Vic' that was carried over from peacetime after WWI. These were already viewed as outdated (and had been discarded by the Germans), and were eventually replaced by the 'finger-four' formation (that the Germans were already using). Yet basic combat flight tactics, such as those mentioned by Wellum, still held true, examples being "The chap who'll control the battle will still be the chap who's got the height and sun, same as the last war" (Brickhill, 1954: 117);[12] and waiting until as late as possible to fire, which meant a much better chance of downing an aircraft, as aces such as Hartmann demonstrated.

"Bader's gospel" (Brickhill, 1954: 173) pushed for new ways of defeating the Germans, such as massing squadrons to confront large bomber formations, and then flying directly into them to break them up. He placed Spitfires above the formations, with Hurricanes below. Here we see the tactic of flying just high enough so that you are as high as possible but not generating a vapor trail (a technique used in multiplayer simgames such as *IL2*). We learn that over the Channel Bader once dived and shot a 109, but resisted following the enemy down to verify his air-kill, "obeying the dictum that it is suicide to follow an enemy down" (Brickhill, 1954: 210). The urge to verify such an air kill would mean (in this case) that one abandons a height advantage, as well as becoming distracted, another tactic that is simulated in serious multiplayer servers where this level of discipline is often the difference between a successful air kill (and a return to the airbase to claim it) versus one that follows with also being shot down.

Bader's novelized biography reflects that he grew frustrated with the propensity for 109s to run away, a common complaint in multiplayer servers when slower early-war Allied aircraft have to contend with faster escaping Luftwaffe aircraft. 109s also handled diving well without coming apart, along with being fast, so they would attack in a steep dive and often escape at speed. Bader jokingly made an addition to one report: "he added as a flippant afterthought: 'and the third one [air kill] I claim as frightened'" (Brickhill, 1954: 211). This annoyance emerges in a simgame such as *IL2* as a reflection that multiplayer servers often fail to track such escapes/retreats, either as a positive statistic, say, for a 109 player-pilot who manages to escape a Spitfire or possibly for a Spitfire pilot who forces the 109 to run in fear. Bader's admission that he wanted to claim a 'kill' because he frightened his opponent occurs within simulators as a contentious phenomenon among players, yet it is one that simgames fail to chart.

The story of Bader's time in the war may present its characters and scenarios in a less than critical manner, but it provides context for a key point of conversation that emerges among players of a game such as *IL2*—the theme of a simtext such as *A Higher Call* (2012), which asks if chivalry or honor existed among pilots as a supreme virtue that separated pilots from other branches of the military. Such a topic is foregrounded in game when a player's aircraft is shot and damaged and he or she chooses to bail out, hanging vulnerable in a parachute. 'Chute-killers' will strafe a helpless player floating to the ground before he or she manages to end the session.

Many multiplayer servers have no rules explicitly stating that this chute-killing is against the rules, but it is often frowned upon as dishonorable, especially by seasoned players who are parts of squadrons with their own rules. It does happen, though, and when it does, a (usually heated) conversation ensues over how historical pilots acted. Certain anecdotes from the war are offered, usually with the most basic understanding of their context or what actually happened. Then someone with the instincts of an amateur historian will start to quote passages and point to books for references that reveal chute killing was either frowned upon or embraced. For instance, While Adolf Galland claims chute killing would be "murder" (1954: 68), anecdotes exist of Poles ruthlessly shooting at German pilots in parachutes during the Battle of Britain, as well as Germans throughout the war engaging in the practice. American pilots were also accused by Germans of doing the same thing later in the war. Even though this was considered a war crime, it had to be explicitly stated by a number of nations to be unacceptable. This is the simgame pointing to the simtext dynamic in action.

One such incident that relates Bader to the chivalry arguments is often mentioned. When he was already a seasoned officer, having been promoted beyond squadron leader to a wing commander, with several squadrons under his command, he was flying a sortie over the Pas de Calais. According to Brickhill's account, he collided with a 109, destroying his aircraft. He parachuted to the ground, but had to leave one stuck prosthetic leg in the plane. After being captured, Bader was taken to a German hospital at St. Omer, where he eventually met another wing officer, the Luftwaffe's Adolf Galland. As mentioned earlier, Galland was eventually to become the commander of all of Germany's air force, directly under Göring. At the time of Bader's arrival, Galland was commanding an airfield nearby, and invited Bader to meet him for tea. In Galland's account he echoes the sentiment, often found among fighter pilots even today, that "the question of chivalry was demonstrated very clearly" by this episode (1954: 68).

Afterwards, Galland allowed Bader to sit in a BF 109, but refused his request to take it for a 'friendly' flight—the obvious risk of escape must have been evident. The Germans allowed Bader to eat with them, and Galland gave him a tin of tobacco. New prosthetic legs were even arranged to be sent from the UK, dropped from an aircraft on a mission that continued into Germany on a bombing run. According to Brickhill, Galland said: "It has been good to meet you. I'm afraid you will find it different in prison camp, but if there is ever anything I can do, please let me know" (1954: 237).

The account of this respectful treatment is often referenced as an example of chivalry among pilots (see Galland, 1954: 68–72 for the full story). When in 1945

Galland was captured and taken to the UK, he met Bader again, and was offered a box of cigars by him. However, Bader "suddenly vanished again, as he had done once before. In 1945 the war went on despite unconditional surrender. War is no game of cricket" (Galland, 1954: 72), an obvious admission by Galland that the war was anything but a sportsmanlike game, especially to men such as Bader.

## Case Studies: IL2 and DCS

A detailed examination into what simgames such as *IL2* and *DCS* offer from within the initial point of entry of the cockpit reveals the degrees to which the history of this space has been simulated, the cockpit's limitations, and its power to engage players beyond gameplay. Both simgames can be organized around two very different modes of play that are often seen in computer gaming, that of the single-player versus multiplayer experiences. Yet their differences are less important to this chapter than the shared, contained space of the cockpit because both modes encourage an engagement with the past, single player often allowing for more imaginative and casual forms of gameplay, while multiplayer encourages competitiveness, and in the most serious, a real desire to survive.

While *IL2* best exemplifies the current complexity of WWII air and tank simgames, a comment on a study-level simulator such as *DCS* helps to see how it adds depth outside intense and competitive multiplayer gameplay. Along with *CloD* and its 'Tobruk' expansion, *DCS*'s WWII planes and campaigns are another example of how history is approached through specific contexts that revolve around aviation and military history. Yet its scripted campaigns provide a greater degree of historical granularity than those offered by *IL2*, following the study-level details of its aircraft with a historical approach to its campaigns.

Both single-player and multiplayer modes encourage the simgame–simtext dynamic, rather than one having more of an influence; in so doing, the single-player option situates a player within very specific historical contexts through scripted mini-campaigns or common mission types. For example, *DCS*'s detailed mini-campaign, *Operation Epsom*, focuses on Spitfires in Normandy as the Allies push south into France, a very generic type of campaign setting that becomes more historically specific through play. This is a paid campaign that provides a guidebook, along with detailed instructions on how to fly the missions, work with wingmen, use radio communications, and so on. These additional simtext elements far exceed the requirements for simply engaging in a dogfight.

The Spitfire-focused *Operation Epsom* also demonstrates the degree to which such a simgame uses historical context both as a gameplay arena and as a learning tool (as does *The Big Show*, discussed later). *Operation Epsom* offers players a free-form experience, rather than missions with specific points to be earned for success; this resistance to offering typical gameplay rewards is programmed to replicate the missions that occurred during June 1944 when the Royal Canadian Air Force (part of the RAF's Tactical Air Force group) fought for control of Caen.[13] These missions were often uneventful, or deemed successful if a pilot went on patrol and returned home. The aircraft such as the powerful Spitfire Mk. IX and its operation become the focus, especially as historical fighter planes embedded in a sortie routine that only sometimes led to combat. Learning the particulars of the aircraft and the roles of their pilots as either a wing commander or a wing man is the focus within such a *DCS* campaign, along with how to situate aircraft and pilots within gameplay contexts as in a scripted campaign.

*DCS*'s *The Big Show* also focuses on the Spitfire, this time recreating missions flown by the successful Brazilian-born French fighter pilot Pierre Clostermann, who flew for the RAF. *The Big Show* exemplifies how history is meticulously interpreted for an experience; in each case, missions are created that mimic events, in a general sense and also at the careful level of attempting to simulate specifics. *The Big Show* demonstrates how the simgame–simtext dynamic encourages players by asking them to find a copy of Clostermann's *Le Grand Cirque* (1948): "Read it, and when you arrive to a chapter that is featured in the campaign, stop and play the mission" (Campaign introduction PDF: 2).[14] Beginning with a traditional simtext, an actual memoir, then following it with directed gameplay demonstrates how the dynamic works for a developer whose simgame can reverse the usual process. In such a way the dynamic proves flexible, both in the types of simtexts encountered (in this case a written memoir rather than cinema) and how the experience is bolstered by this relationship.

The developer of *The Big Show* demonstrates a keen awareness that what is being offered is not a full simulation of everything in the memoir, much less a necessary full correspondence between the game and the past. "The player won't be able to rendezvous with hundreds of B-17s returning from Schweinfurt over Zuider-See, nor can I stress your video cards with 80 plus bandits" (Campaign Introduction PDF: 2). This limitation is down to Eagle Dynamic's game engine (EDGE) and the past state of computer hardware rather than a lack of interest. The developer even mentions a need for "balance," meaning the limitations of games and developer choices that excise parts of the past still provide a "taste" of what it was like to fly a late-war Spitfire over Normandy (Campaign Introduction PDF: 2).

The first mission of *The Big Show* makes demands of players already beyond the expected WWII-dogfight scenario. In *DCS*, the aircraft begin cold, which means players must follow a pre-flight checklist to start their machines. Players must use the proper radio channels to communicate with the tower so that they can taxi and take off. This can be done through a menu, rather than the more sophisticated use of a simple radio and bot-controlled air-traffic-control for *IL2*'s 'Combat Box' server (discussed later). Once in the air, rendezvous points need to be met, as well as squadron leaders located to join in formation, and so on. From this point, the missions are very similar to those found in *IL2*'s scripted campaigns and even multiplayer servers. The techniques used, though, are taken directly from source material offered to players as study guides on how to properly employ tactics for air-to-air combat, escort missions, free hunt, ground attack, and so on. The differences in aircraft and their capabilities along with the roles of pilots in their respective squadrons carry over between the simgames, the experience of playing being bolstered by engagement with outside materials.

*IL2* likewise offers a number of 'scripted' campaigns that are focused on specific aircraft operating with specific missions. There are other examples of these single-player offerings, both official and player-built, but this chapter focuses on a few examples that best represent the wider catalog. *DCS* and *IL2* also both have sophisticated mission builders that allow players to create their own campaigns to play with others, providing players with granular control of mission types they would like to practice. These differ from *IL2*'s larger 'career' mode's focus on spanning longer stages of the war (which I examine later) or its user-created missions for single player or co-op (more than one player). These can be daisy-chained into long and complex events, another difference from the shorter scripted campaigns that act like snapshots of moments from battles in the war, similar to how FPS maps condense larger battles or regions into a manageable and playable gamespace.

Working within these focused constraints, scripted campaigns in simulators such as *DCS* and *IL2* capture particular scenarios that represent the challenges, tactics, and strategies used by the air forces of the opposing nations at different times of the war, in different places, with different aircraft, under different conditions. A quick look through *IL2*'s official single-player campaigns reveal how their contexts capture these particular historical moments as the playable past.

They begin with *10 Days in Autumn*, an early 1941 scenario that signals key gameplay elements for the early war, pointing players beyond the game toward history for clarification. The official description provides an informative, objective POV history lesson as a broad overview:

> This single player Campaign tells the story of a difficult time in October 1941 for the German Luftwaffe on the Moscow front. The Campaign follows the actions of Luftwaffe Group I./JG 52 who were supporting the tip of the German thrust deep into Russia, flying missions from frontline airfields in the Kalinin area. German forces faced seemingly never ending artillery strikes, attacks from Soviet ground forces and sudden VVS air strikes. The intense combat as well as the tough weather conditions demanded maximum effort from Luftwaffe pilots, foreshadowing the looming collapse of the Operation Typhoon. You get to play the role of commander of the second flight in the third squadron (3./JG 52). (Campaigns, 2021)

We see a few notable historical references, such as JG 52. This *Jagdgeschwader* (fighter squadron) wing was known for its use of advanced Messerschmitt BF 109s from the beginning of the war, often recognized by military aviation historians because of its success in the early air-war in the East, with leading aces such as Erich Hartmann flying for this wing. Other notable references such as Kalinin and Operation Typhoon point the player to this critical theater and operation northwest of Moscow where the Germans nearly took the city. Other campaigns jump ahead a year on the Eastern Front when the Soviets began to find success with their resistance, thus equalizing the gameplay for players as the Soviets introduced better aircraft.

The tactics of those players who favor 109s reveal parallels to historically embedded practices by Luftwaffe pilots, such as the use of altitude, the ability to dive with speed, along with the devastation of using 20 mm canons to hit an enemy and escape rapidly. The switch by a player to the VVS requires different tactics, such as turn fighting close to the ground where diving is more precarious and speed is easy to lose. *IL2* offers this development by progressing a year later to Stalingrad, which provides improved VVS aircraft such as the Yak-1 and its ability to turn and to hit hard with its own cannons.

Other conflict zones such as the Kuban area are simulated as well, along with a variety of other types of aircraft such as the American-built lend-lease A-20 Havoc, and the iconic Ilyushin IL-2 Sturmovik attacker noted for its durability and its use within the title of the series. Other campaigns come later in the war with newer aircraft such as the Spitfire Mk. IX, the P-47 D Thunderbolt, and another German favorite, variants of the FW 190. Looking through the descriptions of these regions and aircraft, we see that the developers have moved across the Eastern and Western Fronts through key moments that represent the wider war in the sky, with a focus on aircraft and maps.

The accompanying scripted campaigns also exemplify this piecemeal approach, but with considered focus on the selected periods and their appropriate planes, tactics, and so on. The *Blazing Steppe* campaign places players in the role of VVS fighter pilots protecting Stalingrad from the encroaching Germans, while the *Fortress on the Volga* places them in attacking German 109 G-2 fighters (a continuation from the earlier *10 Days in Autumn*). A move to the Caucasus and the advancing German Army Group A is scripted in *Steel Birds*. This simulates the task of securing the prized southern oil fields. A move to the west in *Hell Hawks over the Bulge* simulates a later event, offering the US 365th Fighter group known as Hell Hawks and their duties during the Battle of the Bulge.

Each of these crafted, scripted campaigns is accompanied by brief but narrative-driven descriptions that add a touch of backstory for the player-pilot, along with instructions on how to succeed and survive. Like the use of maps in FPSs, these campaigns are not comprehensive but impressionistic. They are actually so curated and contained that they operate differently from a textbook description or documentary that tries to cover as much material as possible within a given frame, or uses one example and then analyzes it to explicitly show how it is representative. Instead, these campaigns simulate particular aspects of air combat in specific places limited by game mechanics and playability. For example, the air war over Stalingrad comprised many JU87 Stuka dive-bomber formations, with fighter cover, in far more sorties per day than can be simulated in a one- or two-hour game session.

A more expansive (but still not comprehensive) mechanic can be seen with *IL2*'s ambitious single-player career mode, which has been modded to offer even more flexibility in crafting certain types of activities that represent historical missions. It tries to capture some unplayable elements, through a mechanic similar to how turns work in strategy games. Each day, new missions are offered for squadrons, and the player can choose to fly them or not, the computer scripts running activity in between missions.

*IL2*'s career mode allows a player to begin with a new pilot by selecting a major region of conflict based on the in-game maps—Moscow, Stalingrad, Kuban, and the Rhineland (which equates to the Bodenplatte module).[15] Players then select a side, where they are presented with the map for the region and squadron locations. Selecting a squadron limits the player to particular planes and their corresponding roles, as does choosing the starting phase. For example, a Rhineland career for a US or British virtual pilot moves through a number of specific phases, beginning in September 1944 with a focus on 'Fighting in the Low Countries.' This turns into an 'Autumn Offensive' and later, in mid-December, the 'Battle of the Bulge,' all historical snapshots of battles that limit play to these specific instances.

All the added historical details and in-game references work in the background to situate a player within the context of the simgame as a reconfigured past, each one beginning with a short contextual video that has an animated map and narrator describing the major conflict. In under a minute, the failure of Market Garden is represented as an Allied push from Belgium into Holland that faltered. The other major phases are also briefly summarized with visual presentations that introduce the player to the events. (These also emerge, one by one, as a player progresses through each day's mission.)

A player wanting to fly a P-51 D Mustang will choose a particular American fighter squadron that flew these aircraft, based at a particular airfield, with specific missions. From this point, the game generates a random pilot. These are given names, with back-stories and even a black-and-white photo portrait.

A player can choose to be a new recruit who will rank up successful missions or command a squadron from the beginning as if already a veteran.

Such a narrative-framed career mode offers a player a way to engage air combat but also to think strategically and to plan missions for a specific virtual pilot; these are randomly generated to mimic the sorts of missions faced by historical pilots. Mission success or failure is earned or lost based on certain requirements, and a virtual pilot can be injured or killed, with an 'iron-man' mode determining an in-game death as final. Awards can be attained, and rank can be earned. Along with the initial backstory and portrait photo, a sense of imagined continuity is the extent to which any sort of personal narrative is worked into the career mode. However, a career-focused virtual pilot joins squadrons with pilots controlled by the AI who also have names and ranks. A degree of role-playing is thus encouraged for players, especially when playing as a flight leader who is responsible for the lives of virtual squadron members.

But, again, the focus of *IL2* is on combat tactics and strategies of given aircraft at particular times in the war. Its career mode offers a day-by-day record of missions flown so that players can return to those days. You click on your pilot to see the history of rank and statistics; click on the particular squadron you were flying with to see a historical overview of its origin and role; click on mission plans for a particular day to see who exactly flew, if they survived, if they earned an air or ground kill, or what awards they were given; click on 'headquarters' to see a strategic map of the mission, its waypoints, its targets, and so on. There is even a 'World News' front-page clipping for each major phase for both the Western and Eastern Fronts.

*IL2*'s career mode, while integrated well into the simgame in a focused manner, has also been modded by the community to provide more depth and flexibility so that the role-playing element can be taken even further. The most extensive is the continually updated *Patrick Wilson's Campaign Generator* (2015). This comprehensive mod allows a player to create multiple pilots with different roles, all advancing in the same 'campaign' at the same time. A player might have a pilot who flies for the Americans but also a pilot for the RAF, each with a different squadron; this player can not only choose to have pilots flying for other countries, but also fly pilots on the opposing side. As a mission is generated and flown by a player for a single pilot, all virtual pilots created by that player move forward along the timeline, regardless of whether the player flew them or not. Other tools allow you to incorporate logged information on a virtual pilot, the successes, and the awards, and to easily see them so that 'after-action reports' can be written. This personalized mechanic creates a greater sense of narrative continuity and immersion for players.

As mentioned earlier, a flight 'simulator' such as *IL2* exemplifies how current consumer-based VR headsets create an interactive immersion in the game that relates accurately (to some degree) to the past through an immediacy of engaging with the simulation and the presence that follows. This provides an experience that occurs through elements that readily lend themselves to being simulated, rather than those that prove difficult such as weaving narrative into a combat simulator. While modes that allow careers for pilots also create a sense of continuity for a player, the past emerges with most impact primarily within the rendered cockpit.

At this point, the simgame experience reconfigures the past while simultaneously diverging from the 'realism' of historical context by ignoring the countless lived experiences that are unsimulated. A player is faced with a type of dual-consciousness, with digital-and-analog virtual historicity embedded in simulated machinery and its material counterparts. The cockpit, as a controlling idea for this chapter, thus acts as this twinned space where digital and analog meet, along with imagined configurations, presenting for a player a puzzle that must be solved, both in how to play the game correctly and into understanding the historical contexts for each machine and the places it moved through.

We also see the cockpit's importance when examining the demands it makes on the player; it is a mediating space that determines the success or failure of a virtual pilot. Learning the particulars of engine management, the flight model of a particular aircraft, and how its weapon's systems work must be understood before a player can begin to master an aircraft in a simgame's different modes. This is a critical step for players who want to gain success within a serious simgame, but it also points them outward to explanations of the aircraft's peculiarities—how it was built, used, how it performed, where it flew, and so on.

The different models of the Spitfire and BF 109 exemplify this historically located tension with their critical differences. For example, the Spitfire uses a lever-controlled, pneumatic, differential braking system that requires a pilot to pull on a brake lever while simultaneously pushing the rudder left or right to apply degrees of brake pressure either way. The 109 uses a simpler system that requires toe pressure on the rudder pedals to apply the brakes to either depressed side. There are other examples such as the FW 190's response to the Spitfire Mk IX, or in the Pacific the early dominance of the Japanese's Mitsubishi A6M Zero over the USA's underpowered Grumman F4F Wildcat and its later dominant response with the F6F Hellcat.

Seemingly subtle mechanical alterations to the different versions of aircraft can have a major impact on a player's success, while other historically important changes may have little impact. The importance of taxiing, take off, and landing properly work differently based on the design of particular planes, while other elements point to more critical differences that relate directly to historical combat tactics. Peering from the cramped cockpit of a BF 109 through the window to the left or right, a pilot will see a short narrow wing designed by Messerschmitt for its speed capabilities and compact construction, which allowed for high wing-loading and stability in a dive, but less maneuverability. This looks markedly different from the nimble Spitfire's wing construction, which has been noted for its ingenuity, the elliptical structure providing a distinct wide and curved look quite dissimilar from the 109. It also provided slightly more maneuverability in tight turns, and this became a signature acrobatic trait of the Spitfire.

These subtle differences can be ignored by players, but the handling capabilities (with their historiographies ready to be understood for those curious enough to look) force players to adjust to in-game limitations and capabilities if they want to use the aircraft with any chance of success. This recursive relationship in turn creates a feedback loop that points players to simtexts that clarify these peculiarities. Soon, they learn about the arms race that gave the BF 109 such an early advantage, along with the Spitfire's prescient prewar development and timely wartime variations, and they discover the differing nation's responses for their own aircraft and how they came to challenge the Luftwaffe's most dangerous air machines.

The level of detail and the requirements of players can become quite demanding. The current *IL2:GB* series opts for automated cold-start sequences and displays animations of components in the cockpit, all of which can be adjusted with keyboard or control devices. Rather than provide a deeper level of player interaction by allowing them to directly manipulate these components through mouse-clicks, *IL2* allows for complex engine management through the keyboard or joysticks and throttles to focus on the experience of pilots in the air and combat rather than the important but routine aspects of non-combat flight.

*DCS*, though, as more of a 'study-level' combat simulator, allows for far more granular control of an aircraft with clickable cockpits. *IL2: CloD* (2011) also has limited 'clickable' cockpits. These are not a requirement for serious gameplay, but such features do encourage steps toward new technologies that can track finger movement, such as we see with the Varjo 3. *DCS* augments *IL2* with this added complexity, with the simgames taken together offering a comprehensive experience of flying WWII aircraft, even if both are constrained by the inherent limitations of computer simulators and their distance from the lived experiences of actual historical pilots. The playable configurations, even with these constraints, open up reimagined history as the player enters the rendered environment, a type of immersed space that offers exponentially more immediacy than 2D environments.

While the attention to historically accurate detail in a simgame such as *IL2* begins with the cockpit, a complete analysis of each plane's simulated interior and how well it is modeled on the past is far beyond the scope of this study. This full understanding is also often beyond players, who can approach the simgame and its planes with differing degrees of focus and even one at a time, rather than through exhaustive and comprehensive study. With enough time, just flying the aircraft and learning how to handle engine management, flight dynamics, and weapons' system management itself becomes an education in the WWII air war, especially in how different machines proved capable and incapable in different ways. Yet this remains, metaphorically, above the critical events that drove pilots to combat.

Becoming aware of the cockpit as this curated space, along with its limitations, leads players to broaden the scope of their knowledge beyond the cockpit and thinking about the pilots' lived experiences that are partially simulated—for example, how historic pilots worked in groups as squadrons, were part of a larger war effort through individual and team effort, and how their tasks were driven by what was happening on the ground.

The most relevant example occurs with how formations are used. In single player you can order your squadron into formations, such as the early three-plane 'Vic' that flew very close together in a V formation with the squadron leader at the middle point. This formation had an entrenched history among air-forces, going back to WWI, but proved ineffective when modern aircraft became able to dive from an altitude and 'pounce' at high speed, only to escape, gain altitude, and dive again. In a tight Vic, proper attention to what might be behind you or behind a squadron member was difficult to assess, the entire formation sharing a large blind spot.

A player who is flying with a group will discover this aspect of aviation history, and this might lead to research into explanations of the limitations of flying in such restrictive formations—the benefit being that understanding how formations work in combat scenarios will follow. This leads players directly into the past, especially those key moments that saw tactics change and more sophisticated communication conventions related to commanding a squadron, and will teach them how to follow a flight leader (or how to be a flight leader), for example. Such details illuminate the past, with aviation history as a starting point. Research often begins with learning to fly with a group, rather than solo.

The most important squad-organization change simulated in game was the development away from tight formations such as the Vic into a wider combat spread. With the Spanish Civil War, the German Condor Legion perfected tactics that allowed the higher-speed BF 109s to find success, a wartime turning point in military aviation and also an example of how *IL2* reflects these tactics. The early 109 squadrons over Spain formed up into a two-pilot '*Rotte*' or doubled that into a four-pilot '*Schwarm*,' also known as a 'finger-four' formation, with the squadron leader in front (same position as a middle finger), and a wingman to the left (the index finger on the right hand). The other two members positioned themselves on the right side, staggered like a ring finger and little finger.

An even more radical change that serious players must learn is how to space these positions, changing from flying close together to a looser, wider combat spread that allows each pilot to observe the blind spot of his squadron members. Such a spread during the war was over 100 m, often more, negating an easy drop by an enemy from height onto a member's 'six' (their six o'clock position, or directly behind them). This also allowed for the two *Rotte* elements to separate from each other in combat, while each plane of a *Rotte* remained 'welded' or close together. These two elements could then watch each other's six for approaching enemies. Such a flexible structure also allowed for the confusion and disorientation of combat, allowing the number three position of the original *Schwarm* to become the leader of his own *Rotte* when under attack, with number four now acting has his wingman, sticking close in a temporary welded formation if need be.

Such a simulated introduction to the basics of flight formation within a combat scenario can lead into maneuvers that define air-war tactics for small-scale battles. For a casual player, none of these precedents may ever become fully understood as they were experienced by pilots who lived through such scenarios, but for a player engaging in the most demanding of virtual multi-player servers with a tactical, team-based focus, these virtual interpretations of the past become part of the needed lexicon and praxis for success, even as these practices reconfigure the past along specific lines.

The control of a plane in combat scenarios, the basics of a plane's turn capabilities, or how quickly it can pull from lag pursuit to lead pursuit to place its nose on target to fire are usually the first concerns of a new simulator pilot. In less serious simgames such as *WT*, for example, new pilots gravitate toward finding a nimble plane that turns tightly, an example being the Japanese A6M2 'Zero', thus encouraging players to engage in dangerous circling battles close to the ground (with each other and with the AI). Yet other aspects such as rate of climb, how fast a plane's dive speed is before it suffers some sort of structural damage, how many guns it has, how fast they fire, and how much ammunition is available prove just as critical.

All these variables affect how the plane handles itself in the air, a key factor in translating the historical qualities of a plane to the simulated experience of a player. The maneuvers, such as a dangerous aerobatic 'hammerhead stall' or evasive 'split-S' are often done naturally before their names are learned, and key techniques such as deflection shooting, barrel rolls, flat and rolling scissors become part of a practiced repertoire that has a history of use both in war and in general aviation. Taken together, these techniques allow for more advanced forms of simulated gameplay such as the 'boom-and-zoom' tactics of diving on a lower foe, shooting and continuing past to regain altitude over an enemy who may be losing energy owing to frantic turning. Such critical best practices in how to engage in air combat have parallels with how the air war was conducted in the past, and many of these techniques continue to be practiced today, even with fourth- and fifth-generation jet aircraft.

Capturing these different challenges to simulate air combat finds its most variegated configurations in multiplayer servers, with expert players distinguishing themselves from average or good virtual pilots. Those servers that attract the best players use the most sophisticated forms of modding that exists for *IL2*. While single player is very popular among casual players who can control game difficulty, along with their choices to replay missions (although not allowed in 'iron-man' mode), the multiplayer environment provides modders with a way to increase the competitiveness of the simgame, as well as to engage with history along both realistic and highly reconfigured lines.

While single player in *IL2* allows modders to change the game to a degree that is not accepted in multiplayer, such as using 'reshade' techniques to change the color palette for better (and sometimes artificial) spotting, or even in removing the spinning prop at the nose of an aircraft, modding in multiplayer is primarily the development of demanding campaign scenarios rather than altering core game mechanics. This allows for persistent campaigns to run, either as timed events or for twenty-four hours a day. The active multiplayer count rises and falls according to time zones, with North, Central, and South American players providing a jump in numbers, followed by European, then Russian and Asian time zones having their own peaks. But during these times, one, maybe two servers can be full with up to eighty players each, with five to ten other servers showing lower numbers.

The methods of simulation within single player, career mode, and multiplayer examined in this chapter thus work along two lines of analysis that prove most helpful. First, they function as a way for a player to more intensely enter the configured but curated historical past simulated by the developers. Second, they are a way to understand the process of integrating oneself into a cockpit through a variety of increasingly complex peripherals, especially 'second-generation' VR. This takes us to the multiplayer mode as the most demanding gamespace within the simgame.

## Multiplayer

An examination of a few examples of the most challenging multiplayer servers reveals how they balance gameplay with curated history. As of the revision of this chapter in the winter of 2022, the three most demanding servers for *IL2* are the Finnish Virtual Pilot Server (FS), Combat Box (CB), and Tactical Air War (TAW). Other servers exist that cater to particular focuses, such as the entry-level and very popular Wings of Liberty (WoL), which originally removed weather changes, and provides a helpful GPS icon of your plane's location, engine management information, and structural damage reports. WoL has also proven popular because it offers maps across all the major modules with all the different planes. Other servers, such as Berloga, focus specifically on dogfighting and dueling, while the 1C Games Official Server is the easiest for new players with its lack of engine management, its air start, and its visible plane labels so that spotting is immediate. A number of other servers exist for co-op missions, for a focus on ground warfare, or for recruiting and training.

The current three most demanding servers each have different focuses that reveal how modders can direct the experiences of players' gameplay and frame history through particular developmental choices. The FS distinguishes itself as a 'combined-arms' server, which allows players to choose tanks or planes on the same map. The campaign is dynamic, meaning that player choices matter for the next map. CB offers detailed missions during the late war over the Rhineland, while TAW provides layers of additional functionality for managing a virtual pilot.

While dogfighting is a critical component in these servers, the bombing of bridges, of front-line resources such as depots, of anti-aircraft emplacements, and of vehicles of all sorts proves to be just as important because of how ground attack affects the movement of the front line. This allows for player-controlled attacking and defending of armored vehicles to make a difference on the ground, while aircraft that provide cover help them, along with aircraft that bomb key targets such as far-away depots deep in enemy territory or critical temporary airfields near the front with vulnerable respawning aircraft. A server such as FS also uses paratrooper drops from cargo planes flown by players (although it does not have an infantry component such as that found in Gaijin's *WT*-inspired *EN*). Successes in damaging enemy resources allow for the front line to move, dynamically adjusting until one side has dominated the entire map.

Like FS, CB is a dynamic server, but one that is solely focused on the late war, recreating specific historical scenarios as experienced from the air over the Rhineland. It is not a combined-arms server like FS, but instead each scenario provides a focused snapshot of gameplay that reconfigures past events through the constraints of the *IL2* game engine. These vary, from the 'Bridge too Far' scenario and its Allied convoys that must be protected from bombing runs by the Luftwaffe, to the 'Ardennes Counteroffensive' in which the Germans must push deep through the center of the map, destroying Allied defenses as they go. The context here is the Battle of Bodenplatte, a late-war final defensive measure by the Germans to halt the advancing Allies by destroying their airfields. CB simulates small-scale air combat during this period, beginning in September 1944, through the New Year's Day surprise attack by the Germans, on to the final months of the war in 1945.

These CB scenarios with narrow historical focuses are clarified through descriptions of each map that function as a type of cursory in-game simtext, many of which signal a need for investigation for further understanding. This has little to do with in-game mechanics, yet historical awareness translates to a better equipped player in terms of overall strategy. To this end, CB offers tools that encourage a sense of coordination, creating the effect that a player is embedded in these larger missions; it separates itself from every other server by offering a sophisticated radio function with bot-controlled ground-and-tower communication systems. This addition allows a player to request a call sign; taxi, takeoff, and landing clearance; a mission; a status on the 'picture' of an area (to see what is happening); and to update his or her location for information on how to return to the nearest airfield. Along with these commands, player-flown bombers can provide their estimated time to arrival at a target so that friendly fighters can be vectored in for cover.

A server such as CB approaches its missions within specific historical contexts, but also with the potential for counterfactual reconfiguring. One interesting counterfactual series of missions that could be offered by a server of this kind might imagine a scenario that corrects critical errors made by the Germans in 1942 after the failure of Barbarossa. Because of this prolonged conflict, the air war in the East has become increasingly popular in WWII combat simulation games. While the narrative of Spitfires and Mustangs pushing through Normandy to Berlin alongside massive bomber formations finds much representation in media of the war, the conflict that began in June 1941 with Barbarossa in the East and saw its pivotal point in January of 1943 with the defense of Stalingrad has earned particular focus, especially in infantry and tank warfare. Professional historians have increasingly articulated the importance of the German–Soviet War (see Chapter 5), with the full impact of the air war finding increasingly more commentary. A server such as CB, if its developers were so inclined, could try to recreate such a scenario.

The primary case study examined in this chapter, *IL2:GB*, began by simulating the air war in the East, an important theater both for the game and the war. As mentioned earlier, *IL2*'s first three maps reflect these major points of eventual conflict—west of Moscow, west of Stalingrad, and the Kuban region southeast of Crimea. History of the ground war here acts in the background for players, but is worth mentioning because of how flight simulator players inadvertently become aware of the crucial ground battles through even minimal study. The three German army groups that invaded were each to control a region, the northern pushing through the Baltic States and then to Leningrad, the central toward Moscow, and the southern toward the Caucasus and its resources, primarily oil. At Stalingrad, of course, the mythology of Soviet defense was born.

One curious counterfactual proposed by military historian Joel Hayward (1998) begins by regarding the Luftwaffe's ultimate failure in the East as due to a few devastating operational errors. He argues that Hitler made three critical mistakes during *Fau Blau* (Case Blue) to secure the southern part of the offensive and the oil fields of the Caucasus. According to Hayward, rather than allow the original plan to continue, in which Richthofen would have pushed north toward the Volga and then south toward the Caucasus, Hitler erred when he split the army group, one section heading toward Stalingrad in the north and the other to take the Caucasus in the south. The second major mistake occurred when the German Sixth Army was embattled at Stalingrad and the decision was made to waste valuable resources in taking the city. The last major mistake was refusing any retreat at Stalingrad:

> Wanting to avoid the humiliation of abandoning the city he [Hitler] had publicly vowed to hold, he made one of his most ill-considered decisions thus far in the war: after receiving rash promises from the Luftwaffe's chief of staff, he ordered Sixth Army, which he extravagantly renamed "Fortress Stalingrad," to form a "hedgehog" defense and wait for relief. It would be sustained by an airlift operation, he declared. (Hayward, 1998: 315)

This decision to support Stalingrad at all costs directly affected the Luftwaffe in the region, and it became an "air supply command" (Hayward, 1998: 315).

Hayward poses an important counterfactual by asking what would have happened had Hitler not split Army Group South and instead focused on the Caucasus, rather than Stalingrad, especially for the effectiveness of the air war: "With the benefit of hindsight, it is now reasonable to argue that Richthofen's air fleet could have dealt the Soviet economy a major blow, from which it would have taken at least several months to recover, if it had unloaded as many bombs on Baku as on Stalingrad" (Hayward, 1998: 315). Hayward's counterfactual would have focused the might of Luftflotte 4, the air division assigned to southern Russia on the Eastern Front, along with the entirety of Army Group South, on attacking the Caucasus and depriving the Soviets of its oil resources.

For a simgame simulator such as *IL2*, simulating such a counterfactual would provide interesting gameplay that could begin in the Kuban region with the correct historical Axis versus Allies aircraft at the time but could then move north to Stalingrad after the Caucasus were secured with these later aircraft. *IL2* multiplayer architecture allows for these sorts of reconfigured reimaginings in a unique combination of the ahistorical and historical. In doing so, this would be reflected in new, interesting gameplay challenges.

One of the most demanding multiplayer servers is TAW, which began in 2016, with a development history going back to 2006 and the developers' time spent flying in *IL2:1946*.[16] Out of this early experience, TAW emerged as a dynamic campaign, but one that adds another layer of complexity beyond the other serious servers. In TAW, you not only have a dynamic campaign that is affected by each map session, lasting around two hours, with the front line moving based on successes and failures of each map session, but also track a virtual pilot beyond the basic statistics provided by the default *IL2*-server software. This allows the developers of TAW to make more demands on virtual pilots, allowing them to track particular aircraft earned by virtual pilots in a progression path determined at the beginning of the campaign.

This means that dying in game is more punishing than most other servers, to the point that you lose the pilot and the aircraft, and your rank is reset (or reduced). TAW also removes other player aids, such as all 'technochat' warnings that help with engine maintenance or reveal structural damage. The effect of removing these aids is that players pay much more attention to the state of their aircraft so that they can return home safely, knowing that being shot down behind enemy lines is a capture that will result in the loss of their virtual pilots and all points accrued as that particular pilot (along with aircraft progression, rank, and leaderboard statistics, also lost in varying degrees).

TAW began on the Eastern Front with its first server but now has two campaigns, with the late-war Western Front added in the Rhineland.[17] Recently, the developers added another degree of difficulty by limiting aircraft choice, channeling fighter, attacker, and bomber paths into beginner and advanced, meaning that all virtual pilots should start the campaign as beginners with basic planes determined by their career path. With successful missions, meaning scoring successful ground kills and air kills, plus a return home safely to a functioning airfield, a pilot earns points toward adding more advanced planes. This provides considerable challenge because veteran players can more quickly progress their virtual pilots to advanced ranks with relevant aircraft. This creates a marked tension that means flying in TAW is stressful, but it is rewarding when done well. Again, the focus is on a more serious approach, rather than simply providing quick and easy gameplay successes, as other servers do (and which is what your typical player often wants).

An example of how these early choices function in game can be seen in the exemplary early war competition of advanced Luftwaffe BF 109 Emils versus out-matched Soviet fighter aircraft, such as the I-16 (by Polikarpov, also known as the 'Rata' and 'Mosca'), the early LaGGs (Lavochkin-Gorbunov-Gudkov), and the early Yak-1 (Yakovlev). In most servers, players for the German side would be able to select a 109 E in any configuration offered by the game, which means taking the lightest version of the fighter rather than a beginner virtual pilot being forced to choose the least competitive version. For one Eastern campaign, a rookie player's first Emil had bomb racks, as if meant for a 'jabo' or bombing mission; these slowed the plane because of increased lag, thus, balancing the game in a developer-chosen counterfactual that placed it on an even footing with the Soviet planes.

Moreover, a new Emil pilot may have heavy armor added, which most fighters avoid because of increased weight; it also reduces speed and critical climb rate, along with energy retention and acceleration. These sorts of challenges work with the other planes as well, on both sides, forcing virtual pilots to find success so they earn the best versions of their aircraft. In the Western campaign, this translates into beginner Luftwaffe fighter pilots at first flying the much slower FW 190 A8 Anton over the more dominant and faster FW 190 D Dora, a choice that places the player on a path that may mean they can also fly the nimblest German dogfighter, the BF 109 K Kurfürst, or the fastest and most powerful fighter in the simgame, the jet-powered ME 262.

These difficulties are implemented as gameplay challenges, specific choices by the developers to create an experience that rewards less easily but with much greater impact. Yet much consideration has gone into the historical context of the mission types and, in the case of TAW, the plane sets offered, in most cases directly correlating to those actually used at the time, even if this creates an unfair advantage.

One major hurdle for new players logging onto the TAW server is a message that may tell them they have chosen the wrong aircraft and that they need to register, before booting them off the server. When registering, players have to link their official *IL2* usernames and profiles to TAW, decide which side they will fly for, and, critically, what basic type of pilot role they will fly—whether fighter, attacker, or bomber. This allows them to enter the TAW server without being kicked off, but since TAW is developed as a server run by a third-party it has limited access to actually change core aspects of the game, which does not allow mods to the game engine, the rendering pipeline, or the user interface for multiplayer. A player must choose the correct aircraft assigned to him or her by the career path chosen for their pilots and the one assigned by the TAW developers with certain loadouts. This can cause confusion for new players who think they have registered and are ready, when they actually need to understand what basic plane they can fly. Many are booted out immediately.

Upon returning to try again, when asking why they were booted off, newcomers hear other players simply telling them to go read the manual. This truculence is the opposite to the demeanor of players in more casual servers that prioritize ease of use, with eager players willing to help the confused. By demanding that players register on TAW's server (with the same profile that has to be entered into the *IL2* official website) and read a manual, or at least understand the basics, may be overly demanding (and off-putting), but it is the first step toward a more serious approach that discourages casual players from joining.

The manual is a detailed and dynamic gameplay simtext that changes with each campaign; it explains the core game mechanics, rather than focusing on historical context (which it only minimally features). It is also a fitting example of a written game-manual simtext that exemplifies the way the dynamic works in refining game mechanics for specific historical purposes, often with history working in the background or even obliquely as a type of muted influence.

The introduction states:

> We have created various historical operations using available maps in IL-2 Great Battles to allow players to realistically experience entire parts of the war. The Eastern Front operations take place between 1941–1943 and the Western Front operations take place between 1944–1945. The main goal of this project is to simulate World War II air combat operations from the pilot's perspective with all its harsh realities and magnificent highs.
>
> As such, TAW contains unique features, rules, and limitations that produce a realistic and stressful environment for newcomers, veterans, and elite virtual pilots alike. The emotions of happiness, joy, anger, hate, satisfaction, adrenaline rush, pressure, fear, combat stress, self-preservation, and competition all define the unique atmosphere of Tactical Air War and its unapologetic gameplay. (Tactical Air War, 2021, 'Introduction')[18]

The reference to realism reflects the developers' intention to capture this elusive quality, with the danger of air combat being so distant from the safety of a player who is sitting at a computer and within the confines of a curated game; but they express that capturing an experience is also their goal, what they call "unapologetic gameplay." Rather than being an insensitive refusal to apologize for the horrors of war, this unapologetic posture references the degrees of difficulty that players must overcome on TAW, along with an attempt to translate into game challenges the historic difficulties faced by those who flew fighter aircraft in WWII. Throughout the manual, this refusal to cater to a player base who may want an easier game, or apologize for the difficulties they face, is evident both through careful study of the manual and through the experience of the simgame.

What separates a combat air server such as TAW from the others is that kill streaks, kill-death ratios, and other individual statistics are less important (although they are tracked and form prestige for those atop the leader-boards) than team-based success. That does not mean players still don't try to maximize their individual effort; the server rewards this exceptionalism with its own stat and reward system beyond that provided by the official game. These rankings allow players to see detailed descriptions of their sorties, especially what happened in a dogfight—how many shots hit a target, how much damage was done, and so on. These add up into 'combat points' when a successful mission is finalized after the virtual pilot has returned to a friendly airfield; this in-game currency unlocks more advanced aircraft.

A demand that a player fly his virtual pilot back to a working airfield is another game mechanic that adds authentic tension and depth to the experience, forcing players to think about fuel, navigation, and flight time. Just earning a confirmed kill is not enough. Returning to friendly territory and then finding a working airfield means continued focus is required for the kill to count, often in bad virtual weather, with a damaged aircraft, and maybe a wounded pilot. This return mechanic, along with the full reward of a successful landing, tries to accurately mimic how a successful young pilot who has survived might be offered the latest variant of a plane or asked to join a veteran squadron with the best equipment.

The award of flying the most advanced aircraft works alongside another in-game currency, experience points; these show the rank of the virtual pilot, and provide additional prestige for both the pilot and whoever shoots him or her down. These awards replicate the race for the best combat statistics, especially among German pilots and their increasingly higher requirements as the war went on. A massive difference exists between the total historical number of German air kills versus that of the Allies, as well as the race among German *Experten* pilots to stay at the top of the lists and do what was required to earn the Knights Cross. Such tracking of rank is highly penalized when an in-game death occurs, in stark contrast to other simgames, which often only impose a short time penalty. In TAW, there is a mechanic that encourages "a unique and realistic environment, a special emphasis is placed on self-preservation and the promotion of wise and careful decision making" (Tactical Air War, 2021, 'Lives').

Again, from the perspective of gameplay approaching lived history, the attempt by developers to focus players on not dying in game reflects the 'realistic' desire by historical pilots to survive. To that end, a player only has three virtual lives during the multiple sessions per map, which can be lost during any sort of crash with injury or even by bailing out over enemy lines and being captured. Along with being killed, a capture will end the career of the virtual pilot. Once these are lost, a player typically can't fly for twenty hours.[19] The developers clearly state: "In real-world aerial combat, the most important thing is to survive. Death is final. The penalties for death and capture are therefore very significant" (Tactical Air War, 2021, 'Play Balance').

TAW also has a sophisticated logistics element that determines how many resources each side generates, such as tanks, planes, and pilots, and how many victory points to award for their destruction. These statistics work in the background, dynamically adjusting to gameplay as each side flies sorties. This component has been developed along historical lines rather than for balance, such as the example given in the manual of the German supply problems in the East during its push toward the Volga river. This unevenness encourages players to actually fly (often uneventful) supply missions from a supplied airfield to a damaged or undersupplied one.

The virtual experience of a WWII combat/air multiplayer simulator such as TAW is one that focuses on very curated aspects of the air war, yet still, often in the background, signals specific pathways toward a more traditional understanding of how the past is approached. For example, on a past TAW 'Western Front' campaign (September 24, 2021), a reworked system went into effect that had been trialed a few months earlier on the larger Eastern Front campaign. It offered Market Garden as an offensive push by the Allied side. TAW provided more planes, pilots, tanks, and trucks for the Allies, increasing their chances for success, while the Axis side fought on the defensive. The September push deep into Holland known as Market (the Airborne missions) Garden (the infantry) is also featured in FPSs in the roadmap for *HLL*, while *PS* provides areas around Oosterbeek, Driel, Doorwerth, and Heelsum.

Yet in TAW the conflict on the ground is simulated based on damage done through the air war, rather than through the reported up-close infantry fighting. Bridges, though, can be attacked, as were the key crossings from Eindhoven to Arnhem. And while paratroopers can be dropped from cargo planes, these are minimal events combined with the massive historical airdrops by the Allies that saw over 30,000 airborne troopers jump. Other elements are not simulated, such as the ground war to take the bridges and even the combined-arms approach of FS with its player-controlled tanks. TAW features only the air war because it would be so resource intensive to add other elements.

Market Garden was followed by the German counter-offensive (known as the Battle of the Bulge), which remains no-more than a title in TAW. Instead of any clarification over the initial Allied defeat at Arnhem, the potential for a German victory during their counter-offensive, and how the Allies eventually broke the 'Stalemate on the Rhine' (TAW's third and final mission of the campaign), TAW instead presents detailed variants of aircraft present during the events. These variants are not exhaustive, limited as they are to the aircraft offered by the simgame's developers. And while *IL2:GB's* full plane-set has increased significantly from the first Stalingrad module, they are still lacking for both fronts.

For example, the late-war VVS Yak-3 has yet to be modeled, which would give the Soviets a dominant plane in the East. Other notable planes have recently been addressed such as the RAF Mosquito, which arrived before the Normandy release. The promised Allied cargo plane C-47 Dakota has also just been released, this plane sorely needed as paratrooper transport comparable with the German JU-52. And yet, in the end, game-engine limitations have acted as the primary factor in how the air war is simulated, *IL2:GB* performing much better in small-scale squadron-against-squadron types of conflicts than the massive bomber-wing attacks by the Allies with their escorts, and the often-smaller German defensive sorties.

This limitation has not always been present. In a critical moment in the series' development history, the developers of *IL2:GB* opted for a newer Digital Warfare Engine rather than the older engine for *Rise of Flight* (2009) or the engine that runs *1946* and *CloD*. Yet the engine for *1946*, for example, better handled many more objects in the air for a number of reasons, primarily that its rendering demands were far lower. One server that simulated such large-scale attacks was 'Scorched Earth Online War' for *1946*. This co-op-based server allowed for organized missions that dynamically adjusted to the successes and failures of the combatants. These were organized by squadrons and covered a wide range of theaters, with virtual pilots progressing (or dying) throughout the entire campaign. It allowed for a number of complexities not seen in the current *IL2* game engine, such as commanders and sub commanders who issued orders and missions for both the ground and air.[20]

## Tanks and Ships

Other vehicles such as tanks (and to some degree, ships) feature in WWII simulators as well. Tank simulators have a long history that dates back to the very beginning of the video game industry, when *Battlezone* (1980) emerged in arcades as a two-stick, wire-frame game with a perspective from within the interior of a futuristic tank. Since then, the number of computer games with some sort of tank simulation has far outnumbered flight simulators because they often accompany infantry-based games.

Tanks feature prominently in hybrid genres, including real-time strategy games such as the *Steel Division* series (2017) and its god-like or, when zoomed in, third-person perspective. We also see this in FPSs such as *EN*, which allow players to control a tank as a gunner, driver, or commander but with minimal simulation of complex system management. Other popular games such as the *BF* series have featured WWII tanks and other vehicles. And with modern war games, the offerings have increased through the decades-long arms race during and after the Cold War. The more serious simgames that focus on WWII tank warfare are limited. Some of the most demanding are *IL2: Tank Crew - Clash at Prokhorovka* (2019) (TC), *Steel Fury: Kharkov 1942* (2007), and *Steel Armor: Blaze of War* (2011), which provide focused and challenging tank-based simulators. More accessible games such as *WT*, along with *World of Tanks* (2010), provide a wide range of vehicle selections from differing nations with different degrees of complexity.

*TC* is integrated into its *IL2:GB* simulator with a massive single map, Prokhorovka, and a limited but expanding tank list between Soviet and German sides. It exemplifies, as do flight simulators and their contained cockpits, how the interior of a tank hull and turret provides a unique experience for players, especially those who bolster their simgame with peripherals such as VR. These sorts of sitting simulators with ready-at-hand devices mimic well the arrangement that is being simulated, lending themselves to more immersed gameplay. *TC* is also a demanding simulator, with detailed interiors and limited game aids. When it is played as a 'combined arms' experience, meaning aircraft are added (and flown by humans), an increased complexity in strategy and tactics is offered, especially in the most demanding of multiplayer servers.

This use of combined arms requires a sophisticated and complex development of both air and ground elements, most recently utilized in the FS server for *IL2*. While the air war in this server requires the *GB* modules from Stalingrad up to Bodenplatte (and recently Normandy), the ground elements use the stand-alone simgame focused on tank warfare, *TC*. This ground focus centers on a large map around Prokhorovka, the scale of tanks demanding that detail be paid to terrain objects seen up close.

Like that of an FPS, this shift in scale and focus from the air to the ground means a reconsideration of both the resources demanded by the game engine and the amount of detail this allows. This fidelity begins with the vehicles representative of those driven by the Germans and Soviets on the Eastern Front during this portion of the war, with Tigers and Panthers facing T-34s and KV-1s, among others. And while *TC* offers the Prokhorovka map, the assets can be used on any of *IL2*'s air-war maps, thus allowing a server such as FS to provide its unique gameplay (as previously noted). As with the operation of aircraft, a number of different pathways from simgame to simtexts is encountered for tank simulators, involving how to operate the vehicles as well as the contexts in which they were used. The successful challenge to the German Panzer III and IV by the Soviet T-34 is a historically relevant curiosity that leads a player to understand German setbacks against Soviet armor and their move from the Panzer IV to more heavily armored and armed tanks (which proved more difficult to produce, transport, and maintain).

Along with the historical emergence of the Panther and later Tiger II, the Battle of Kursk becomes an important centerpiece for the game. Alongside Stalingrad, Kursk, and the failure of the German Operation Citadel to recover what was lost at Stalingrad, players experience a more balanced gameplay that points towards this critical moment when the German push east faltered. The experience of players as they learn how to use these machines, attempt to understand how to use them tactically, and situate them as historical objects with particular pasts, comprises the overall experience of such a simgame—which is clearly located in its historical past.

Switching from the cockpit of a plane to the interior of a tank thus finds parallels as a player adjusts to a new enclosed space. Key differences in function require a tank player to position him or herself in either the gunner, driver, commander, or machine-gunner position, with only the commander being able to open the hatch to take a position outside the tank. The interiors are modeled with accuracy, and the animated controls are designed to replicate the overall requirements of operation. The confining and claustrophobic effect of peering through a narrow sight window and not knowing who might be to the side or behind speaks to the dangers tank crews faced (and still face) from anti-tank infantry units or a tank that is outside the narrow range of visibility. To this end, the experience is similar to a flight simulator, in that key functions are simulated with a greater degree of accuracy than those found in arcade versions. Players can also utilize tactics and strategies taken from best practices in WWII tank warfare, such as using a ridge line for a commander to peek over, with maybe just the top of the turret visible so that a few feet forward would bring the main gun into firing position.

These contained spaces and their mechanical challenges, situated as they are in specific gameplay scenarios based on wartime use, place such simulators at the forefront of current VR-driven gameplay. Other types of WWII simulators, though, lend themselves less to these immersive experiences. For example, while air and land are highly represented, simulating the war at sea within simulators has been less successful than in other genres, such as strategy games. *UBOAT* (2019) blends strategy with a variety of other genres such as resource-management games along with a third-person, cross-section perspective of a manned submarine. This focus on managing the activities of a crew in preparation for combat reflects the tedium, while reducing it in favor of gameplay.

While the bulk of such a simgame focuses on a wider perspective of ship management, it also provides a switch to the first-person perspective that is found in earlier submarine games such as *Wolfpack* (1990). Titles from the *Silent Hunter* (1996) series also take a blended-perspective approach, while other titles situate submarines as abstracted units in a larger naval force (see *HOI4*, in Chapter 5). This combination of a wider, strategic focus thus finds parallels with FPSs and simulators. But even managing a single ship's or submarine's many systems poses the same problem as managing any large military vessel, much less a fleet. *World of Warships* (2015), along with naval vessels within *WT*, offers third-person perspectives that condense the many systems and subsystems into simplified and abstracted forms of control. This distancing steps away from the serious use of a simulator to replicate degrees of realistic simulation and to generate an individuated experience. These high-level perspectives lend themselves to system-management simulators, and are at home in strategy simgames.

Simulators with steep learning curves such as *IL2* that focus on the experience of individual persons rather than large weapons and systems management teams, and even more so *DCS*, can also serve as training tools for study-level practice. The Lockheed Martin-developed *Prepar3D* (2010) flight simulator takes this training focus a step further, with a steep subscription price and cost for individual planes. *X-Plane* (1995) also allows for this focus on training through its many versions, while the most recent *MFS:2020* has less of a learning curve, being designed for the consumer market and casual fliers. *MFS*, in particular, has teamed with Asobo Studies to use photogrammetry from Bing satellite data to render the entire world in recognizable 3D, its streaming service allowing pilots to pick and choose where they would fly and to see terrain, cities, rivers, and oceans rendered as recognizable objects.

The use of such tools as training systems reminds us that they are also able to construct simulated gameworlds. Rather than focusing on how *MFS*'s photogrammetry allows for actual navigation along, say, a coast in New Guinea or any other remote area (which it does), we should note that these tools open an environment to a player/pilot with a variety of highly imagined effects. When narrowing the scope to how a past event is configured (rather than how well it trains someone in the present), we see such simgames encouraging an encounter with the objects of the past in unique ways that foreground gameplay experience.

## Conclusion

As noted in Chapter 3 on shooters, thinkers have argued that the experience of playing historical computer games is quite similar to that of historical reenactment, and that we see this most with the visuals of digital video games rather than through any embodied elements. This is generally the case, except with simulators.

An argument can certainly be made that reliable, accurate, and realistic "human interaction" (Rejack, 2007: 414) with the past is the core element in which digital computer games fail to recreate a convincing embodied experience when compared with reenactment. However, with simulators a digital simulation of embodied action reconfigures (rather than reenacts) direct links with history through encounters with virtual machines (WWII planes) and the tactics used by aviators. Both of these focus on technologies as extensions of human beings (both for the historical pilots who lived and died within the actual machines and who used the tactics in life or death situations, along with the players today who learn of these through simulation and study). In this way, we have digital simulations of analog technologies (again, the planes) and immaterial technologies (tactics).

As this chapter has argued, the limited and constrained environment of a player at a computer that is simulating aspects of WWII aerial combat, and its accompanying dynamic, forms a unique mediated experience that blends history and gameplay into a unique gameworld. Yet in some cases such simulators lead to embodied experiences. These have traditionally been in the form of aviation or tank museums, heritage sites, and memorials, but taking a more active approach, restoration projects of WWII aircraft offer time in genuine warbirds for individuals (and players) who want to experience actual flight. These can be found in places such as the UK's Goodwood Aerodrome, which also offers a physical simulator experience built around an actual cockpit of a Spitfire with a projector and a wrap-around high-fidelity screen. This scale simulator is built on hydraulics to replicate the feeling of movement. It is primarily a training tool for pilots learning to fly Spitfires today, but is open to the public for anyone to buy time in it.

Along with Goodwood, the public can find other physical simulators, and even purchase brief rides in WWII aircraft at a number of other airfields. The Biggin Hill Heritage Hangar in the UK is another historic place that restores Spitfires, along with other planes such as the Hurricane and even a BF 109. The public can tour the hangar to view machines that are being restored, a type of material analogue to the game *Plane Mechanic Simulator* (2019). As at Goodwood and other memorial sites, the Heritage Hangar offers rides in two-seater Spitfires, an expensive but powerful example of how the lived experiences of historical pilots finds a contemporary use for both a paying public interested in embodied experience and pilots wanting to train to fly.

Such experiences and training, though, are in the context of an appreciation of the past rather than training for any wartime scenario. Spitfire and Hurricane pilots today, along with the variety of pilots for other WWII aircraft, fly as enthusiasts rather than as airmen and women in preparation for combat.

The past, in this sense, is reconfigured but within material, embodied space, with all its challenges and particular dangers but without the guns and ammunition and potential combat.

Still, dangers exist far beyond the experience of a VR pilot. At Biggin Hill, for example, all persons paying to fly in a Spitfire must watch a training video that explains the dangers of such flying, along with how to unbuckle straps, open the small cockpit door, and exit a still flying aircraft with the hope your parachute will deploy.[21] Such potential for harm separates the two experiences of the digital computer game and embodied material flight in a critical manner, and one that points to a key aspect of this study—that simgames are predicated on a reconfigured imaginary gameworld grounded in the past but are safe from its dangers.

# 5 Simgames: Strategies

This final chapter focuses on a type of simgame that provides a broader scope than shooters and simulators: 'grand' strategy games (GSG). The broader genre of strategy game is exemplified by Sid Meier's *Civilization* (*CIV*) (1991) series and has entered professional academic discourse as worthy of analysis and a favorite of historical game studies scholars (see Chapman, 2013, for one example). While many popular strategy games beyond *CIV* have been released, such as the *Age of Empires* (1997) and the *Total War* (2000) series, historical GSGs take the genre one-step farther with historical depth and complexity in game mechanics. Yet, they have failed to achieve the numbers of the most popular types of PC games on Steam. But this niche subgenre of 'grand' strategy has improved its player counts, with Paradox Interactive's *HOI4* second only to *CIV6* (2016) at the time of revising this chapter in the early winter of 2022.[1]

Paradox provides the most extensive list of challenging simgames in this genre. They have released several series, such as the popular *Victoria* (2003), *Crusader Kings* (2004), and *Europa Universalis* (2013). With *HOI4*, one of their most popular GSG series, they provide a global perspective on WWII that functions at the level of warring nations, with more focused control that allows for commands of armies, navies, and air-forces. *HOI4* proves most helpful because as a complex WWII simgame it blends historical reconfigurations with counterfactuals. Even more critically, as expansive as it is, *HOI4* reflects the trend in simgames to maintain glaring lacunae rather than simulating the worst aspects of the war, such as war crimes; these lacunae become obvious beyond those missing in shooters and simulators because of how a GSG such as *HOI4* addresses (or fails to address) murderous political policy and its effects.

This chapter argues that a tension ultimately exists between curated history and morally acceptable gameplay, one that most clearly emerges in a GSG such as *HOI4* because of how comprehensive it appears. Paradox provides different scales for its simgames, with the *HOI* series sitting in a middle area, both at the scale at which a player is granted control (i.e., that of a nation, rather than a family dynasty, culture, or even a planetary civilization) and also in its constricted timeframe, which is located a few years before and after the war.

This chapter examines *HOI4*, then, not just because it is the leading WWII strategy game that covers these important years, but because it allows players to choose a nation and manage it from the widest possible scope of its government down to detailed control of military units with given specialties and weaponry. Another interesting, if less developed game, *Making History II: The War of the World* (2010), was co-developed by the historian Niall Ferguson. It provides similar gameplay with a less developed overall look and feel and more limited gameplay functions.

In *HOI4*, the greatest granularity in perspective exists in the detailing of sea, air, and land aspects of the military, but players never find themselves in cockpits as they do in simulators. Rather, along with combat, they control diplomacy, the economy, espionage, and so on. These occur through either a historically located scenario or one that is similar to the alternative histories we see in popular fiction and film. What is most revealing is how *HOI4* allows a player the flexibility to reimagine major events from the past, thereby allowing for a type of reconfigured history and also for creative play that, when modded, creates any number of counterfactual scenarios from the plausible to the highly improbable. With mods, the game can even be fully converted into a fantasy setting, such as a mod that allows for the Warhammer 40k intellectual property to be played.

This type of complex GSG as exemplified by *HOI4* also works as a fitting example for this book's core dynamic because of how history is simulated within the game, in that its AI features are not designed to exactly replicate key events if a player lets the AI make all decisions. For example, the nationalists might lose in Spain if players left the game to run on its own, while a conquering Germany might not push all the way to Moscow or see the disastrous destruction of the Sixth Army west of Stalingrad. Players, if they choose, can try to replicate historical events, and the game allows this framing up to a point even as it provides unexpected turns. In *HOI4*, the focus is on

flexibility rather than linear movement through the events. This chapter ultimately foregrounds how 'national focuses' are worked into the principal nations
as constraining elements through wartime events, and how they govern high-
level strategy, while tactics are randomized because, in many cases, players take
control and make changes that can drastically alter events.

For example, one early ability to reimagine a different past is to ask what
would have happened if Czechoslovakia had resisted the acquisition of the
Sudetenland. In one scenario, this creates a problem for an embattled Germany,
which most likely would not have rushed into the Soviet Union. They would
have consolidated their power in Europe, while Czechoslovakia remained intact
and held out in its well-fortified mountain bunkers. This one possible counterfactual can lead to many other unknowable outcomes, such as a Germany that
delays an attack on Poland, giving itself more time to arm itself and consolidate
grain and oil imports from Russia. Without an attack on Poland, Chamberlain's
appeasement can be reassessed. The Normandy invasion would perhaps be
avoided, and the Soviet Union would surprisingly improve its relations with
Germany. The UK would then become an unwitting possible ally of Germany
(until the horrors of National Socialism were uncovered), the 'cold' war moving
beyond 1946 without Europe being destroyed. This sort of counterfactual
scenario is common to the game, with many being proposed and played.

In *HOI4*, different broad-scale choices that influence a nation's actions at
the highest levels are playable. These are akin to political ideologies, economic
philosophies, and military practices, all of which combine into a nation's
posture, attitude, and belief system, all of which also help or hinder the war
effort. These become highly important in game because of what they simulate
and what they ignore, with the German national focuses representing the most
difficult case of missing lacunae. But other nations also have areas of absence,
such as the missing imperial pursuits of the Japanese and their racial policies
toward the Chinese, Soviet brutality as a response to Germany's war of annihilation, US and British bombing of German cities in Europe, and the USA's
use of nuclear weapons in Japan.

In foregrounding the effects of these curated national focuses, this chapter
thus examines how the concept of 'total war' is simulated (or not), allowing for
any number of problematic areas to surface, often as lacunae that can only be
filled with study outside gameplay. These 'fantasies of contorl' or examples of

'dark play', as some scholars note (discussed later), foreground GSGs such as *HOI4* as emblematic of how the past is both sanitized through erasure, as well as opened to potentially egregious forms of modded play. Such a GSG works squarely within the dynamic even more so than shooters and simulators because of its focus on broad history, rather than just the machines of war. It encourages an investigation into the past as a critical part of gameplay, enough so that these lacunae become evident with even a cursory glance outside the simgame.

To that end, this chapter also examines a few exemplary simtexts that redress the lacunae missing from *HOI4*, such as those by serious scholars who attempt explanations for some of the war's most difficult topics, especially the German war of annihilation in the East. It works through the national focuses of the major belligerents, demonstrating how the game allows players to follow historical paths, or not. Its most detailed analysis is of the German–Soviet War, showing especially how the Eastern Front is now a major area of interest in simulated gameplay (which as already noted can be seen in simulators as well as in shooters). It ends with a detailed analysis of the German national focus tree and how it is devoid of any reference to the most horrific war crimes that happened in Eastern Europe and in the Soviet Union.

## Total War Unaddressed

As a way to understand the impact of what is simulated and what is not in a GSG such as *HOI4*, we can begin with 'total war,' a concept that works across popular computer games, as well as within serious professional military history.

Among gamers interested in strategy simgames, the concept forms the title of one of the most popular real-time strategy series, *Total War* (2000) (*TW*). Its early successes provided players a way to manage the armies of feudal Japan, ancient Rome and Greece, and medieval Europe, and its most recent successes translate the grim fantasy world of Games Workshop's tabletop war game *Warhammer Fantasy* (1983) to the computer game system: *TW: Warhammer* (2016). While the concept of total war is explicitly stated in the title of the series, such simgames fail to simulate many problematic aspects now associated with war in its most comprehensive form.

The concept of total war has a long historiography outside computer gaming; it is grounded in military history through Carl von Clausewitz's

*On War* (1832) and later Erich Ludendorff's *The Total War* (1935). Its guiding principle describes the phenomenon of a totalizing type of warfare that is ultimately without rules and is waged against more than armies. Ironically, the *TW* series has very little of this type of playable violence that reaches outside conflicts between armies. Granted, a player can position conscripted peasants in *TW: Rome* (2004) at the front of an army, sacrificing them as a tactic to slow the enemy, and after a battle a player can click a button to execute prisoners or even sack or raze an entire settlement (which, although this is not stated explicitly, would eradicate the entire populace). However, such real-world wartime violence in which civilians are targeted is often abstracted to the point of little impact or outright ignored in computer games, because of concerns about simulating war crimes when providing in-game agency to players.

As I mention later, this omission provides a contradiction. Yes, simulating war crimes in a simgame is problematic because it might provide indefensible player agency, but the erasure of such war crimes also potentially removes horrible truths that should be remembered. Thus, such difficulties remain unplayable even when players are inspired by the dynamic to find clarity over events that are simulated (or not) within a historical simgame. Many such moments of clarity can arise to form a wide tapestry of historical understanding for an event such as WWII.

To take just one example from this chapter, before the beginning of Operation Barbarossa and the German invasion of the Soviet Union, Hitler challenged his generals and explained:

> We must forget the concept of comradeship between soldiers. A communist is no comrade before or after the battle. This is a war of annihilation. If we do not grasp this, we shall still beat the enemy, but thirty years later we shall again have to fight the Communist foe. We do not wage war to preserve the enemy. (Quoted in Kershaw, 2008a: 599)

The blending of military tactics with political and cultural strategy can be seen when we view this statement about not preserving the enemy through the lens of total war. In combining these concepts of totalizing annihilation, with war acting as the connecting tissue, we see how addressing the true horror of such an endeavor remains problematic.

In failing to offer this horrible aspect as playable content, such simgames also fail to address the depth of understanding provided by other forms of historical study beyond play, such as the literary impulse for representing the varieties of the human condition, especially the agonies of suffering as seen in psychologically complex characters or the cinematic spectacle of war at its worst, or even professional histories that carefully chart the most complex of causes for the war, and its worst results.[2]

Just as much, philosophy and its probing questions are outright ignored. To take only one such example, of which there are many reaching back to the critique of the Enlightenment, Hannah Arendt's *The Origins of Totalitarianism* (1951) explores the critical concept that challenged thinkers after the war's end, even working it into her title. She pivots away from the perspective of total war to what she calls the "final crystallizing catastrophe" (Arendt, 1979: xv) that saw a war of annihilation waged, with the Jews as the primary target. She sees this sustained attack plaguing the Jews who were consistently threatened with dispersal as going back to their Babylonian prehistory, to the Romans, and through their medieval history, only to encounter its most pernicious secular form in National Socialism and its Final Solution. Götz Aly, a German historian, responds to Arendt's work on the subject by foregrounding these horrors within a modern context of hyper-rational policies by National Socialists with clear "utilitarian goals" (Aly and Heim, 2003: 3) that are discernible and therefore explainable. The motivations are complex and far beyond any simgame to address, with our literatures and philosophies still struggling to quilt together an answer—ultimate evil or explainable (even if deplorable) rationality?

The problem of totalitarianism for nuanced and complex thinkers such as Arendt and Aly is explored in a manner outside the scope of simgames, failing to reach difficult concepts such as ideology, racism, imperialism, empire, and antisemitism, all of which converged in the murderous policies of Hitler, but also in those of Stalin and the Japanese challenge to Western imperialism. The historiography that critiques this sort of power is daunting, and these difficult subjects have no presence in simgames. Even the military concept of total war, which is used blithely as a title, offers very little clarification in the way of game mechanics in the *TW* series, or in the case study in this chapter, *HOI4*.

## Power of Individual Stories

The most challenging turn of the simgame–simtext dynamic occurs when players are confronted with historical lacunae during gameplay that are only clarified with outside study. These missing pieces patch the gameworld tapestry, situating a reconfigured past within the context of a simgame. A considerable difference, though, exists when thinking about the large-scale elements that are undersimulated in shooters and simulators and the blatant lacunae that exist in a GSG such as *HOI4*, a simgame that attempts a more comprehensive inclusion of the major elements that defined the war.

The dynamic not only clarifies how to have success in game by driving a tank or flying a plane or managing a nation, constrained as these are by curated historical contexts, but it also emerges in *HOI4* as high-level political and military strategies, an analogue of looking outward to other sources for the broadest understanding of the war and its focused events. As noted with shooters and simulators, the archive encountered by strategy players outside gameplay is beyond the control of professional historians or cultural gate keepers, but is still apparent in simtexts that attempt to describe the most complex motivations and causes for the war.

Such content from the public sphere may be well considered, careful, and aware of the dangers and horrors of war, or it may be designed for political indoctrination of the worst sort. Just as prevalent across both professional and popular simtexts, the dynamic may also point the curious player to stories of individuals, and here the power of literature, film, and other mediating forms of storytelling emerges in examples that show war affecting human beings, as well as soldiers as heroes or villains—these two perspectives often in tension but also, in the most nuanced simtexts, at work together to complexify simplistic reductions (see examples in Chapter 2).

Such human stories of the past shift the focus from machines or abstract processes to real people, often flawed even when extraordinary. While hybrid simgames have yet to find a way to harness such stories with the same psycho-logical depth as literature, they have captured the spectacle of cinema. How to tell human stories powerfully is a challenge within game spaces, one that film and cinema has already accomplished, many filmic techniques being incorporated into computer games in varying degrees from cutscenes to dramatized narratives. Even more so, the most demanding of these (i.e., simulators), are still reliant on either the steep learning curves of mastering machinery and their tactics, or, in the case of strategy games, in presenting complex but abstracted processes that allowed nations to manage the conflict.

An obvious but problematic way for historical simgames to accept this challenge of incorporating stories with psychological depth, while still retaining interesting gameplay, would be to find the previously mentioned lacunae and to simulate them. Such a task clashes with several potential problems seen clearly in a simgame such as *HOI4*, the least problematic being the simulation of past elements that create boring gameplay. As mentioned in earlier chapters, many examples can be found, such as the mundane tasks that comprise the tedium between battles from patrol duties, to cleaning equipment, to taking tests. In *HOI4*, simulating such minutiae would limit the expected broader focus for gameplay.

The most problematic combination for engaging gameplay of playable psychological depth combined with proper historical breadth emerges when thinking about the importance of collective remembrance for the war's worst offenses. As mentioned earlier, playable Nazis is one such lacuna, as is incorporating the many crimes committed during the Holocaust. These are blatantly missing in computer games to avoid giving agency to anyone who would fetishize human suffering or would embrace the graphic violence enabled by the political agents of National Socialism or other agents of war crimes. While the attempt to obliquely represent such troubling aspects of the war through specific Wehrmacht units can be found within FPSs, dampening effects often remove any agency and understanding of how, say, the Waffen-SS operated. This technique works through erasure of their deeds or, nearly as problematic, through reconfiguring Nazi tropes into something else, yet recognizable.

A way to responsibly structure such lacunae into simgames would be to work along a continuum that seeks stories of individuals and their lived experiences at one pole, with the opposite pole occupied by the broadest views of the war as teaching objectives. For example, regarding the lived experiences of the common German soldier, the myth of the innocent (or clean) Wehrmacht suggests that they were not responsible for the campaigns of annihilation by the SS and Nazis against Jews across Europe into Poland, the Baltic States, Ukraine, and Russia. This appears plausible at first glance, because it is sensible to believe that some common German soldiers fought (or were forced to fight) for various other reasons besides the political indoctrination that led to atrocities against civilians, particularly the Jews.

Such a selective-memory narrative provided relief for postwar Germany and its surviving soldiers, some of whom may have been honorable during the war, while at the same time distracting from the broader perspective of how ordinary Germans, along with their primary fighting force, the Wehrmacht, allowed and aided war crimes and, according to thinkers such as Wolfram Wette, were conditioned through years of prewar cultural prejudice (see Wette, 2006, and how this 'entanglement...' discourse has a detailed historiography that presents a newcomer with difficult material that has to be parsed). Simulating both how a common soldier might be fighting without supporting National Socialism or, at the opposite pole, simulating how others were conditioned to accept such racist and violent policies could demonstrate the complexities involved in German society at the time—and what led to its worst war crimes.

The war can also be approached from the widest perspective, beyond even that of officers, generals, and national leaders, examining the forces that drove nations to war, such as economic pressure, the politics of the previous conflict, nationalism, political rhetoric, and racial prejudice. The danger in such extreme abstraction is that it utilizes a type of anti-humanism, removing human actors as primary mechanisms and allowing a type of totalizing determinism that skews the event away from its effects on living people. GSGs such as *HOI4* allow for this broadest level to be played, even as it introduces a limited human perspective at differing scales. Yet just as a narrow focus on what soldiers and civilians experienced produces glaring lacunae (such as how the common German soldier, their officers, and their military staff thought and felt about Jews, Bolsheviks, Slavs, and Soviets), the broader focus that would abstract such murderous prejudice is left out of *HOI4* as a playable game mechanism.

A major lacuna avoided in game is the propaganda techniques that demonized and dehumanized the enemy across all the major nations—a prejudicial depiction of the enemy being translated into prejudice against an entire people or culture. While the worst case is Goebbels' propaganda machine that maligned Jews and tied them to supposed 'Asiatic' Bolsheviks as the primary enemy of Germany, as well as maligning Eastern Europeans and

Soviets as inferior 'Slavs,' Soviet propaganda against Western capitalists reaches back to well before the October Revolution. The representation of Germans as inhuman conquerors who would show no mercy was one of many inflections that emerged during the Russian ideology around its Patriotic War, one that continues today as a way to remember the aggression of the German invaders.

US representation of the Japanese is another example that reveals overtly racist arguments for war through a variety of media, along with the removal of US-Japanese citizens to internment camps. The Japanese also channeled hatred for Western colonialism in its representations of the USA as anti-Asian, while at the same time utilizing racist representations of the Chinese as justification for its own crimes and imperialist aims. The British, Italians, and French demonstrated their own inflections, which extended back to colonial practices. The worst of these prejudicial motivators are excised as gameplay mechanics in *HOI4*, even though they comprise a major part of any broadscale understanding of the war, but some forms of historical framing do exist in game that can drive a nation toward liberal democracy, fascism, communism, or a vague position of independence.[3]

## Dark Play and Fantasies of Control

In most WWII simgames, the lacunae that hide the missing parts of total war do so to avoid providing agency to players for the worst kinds of war crimes. Yet developers and players still find ways to push boundaries. The concept of dark play is foregrounded in an anthology on the subject, examining how games allow players to engage in questionable play, sometimes after thoughtful consideration and awareness. Such dark play can also be considered a type of questionable performance, especially within such a context as WWII. I consider such concepts, along with fantasies of control (discussed later), as the potential dangerous extreme of simgames.

The editors of *The Dark Side of Game Play: Controversial Issues in Playful Environments* recognize that in computer games "we can be assassins, megalomaniac super villains, mafia members, criminal bikers, vampires, werewolves, and even Nazis" (Mortensen, Linderoth, and Brown, 2015: 4). This list of playable agents, ending with Nazis as the worst offenders, is telling because, as historian

Ian Kershaw notes, what continues to challenge us is "the question of the essential singularity of Nazism" (2008b: 21). Nazism as both an historical reality and a potentially problematic gameplay element points us to what others have called the 'limits of play,' as Adam Chapman and Jonas Linderoth do in their article that analyzes its use (2015). The editors note that other forms of dark play exist, from players choosing to bring grief to others to games that overtly work against players. The potential areas of investigation, as the anthology shows, explore death as a dominant mechanism in digital games, as well as demonstrating concerns over how children are represented as non-player-characters and the potential for simulating abuse.

Rather than stop at an answer to what may seem a complex but expected question about how Nazi imagery and ideology have been used (or erased) as an alarming example of dark play in computer games and to what effect, Chapman and Linderoth ask a more nuanced and difficult question, "how do designers get away with it" (2015: 139)? The approach they use is taken from Goffman's frame analysis, in particular the idea that games frame a player's experience of a particular event's original meaning by transforming, or 'keying,' it in one of two opposing directions, one that 'upkeeps' the meaning away from what we consider to be a realistic understanding, or one that 'downkeys' this less realistic experience for one that is closer, problematic as that can be, to a real past (Chapman and Linderoth, 2015: 141).

The implications are that the transformation, if it leads closer to what happened in the past, presents realistic elements that might be harmful to a player. The opposite keying would trivialize these problematic elements by removing them from a realistic context. As the authors note, the former makes a player responsible and thus guilty, while the latter encourages a mocking distance, a type of culpable irresponsibility. The option by developers of erasure, as in the lack of representation of playable Nazis or the Holocaust in computer games, is the end result. Attempting to realistically simulate aspects for players of such horrific elements crosses lines of play into a dark performative experience that might encourage graphic fetishism in human suffering or possibly remove it from its realistic past into the realm of casual entertainment.

Yet still, as Chapman and Linderoth argue in their analysis of WWII games, the Nazis are still playable even though they are often replaced by generic Wehrmacht soldiers bearing the Iron Cross rather than the swastika.

They follow Goffman that different media have different frames for the same event; in this case, Nazis, the SS, and their insignias, swastikas and so on, are all openly depicted in film, yet not with anywhere near the same representation in games. The authors suggest that something inherent in games trivializes serious themes, offering play instead of reality, often as a way to remove harm from the experience.

In doing so, the consideration of complex and nuanced themes, as found in serious literature, is avoided to be replaced by a degree of playful agency in what the authors call games' "special status as cultural objects, in that they can be considered as value thermometers of a society" (Chapman and Linderoth, 2015: 150). Their conclusion is that investigating the limits of dark play in games says more about society than it does about the particular games themselves.

The developers of *HOI* have explicitly stated their position on such elements of dark play:

This is a firm reminder that bears repeating!

There will not be any gulags or deathcamps (including POW camps) to build in Hearts of Iron 3, nor will there be the ability to simulate the Holocaust or systematic ethnic purges [...]

NOTE: Strategic bombing in HoI will be abstracted and not allow you to terror bomb civilians specifically. Chemical weapons will also not be included in the game. Any threads that complain about this issue will be closed without discussion.

NOTE: There will not be any swastikas in the game, because it IS illegal to show them in Germany and various other countries. Same goes for other Nazi symbols (e.g. related to the SS) or Nazi propaganda material, including songs etc. Any links posted to a mod which includes a Swastika or other illegal Nazi symbols will be deleted. Any threads that complain about this issue will be closed. (unmerged[9046], 2011: online)

Paradox Interactive, at the time of the third version of *HOI*, provided this clarification to step away from the hazards of players modding the game along reprehensible lines. The fourth version maintains this erasure, even as mods complicate such full erasure with elements that inch nearer to those that would be banned (discussed later).

But the fact that these rules needed to be stated demonstrates how difficult this terrain has become. It speaks to how such a simgame works across boundaries that separate a military strategic simgame, with its focus on tactics and strategies, from non-military mechanisms used in war. Ideologies that drive belief systems, together with the politics of mass murder or genocide, move from strategy to simulation in a way that speaks to the terrible potential of dark play.

*Historia Ludens: The Playing Historian* (von Lünen et al., 2020) is another helpful examination of how play and history converge in games. It clarifies how dark play can still emerge even though developers overtly ban certain elements. It works through a variety of issues related to historical game studies, several of which relate to my study because they foreground how play and history intersect, with the player ultimately gaining more agency with new tools. An insightful examination into how modding allows players to change games (Salvati, 2020) demonstrates the power of these new forms of player agency that offer experiences examined earlier, such as flying a WWII aircraft; yet as the author notes, these also sometimes reinforce dangerous ideologies. Salvati calls these 'fantasies of control', a recognition that with mods players can simulate imagined worlds, or fantasies, directly under their own control, which allows for real-world prejudices to be enacted within the digital space of computer games.

His examples are clear warnings of the power of modding, such as a mod for Paradox Interactive's *Europa Universalis IV* (2013) that encourages religious wars of extermination. He writes:

> Far from an isolated case, the practice of modding strategy games to include explicitly racist, ethno-nationalist, or neo-fascist themes (often defended by their creators on grounds of comedic irony or free expression) has become something of a cottage industry in recent years. (Salvati, 2020: 156)

Salvati lists examples, such as segregated space colonists in *Stellaris* (2016), to the insertion of Adolf Hitler as a leader of Germany in *CIV6* (2016). His critique is important, especially in today's geopolitical climate in which polarized political positions are given voice across media platforms.

He reiterates an important question (found online) that asks if strategy games attract a particular type of player who are sympathetic to fantasies of control. The answers point to how these games might reinforce nationalistic notions, or even satisfy players who want to "indulge in fantasies of blood and iron" (Salvati, 2020: 158). Other suggestions center on how imperialism and empire are themselves reinforced through mechanisms of control embedded in the games. Players take the role of a god-like force directing nations, armies, and economies. They literally plan and execute the destruction of their enemies at the highest level of existence, in some games such as *Stellaris* (2016) this being interplanetary civilizations.

Salvati finds the links between right-wing ideology and games extending into the tools used, such as the communication application Discord or even the game-distribution platform Steam, and to real-world activity that furthers political aims. The movement from a popular game release to a mod that offers racist, misogynistic, or overtly graphic gameplay, and then to real-world recruiting for groups such as the 'alt-right' or more extreme neo-fascist thinking reflects the dangerous dark side of the dynamic analyzed in this book. A player influenced by the simgame–simtext dynamic may just as likely encounter texts meant for ideological indoctrination as for careful examination of a historical context. Salvati recognizes that a critical approach such as Alexander Galloway's sees in these unfortunate connections between games and ideology a link that shows how culture emerges within games, rather than games being the originator of such ideas, and that for a thinker such as Galloway the most pervasive form of control embedded in games comes from how their code organizes gameplay (rather than how they reinforce political ideologies) (see Salvati, 2020: 164–66).

*HOI4* can also be modded, and thus risks becoming a platform for fantasies of control and dark play. Most mods avoid these delicate issues. Some, though, as Paradox's forums demonstrate, can attract what appears to be a right-leaning tendency, with Paradox forced to ban threads as well as purge mods. Some of the more well-known mods avoid outright banning but still offer the potential for dark play and fantasies of control to a lesser degree. 'Millennium Dawn,' with its reach into the twenty-first century, offers the potential to encourage right-wing resurgence within liberal democracies as we see today in North America and Europe. This is problematic beyond others such as 'Kaiserreich,' which asks what would have happened had Germany won WWI, or 'End of a New Beginning,' which reaches back three centuries before the war.

To differing degrees, these types of total-conversion mods offer cultural, political, and ideological elements that have been excised in *HOI4*, especially those that relate to war crimes. The mod 'Deus Vult' demonstrates the length to which this can be taken and still avoid being banned. It offers a conflict similar to the Crusades, in which Jesus Christ acts as a field marshal and encourages wars of religion, with all their bloody justifications and outcomes.

## Professional Histories

The types of simtext histories a WWII GSG player might encounter to fill the missing parts within a simgame such as *HOI4* range from the broadest scope such as the William Shirer's popular *The Rise and Fall of the Third Reich* (1960) to more recent descriptions that cover the entire war. These also focus on particular battles, with historians writing for the popular sphere including popularizers like Antony Beevor and Stephen Ambrose. Along with these accessible simtexts, more difficult academic monographs written for professional historians occupy the far end of the continuum. Any of these simtexts can fill in missing details, as can introductory accounts readily available in online sources.

As noted already, however, less thorough material might initially come to hand when someone starts the interpretative process, especially if they begin with online research. For example, YouTube videos have become ubiquitous to the point they are often the first steps by players who are investigating events such as WWII; documentaries also form a critical part of the simtext archive. Along with these digital popular-history simtexts, written historical accounts are still being published and offered online in digital format, increasingly in the popular sphere.

A more detailed look at a single popular simtext by Shirer demonstrates how ideas within it emerge as directly relatable to gameplay, while also separating its level of analysis from gameplay. Shirer's work is exemplary as a middle-ground simtext that falls between the most easily consumed digital texts and more recent work written for professional academics, especially for this chapter and its focus on the European theater and what happened in the German–Soviet War. For a simgame such as *HOI4*, it presents broad history and counterfactual scenarios that are playable. With this general approach, found in accounts such as Shirer's and many others, player-readers encounter simtexts that not only provide a general history, but also reveal lacunae missing in GSG gameplay.

Shirer was in a position to deliver an account that acted as an early touchstone reference text; while dated, it is still widely known. Having witnessed those critical years as a correspondent who was often based in Germany itself, he had a unique perspective on events. He was even present at key moments, such as witnessing Hitler's demand for France's surrender in the same place that Germany had admitted defeat in November 1918 (Shirer, 1960: 742–43).

Two decades after the war, Shirer's monograph provided a comprehensive account that showed how Germans reacted to many of the major moments of the prewar and later war years. His book details the event by exploring a wide range of subjects, such as the rise of Hitler, the birth of the Nazi party, the last days of the Weimar Republic, the outcome of the war, and the horror of what ensued with the New Order, all expected topics within a comprehensive historical account.

Each of these areas is ripe for investigation by an interested player who is taking a first foray into professional history. These areas provide a basis for answering key questions—such as how events affected each other—and also fill in missing gameplay lacunae related, in particular, to the ideological policies of National Socialism. Detailed historical accounts such as Shirer's from a non-military historian are even helpful when mining such difficult terrain as to why battles were won or lost, and players interested in such investigations will find that a historical simtext can do more than reveal the strengths and weaknesses of military tactics and strategy; it can address topics that are off limits for gameplay.

For example, one key aspect of understanding the war is accounting for the outlook of leaders, and the effects they had on the lives of ordinary people. This psychological level of analysis separates such a book, along with subsequent and even more rigorous historical accounts by authors such as Ian Kershaw (discussed later), into the difficult terrain of causal motivation for individual actors. An account such as Shirer's is notable because, through it, he draws portraits of individuals such as Hitler and those closest to him through the perspective of one who witnessed many of the events at the time. In doing so, Shirer's simtext extends beyond the initial range of subject matter that is closest to a simulator such as *IL2* or even a strategy such as *HOI4* (i.e., military aviation simulation and totalizing war) and attempts to answer complex questions about causation and motivation in the minds of individuals. A process of interpretation is required to parse such arguments, many of which find common ground with literary techniques that describe the motivations of characters.

In Shirer's book, a reader learns that Hitler "was possessed of a demonic personality, granite will, uncanny instincts, a cold ruthlessness," but also "a remarkable intellect, a soaring imagination" (Shirer, 1960: 6). He describes the young Hitler as a dreamer who refused to work so that he could spend his days listening to the epic operas of Wagner. An account such as Shirer's, written in the middle part of the twentieth century, could still focus on the dominant personality of a national leader, even sincerely muse about his "peculiar genius" (Shirer, 1960: 42), while later historians often forgo such focuses on the individual for more nuanced complexities to explain the rise of dangerous leaders. New historical trends, as well as changes in literary and critical theory, have moved discourses away from viewing individuals as such important forces, with the myriad cultural processes and their stratified artifacts, often unseen or unheard, being just as important when attempting to understand the past.

For a non-professional-historian player who is interested in the war, such a representation of Hitler as Shirer's might trigger a need for explanation. Shirer is by no means sympathetic to Hitler or his policies, often noting aspects that make him one of the twentieth century's most villainous individuals. Yet in his depiction of Hitler as the prime perpetrator of Germany's downfall, as well as the driving force behind its most pernicious acts, he represents Hitler as a historical figure of importance in the same camp as Alexander, Napoleon, and Bismarck, and thereby valorizes the class of 'great men' in a way that appears antiquated today, yet is a common simplification in the public sphere and among players.

Shirer also foregrounds Hitler's *Mein Kampf* (1925–27) as a particular book of prophetic importance, primarily as a reflection of Hitler's thinking prior to the war. The validity of this insight, that so much of what Hitler desired could be found and understood before the war, reflects the value of such a book for Shirer, rather than any value in its ideological message. But these connections require interpretation on the part of player-readers so they realize that Shirer's exposition on *Mein Kampf* is a damning literary and philosophical critique. With careful reading beyond what is expected from a casual simgame player, they can piece together Shirer's condemnation of National Socialism and its effects even before arriving at Chapter 27 and its horrific account of the Final Solution.

*Mein Kampf*, as Shirer notes, contains the pernicious thinking that Hitler would later transmute into National Socialism, especially the core sickness of its *Weltanschauung*, its deplorable racism. It also outlines Hitler's project for *Lebensraum*, or living space, that he planned to acquire, not by colonial means across the seas, but within Europe—regarding it as an analogue for what occurred in North America and its genocide of native Americans (Shirer, 1960: 308). Shirer speculates that "had the foreign statesmen of the world perused it carefully while there still was time, both Germany and the world might have been saved from catastrophe" (Shirer, 1960: 81). Couple that with the book's blatant antisemitism, according to Shirer, and one can perceive an ideology forming that would later see concentration camps turned into extermination camps.

Yet the difficulties in determining someone's motivation, or how previous actions such as writing a book might have been prophetic (and might have served as a warning), prove less helpful in clarifying gameplay than when players see historians speculate about counterfactual possibilities, especially those that can be simulated in GSGs. A work such as Shirer's utilizes counterfactuals as mechanisms of historical analysis, an impossible-to-resist impulse that occurs even when someone who is open to fruitful speculation thinks carefully about such events. These counterfactuals can be modeled in GSGs such as *HOI4*, a way to simulate aspects of alternative history or to replay events as they unfolded. Such speculation, as already mentioned by Ferguson, is resisted by many traditional historians, although he and others encourage it as a generative use of the imagination inspired by sensitivity to historical complexities (Ferguson, 1997: Introduction).

Reading through Shirer's account, a reader encounters a number of speculations that he or she might want to use as a frame for *HOI4* gameplay. He notes key moments that could have avoided the war, such as the window of opportunity that the Allies had to defeat Hitler before the German military could pose a threat, which was any time before Germany reoccupied the Rhineland in 1936 (Shirer, 1960: 211).

Shirer's observation that had the French Chief of the General Staff, General Gamelin, given the order to challenge German troops as they moved into the Rhineland, their generals may have given the order to fall back. Shirer argues that with initial resistance by a determined French, this would "have been the end of Hitler, after which history might have taken quite a different and brighter turn than it did, for the dictator could never have survived such a fiasco" (1960: 364). Such a speculative conclusion demonstrates the power of counterfactual thinking, even if the scenario might have been an impossibility (thanks to the lack of a determined French military staff, perhaps). But, as mentioned later, this sort of non-historical preparedness is available in game as a powerful counterfactual, with specific French national focuses offered in *HOI4*.

Likewise, throughout Shirer's early account he represents the British and French response to Hitler as a series of miscalculations that have since been analyzed in numerous histories as the Allies' moral failure to admit or resist the rise of fascism in Europe. Chamberlain's appeasement along with Gamelin's pacifism is a common topic. Writing from Berlin at the time, Shirer argues that had the British prime minister specifically, and adamantly, informed Hitler that Britain would rush to Czechoslovakia's aid, "the Führer would never have embarked on the adventures which brought on the Second World War [...]. This was the well-meaning Prime Minister's fatal mistake" (Shirer, 1960: 364). Again, unlike a pacifist French military, a Chamberlain with a will like Churchill's works only in the realm of alternative-history counterfactuals, rather than plausible history, such as the British national focus that brings Churchill to power early to address the German threat (discussed later). A player using such a counterfactual in this example can take control of the British government and from the beginning direct Britain toward the sort of intervention that Churchill championed and Chamberlain resisted. He or she could set a goal that a major victory point would be the survival of Czechoslovakia at all costs.

In detailing the curious impact that Chamberlain's appeasement had on paving the way for Hitler's early successes, especially in Czechoslovakia and Poland, Shirer argues that the people of Germany were at this point still very hopeful that Hitler would bring peace, being unaware of the enormity of his plans of conquest for Europe—and the crimes and disasters that these would bring about. Certain generals, such as Franz Halder and Erwin von Witzleben, were willing to oppose Hitler according to Shirer, and could have acted at a critical juncture when Hitler was planning his invasion of Czechoslovakia.

But, according to Shirer, "Chamberlain's trip to Munich certainly cut the ground from underneath their feet" (1960: 413), arguing the contentious proposition that a prewar resistance movement within the Wehrmacht could have resisted Hitler if given the right circumstances. Such speculation about Chamberlain's delusion in making Hitler a true friend of England and his insistence on peace forms the center of this account of human folly, which Shirer unfolds as high-stakes drama.[4] Chamberlain returning in apparent triumph and waving his misguided letter, believing he had avoided war, hints at what might have happened had the Allies stood firm at so early a point with no reliance on theatrics or the good will of Hitler.

What is most curious as a critical counterfactual is that, according to Shirer's interviews with German generals after the war, that had the Allies attacked from the west while Germany was moving into Czechoslovakia, "Germany would have lost the war, and in short order" (Shirer, 1960: 423). This is based on the number of divisions each side had, with the Allied forces vastly outnumbering the Germans. According to this line of thinking, a firm France willing to engage, a Britain willing to stand up to Hitler, and with the thirty-five Czech divisions, behind their highly defensible mountain fortress bunkers, the combined Allied force would have stood a good chance of resisting (Shirer, 1960: 416a). Such a counterfactual is interesting to replay in a simgame such as *HOI4*, where one can create the scenario of a well-prepared, armed, and emboldened France, Britain, and Czechoslovakia. What is not simulated in such a simgame is the narrowest level, that of human beings and the war's effects on them. Shirer recounts more of the dramatic moments with the elderly Czech President Hacha fainting after his meeting with Hitler when he realized the fate of his country. The broadest understanding of actions of such events, at the macro-level of armies and nations, fails to simulate its opposite with this narrow focus—an old man fainting.

Such speculative analysis from a journalist turned historian provides insightful examples of how players can reconfigure key 'what if' moments that can be translated into strategic gameplay. Players are now in a position to model such scenarios with computer systems, not replicating exact details, down to the granular level of individuals within cockpits or trenches, but within wider simulated spaces that allow for different degrees of verisimilitude. A simgame such as those within the *HOI* series, however, allows for very specific scenarios to be played, such as those I have mentioned.

What is profound about these counterfactuals is not only that they spark a curious interest in modeling outcomes through simulation, but also that they hint at answers only found through deeper study and investigation. For example, Shirer also offers another key moment, that of an apparently duplicitous Hitler invading Poland (1960: 634). He asks why the well-armed French army didn't attack as it had promised. He gives his reasons, first among these being defeatism, along with other key issues such as concern that Germany would bomb its cities. But by looking at the number of divisions and their placement, one can follow his line of thinking that a determined France could alone have taken over western Germany before Hitler's forces had finished in Poland. Again, such a strategic scenario can be simulated in *HOI4*, with a counterfactually determined France backing its ally rather than refusing to come to its aid.

This reconfigured potential within a GSG such as *HOI4* allows for an involuntary education, as Ferguson might hope, with such speculations providing a type of inadvertent consciousness-raising in that players become better aware of the mistakes of the past that led to war. But such lofty aims obscure a more mundane process: a player unaware today of what occurred in the past, or what might have happened, performs preliminary research by engaging simtexts to better understand strategic gameplay. The counterfactuals may be experienced first, the texts follow for clarification, and historical context is clarified last. Of course, with enough study players might reverse this, and begin to simulate key elements that they consider might have changed the course of the war. Shirer's simtext is full of these potentials.

This directed aspect of the dynamic, though, does not mean, as educators interested in *Bildung* and *paideia* might hope, that such encounters with simtexts always create a more aware liberal subject who is better prepared to counter the sort of horrible totalitarianism seen in the war. What might just as easily occur is an encounter with simtexts that, in the least-worst case, provide misinformation or, at worst, indoctrinate through propaganda that runs counter to liberal democracy. And just as any encounter with a text requires interpretation, simgame developers must contend with aspects that go beyond entertainment into problematic areas, such as the celebration of war crimes or even their justification today. To that end, as already noted, a simulator such as *IL2* bans the swastika from both its German aircraft and from any user-made skins. Even more so, *HOI4* removes any reference to the Final Solution from its simgame, a pointed erasure that, while disallowing any type of gameplay that would encourage genocide, forgets one of the worst offenders in the modern crisis of rational, Western society.

Shirer's account of the war crimes of National Socialism are primarily condensed in one chapter at the end of the book. In it, he notes that "no comprehensive blueprint for the New Order was drawn up" (1960: 937), an acknowledgment that is also noted by other historians who have had to piece together the canvas of war crimes championed by Hitler and others. A chapter such as Shirer's, within a broader general history, acts as an introduction for players who wish to solve the mystery of such a glaring in-game lacuna. He notes key difficulties (later to be ignored by *HOI4*), such as labeling Jews as '*Untermenschen*,' and how this directly related to the war crimes committed upon the Jewish population of Eastern Europe and Russia. He also addresses the practice of forced slave labor, with concentration camps eventually turning into extermination camps; likewise, he considers the treatment of prisoners of war, especially the Soviets, with the starvation forced upon them being another inhumane practice that had direct effects on war effort (it reduced the supplies needed to support these prisoners of war), something also ignored by simgames. Conversely, this abuse had a direct effect on how German prisoners were mistreated by Soviets in revenge, which recursively fueled German hate propaganda against the brutality of supposedly animalistic, inhuman, 'Asiatic' Russians. All of this has no playable function in *HOI4*.

Shirer's short account of the Final Solution, compared with more detailed accounts by later professional historians, foregrounds some of the most atrocious policies excised from *HOI4*. He mentions the *Nacht und Nebel Erlass*, a policy that directly 'disappeared' undesirables from the western regions as an act of terror, as if into the 'night and fog.' He mentions the crimes of the four *Einsatzgruppen* (A, B, C, D) in the East as a key mechanism of the Final Solution, using interviews and descriptions in a journalistic fashion, juxtaposing detailed accounts of murder with statistics of persons killed. These techniques for 'liquidating' human beings early in the war began with shooting, then the use of gas vans, the early precursors to what would happen on a larger scale in the extermination camps—all unplayable.

This topic's difficult nature challenges any notion of working such material into suitable gameplay. To approach it historically with care exposes a player to a vast range of literature. Shirer's early account is not exhaustive, yet he treats the topic with an appropriate awareness of the scope and horror of what the Final Solution meant for those who suffered under it. The suggestion that any game should allow players to implement anything like a Final Solution, or concentration or extermination camps, and death squads is outright rejected by Paradox (as well as by developers of other WWII strategy games), but may have to be addressed as more forms become popular with indie game developers, and as VR play increases.

This missing subject matter within *HOI4*, alone, opens a player to an entire literature of grievance about the Jewish Holocaust, or what is called the *Shoah* by Jewish thinkers who, like Arendt, situate it within a long history of persecution. This missing gameplay canvas (and one specifically erased) is the most sensitive and telling example of how public memory of the event is still with us as a powerful site where care needs to be taken. As late as the 1990s, historian David Irving lost a defamation lawsuit against an American author, Deborah Lipstadt, and her publisher, Penguin, for her claims that Irving was a Holocaust denier. He lost, and in so doing was also discredited as a historian. Literature exists that details this trial and what it means for history as a discipline, as well as how the Holocaust is perceived today (Evans, 2002; Lipstadt, 2006; Pelt, 2016). Such an impactful case demonstrates how powerful this subject remains.

Without addressing Holocaust denial, we can see that the historical archive that details the crimes committed by National Socialism is vast, and these crimes are entirely absent from computer gameplay. Yet the most considered of WWII scholarship attempts to answer these difficult questions that gameplay cannot approach. To take one example, recent work such as Götz Aly and Susanne Heim's *Architects of Annihilation: Auschwitz and the Logic of Destruction* (2003) provides detailed descriptions of the rational processes involved in the killing of Jews. This stands in stark contrast to arguments that focus only on the evil of Hitlerism or suggests the crimes are somehow incomprehensible.

Ian Kershaw's work, including his detailed biographies of Hitler, addresses these complex issues, and will challenge any interested player. A nuanced approach can be found in Kershaw's *Hitler, the Germans, and the Final Solution* (2008), written by a historian of Germany and the war rather than a Holocaust historian, but who over decades has treated this most difficult subject with care. It is an example of how the historiography of German involvement in WWII has moved through different stages, with different points of interest; yet even so, today, the crimes of the Nazis and their effects on our understanding of the Holocaust have not diminished but grown in scope.

In looking at Kershaw's research agenda over the past several decades, we see a focused interest emerging in the consciousness of German people and how it led to Hitler, and antisemitism. The latter has developed as a research field among a number of historians (many German) and has proven fruitful, especially in unraveling the details of how it formed. Kershaw has examined his early argument that 'moral indifference' proved just as harmful as overt hatred when explaining antisemitism in Germany:

> The term 'indifference', I insisted, did not mean neutrality, but carried nega-
> tive overtones—those of shrugging one's shoulders or turning one's back on
> an evil in recognition that one can do nothing about it, and in the feeling
> that other concerns are more pressing or overwhelming. (Kershaw, 2008b: 7)

Beyond indifference, in Kershaw's understanding, the role of the state comprised many other agents that proved to be critical issues when understanding the worst aspects of the war. This debate often decentered Hitler as a prime agent, not lessening criminality on his part, but highlighting other strata that proved just as harmful.

This broader scope has also worked alongside a push to encourage a historicization of National Socialism in the same way that historians have examined other eras, such as the French Revolution or the Reformation. This has meant normalizing the events "with cool rationality, free from emotion" (Kershaw, 2008b: 13). Still, the momentum in foregrounding the reprehensible nature of Nazi war crimes has continued, according to Kershaw, even as structural elements from society to individuals have shifted the focus away from powerful personalities to more abstract forces. At this point, readers have had the chance to wade into the most difficult structural and formal analyses that attempt to understand the motivating causal factors for a nation's crimes during total war.

Kershaw is quick to note that such attempts at full understanding are still resisted by those affected by the events, primarily because the event is so embedded as a defining part of modernity:

> The Holocaust and attendant crimes of the Nazi regime have loomed ever larger both in historical writing and in popular consciousness—so much so, indeed, that the Holocaust can now plainly be seen (something not so plainly apparent in the 1970s or even 1980s) as a defining episode of the twentieth century. Among the various reasons for this development is the opening of the archives of the former Soviet bloc which has prompted a much sharper focus than had ever been possible during the Cold War on Nazi crimes in eastern Europe—the epicentre of the horror. (Kershaw, 2008b: 16)

Rather than ignoring the war's most painful and undersimulated element, professional history and popular perceptions of the events have embraced it across varying media as one of the key moments and places of the past century—Kershaw's 'epicentre of horror.' Filling such obvious gaps within a simgame like *HOI4*, though, proves highly problematic, and may never be possible.

## National Focuses and Counterfactuals

A detailed examination of *HOI4*'s national focuses reveals lacunae relating to the worst offenses, while still providing players with enough counterfactual choices so that both gameplay and historical understanding can occur within the simgame–simtext dynamic. We see this when players engage in historically focused campaigns and must choose motivating factors, even in a game mode that uses historical constraints for all the nations in the war except the one the players choose, or even in randomly generated scenarios for all nations that create non-historical games where all manner of counterfactual events can occur.

The first mode forces all AI-controlled countries to choose national focuses in the correct timeline of events, and also forces them to follow historical paths, in most cases (deselecting this for the AI allows for a non-historical option for all nations). If a player chooses the historical paths for the AI but decides to choose non-historical actions for his or her country, counterfactual scenarios emerge that can drastically change the outcome for the player's particular country and the entire war. All three modes provide different levels of gameplay challenges with counterfactual potentials.

By simulating this combination of actual historical events with probable or improbable alternative outcomes, history can be reconfigured. A type of playable gameworld is contained within a gameist mode of counterfactuals, rather than a fictional or historical mode, that then points back to simtexts and their traditional process of interpretation. This chapter's final section will show, though, that these sorts of strategic and tactical counterfactuals in the most complex and demanding of WWII GSGs such as *HOI4* are problematic because of critical lacunae that the game overtly fails to simulate. These lacunae, as noted earlier, are a response to what some thinkers call the problems of dark play or fantasies of control; they comprise the missing historical pieces with which the simgame–simtext dynamic ultimately confronts a curious player, for better or worse.

*HOI4*'s inherent malleability in shaping historical or non-historical gameplay provides players with a method for reconfiguring history through strategic choices that affect the outcomes of the war. As players choose a nation and begin to make decisions (either within a historical frame or one that seeks a non-historical outcome), they work through a turn-based system that speeds along at predetermined rates, as well as slowing down to hours or rushing through days and weeks. History here works as a modulated flow of time that defines the player experience as different from shooters and simulators. Player decisions are punctuated with in-game news stories from around the globe, events such as the Spanish Civil War or Germany retaking the Rhineland appearing as brief alerts, all adding to an increase in tension that must boil over before most nations enter the war.

This timeframe is condensed and flexible. For example, a player can choose to begin early in 1936 to better prepare for the coming conflict. Such an early start allows for a number of interesting counterfactual scenarios, especially in nations that will be directly affected by the actions of the primary belligerents but were unprepared owing to political decisions, such as the lethargic military leadership in France, the desire by England's Neville Chamberlain to achieve peace with Hitler, the decimating Soviet purges enacted by Stalin, and the USA's staunch isolationism until Pearl Harbor. A later start date of 1939 places a player right on the brink of war, which allows for immediate tactical play. The simgame then focuses play on the next five years, but can reach 1948 with gameplay mechanics such as researchable technologies. A player can carry on and let the game run through later years to simulate the beginning of the Cold War, with the AI continuing to make tactical choices. Mods can also extend gameplay so that technologies and focuses are developed up to the 1970s.

Many counterfactual scenarios are open to players, from tactics such as Germany attempting to land paratroopers on the shores of southern England to broader strategic choices, such as Germany never attacking the Soviet Union, or doing so later or in a different manner—by focusing solely on Ukraine, Crimea, and then the Baku oil fields, for example. Such choices for the AI, while counterfactual for the player, begin with national focuses that offer such potentially war-altering changes.

A player can also create a custom game that allows for granular control from the beginning, such as making a particular nation stronger or weaker (such as a war-ready France) or choosing what type of political organization a nation will have (such as a democratic Germany or fascist England). Foreign policy decisions can be made for nations as well, which allows a player to determine how an AI ally or enemy will behave under certain scenarios. You can change war goals, for example, or whether a country will or will not send expeditionary forces. A player can select or deselect whether coups will occur, allowing difficult civil wars to be avoided for counterfactual scenarios (if a democratic Germany ousts Hitler, for example). What is most interesting, though, is how to combine these with counterfactual scenarios through national focus choices.

The simgame provides a uniform basic focus tree for all secondary nations, with all the major combatants receiving unique trees, and other secondary nations as well. If a player chooses, for example, Brazil, he or she (as with most of the secondary nations in the game) will have five major branches that represent the broadest potential strategies. These are structured as military, economic, and political decisions. The military focuses of 'Army Effort,' 'Aviation Effort,' and 'Naval Effort' give players military advancements on technologies in land, air, and sea; these equate to the historical arms races that occurred between the major belligerent nations. A focus on 'Industrial Effort' increases the capacity to build factories for civilian or military uses, while 'Political Effort' increases political capital that can be used in game for a number of activities, from the creation of laws to the hiring of advisers and the making of critical decisions. The political focus is broken into two major sub-branches, a 'Collectivist Ethos' and a 'Liberty Ethos,' which are exclusive. Choosing the collectivist route divides into 'Nationalism' and 'Internationalism' sub-branches, each allowing for a nation to move toward fascism or communism; both of these can eventually lead to 'Ideological Fanaticism.' The liberty route leads to a choice between 'Neutrality' and 'Interventionism.'

While the base game offers unique trees for the seven primary nations (France, Germany, Italy, Japan, Soviet Union, Britain, and the USA), paid downloadable content (DLC) offers additional features that adjust these unique trees, as well as offering other nations' reworked focused trees, providing interesting counter-factual scenarios while still excising the previously mentioned difficulties (and others) that define the worst parts of war. This increased level of selective granularity with national focuses, combined with entirely new mechanics to create differing scenarios, changes the game from focused primarily on the management of militaries to wider strategic interests that can influence the war.

For example, the 'La Résistance' DLC offers a radical new way to play the game that no longer relies on military might. Instead, espionage provides a player a way to create intelligence agencies whose agents perform intelligence and counter-intelligence operations. These agencies are funded from the game's version of capital, its civilian factories. So rather than a player building military factories to produce more equipment and weapons, a nation that feels protected from the immediacy of invasion can focus on building civilian factories, then a spy agency. This DLC also expands the French, Spanish, and Portuguese focus trees. A player can choose to put his or her resources into espionage missions and broader operations along a number of lines, such as creating resistance movements, encouraging collaboration with other governments, capturing enemy agents, and freeing friendly captured ones. Military secrets can even be gained through cracking codes, as well as inserting agents into key positions. These spy-based game choices act as unique counterfactuals outside direct military, tactical, and strategic intervention without hinting at the crimes of historical secret police organizations.

## A Few Examples

A close examination into several of the most interesting nations' focus trees reveals creative, counterfactual possibilities, along with glaring lacunae. How the war on the Eastern Front and, especially, how Germany is played provides the most interesting case study for this chapter's analysis, but a cursory look at a few others reveals how they simulate these issues as well.

The 'La Résistance' DLC provides opportunities for non-historical play for Portugal and Spain that allows them to more directly influence the war at the highest levels, especially with France taking a stronger leadership role. Portugal can choose focuses that more directly align itself either with the Allies or Axis, but its most impactful possibilities stem from the 'A Royal Wedding' focus and the reinstitution of the monarchy. This allows for the sub-branch 'Monarchist Uprising in Brazil,' which, if left unattended by a distracted (or interested) player, could lead to 'The Empire of Brazil.' With proper care and focus that keeps control in Portugal, the monarchy can be fully reunited with its former colonies, in 'The Kingdom Reunited.' If successful, this grants Portugal all the resources of Brazil and huge influence in South America. With a focus also on naval development, Portugal can then influence the shipping lanes in the Atlantic and Mediterranean and add pressure to its enemies.

Spain is also affected by the 'La Résistance' DLC, with a unique focus tree that simulates the impact of the Spanish Civil War, as well as providing the country with the mechanisms to engage in curious counterfactual scenarios far beyond its historical role. The complexity of choices before the Civil War, the specific choices during, and then those afterwards reveal a complex focus tree that allows Spain to move from a position of neutrality to a major belligerent. Spain proves to be a unique nation, thanks to its early internal conflicts, and this allows a player to engage in politically determined combat scenarios. Events trigger the Civil War very quickly, at which time the northern part of Spain is dominated by nationalists with two small pockets controlled by republicans (who primarily dominate the central and southern parts of Spain).

There are branches that allow for resistance to republican Spain through traditional Falangists challenging monarchist Carlists, who themselves can become united through shared nationalist movements that lead to Spanish fascism (and an obvious more direct alliance with Germany). This unification sub-branch pushes Spain to be more directly involved in the war, beyond the creation of the Condor Legion as a prewar proving ground for the Luftwaffe. Another possible counterfactual is for nationalist Spain to join the Allies, which has drastic changes for the European theater in game, forcing Germany to open another early front, but also allowing the Allies to easily move troops into Europe. This creates a scenario for a nationalist-inspired Spanish monarchy to be revived. These possibilities detail just the nationalist sub-branches; Spain also has granular choices for republican and communist focuses, each of which provides just as much potential for non-historic gameplay that has powerful in-game impacts.

A new player with no knowledge of twentieth-century Spanish history may quickly move through the focus tree without paying much attention to the details, the events, and their impacts. This leads to two disruptive in-game moments—mini-civil wars within the larger contest for Spain. Right-leaning factions may split if a player who has begun along a nationalist route has not taken the 'Fuse the Parties' focus, which is meant to align these similar anti-republican groups under Franco. If aligned, this solidification avoids the first of two smaller civil wars, which would have been led by monarchy-supporting Carlists. A player soon learns that he or she must remove the disruptive republicans from the north of the country, and do it quickly so the Carlists do not revolt, angry that such turmoil is continuing. The second mini-conflict occurs within the republicans themselves, when anarchists revolt in the east. If both occur, Spain is broken into multiple warring factions.

The Spanish focus tree allows a player to encourage any of these scenarios. A historical play through as a nationalist is easiest, especially when accepting troops from Germany, Italy, and even Portugal. The creation of the Condor Legion also provides a boost, although the republicans will be supported by the Soviets. For the nationalists, with Franco in control and a secured north no longer an issue, engagements by better equipped and trained units seasoned in Africa allow for a push toward Madrid, and then south and east.

Once Spain is under Franco's control, still within a historical frame, a player can engage a powerful counterfactual that asks what Spain could have contributed to the war had it not remained neutral. A fascist-leaning or even non-aligned Spain might have risked the ire of the British and easily taken Gibraltar. In one scenario, its veteran troops, even suffering the fatigue of the earlier civil war, could have justified war against Portugal, which would not have been ready to resist. Since *HOI4* offers a winner the right to annex all states or to puppet a defeated nation, a puppet Portugal would then provide resources and manpower, yet still retain control of (and the responsibility of managing) its colonial holdings. Such a scenario could have given Spain a more direct role in the Mediterranean. In a further counterfactual scenario, a belligerent Spain that has angered the British might be inclined to help Italy in Greece. Taking action in this region might have also helped the Axis with Malta, Crete, and North Africa, with what would then have become a closed back door helping a weak Italy to prevent the Allies from entering Europe.

As the *HOI* series has progressed through its different versions, and most specifically as the fourth version has developed through DLCs with new mechanics and focuses, a shift has continued that has allowed for more granular control by players, while also broadening play into wider strategic game mechanics. This can be seen with focuses applied to minor nations and also adjustments for major nations. The 'Man the Guns' DLC works along both of these differing scopes. It adds focuses for a nation such as Mexico, which played a small role in the war; yet it also expands the focus trees for both the USA and the British Empire, allowing them to be played in drastically coun-terfactual manners. Along with these developments, new mechanics for naval warfare continue to allow for more detailed control of navies, balancing tactical warfare with the strategic on the high seas.

Both the American and British focuses demonstrate the degree to which the simgame allows for flexibility between historical and non-historical play. The USA can 'Suspend the Persecution' to move toward communism or place 'America First,' focusing on a fascist USA. Both of these have drastically different, non-historical outcomes that would affect how the USA is used beyond its early game neutrality for its mid- to late game critical role. Both lead to civil war. The communist path allows for an early desegregation of the army, with major economic restructuring strategies to implement radical demo-cratic socialism, with a movement toward militarism and outright communism. These lead to possible 'USA–USSR Economic Cooperation' and a potential clash with European democracies under threat of fascism, as well as possibly leading to conflict over 'Shatter the Empires' because of the Allies' remaining colonial interests.

The fascist sub-branch for the USA has a potentially similar disruptive effect, especially with its economic and military strategic focuses. These allow for draconian new immigration laws with an 'Empower the HUAC' (The House Committee on UnAmerican Activities) focus. Along with these laws, changes to voters' laws create the Silvershirts, a league of fascists determined to pursue US world dominance. This counterfactual reimagining continues with economic choices that create prosperity and privatize industries, while still maintaining a connection to governmental oversight. The famous Nazi-sympathizer Charles Lindbergh can even be sent to learn from Germany's prosperity.

These sorts of overt revisionism are exemplified in 'Honor the Confederacy,' a reimagining of a US that retells the story of the South's loss in the American Civil War of the 1860s as a way to valorize the US South's rebellion. All of this leads to the 'War Powers Act' and overt American aggression, such as the seizing of Cuba or an attack on Mexico. This changes 'Manifest Destiny' from default control of the Western Hemisphere into 'North American Dominion,' with eventual aggression toward Canada and more direct control of Central and South America. This leads more easily into strategic dominance of the Pacific, and eventually Asia.

The expanded British focus tree allows for just as many drastic counterfactuals, with the expected historical 'Reinforce the Empire' running up against a more democratically leaning, status-quo branch, 'Steady as She Goes.' Even more so for the early game than in the USA, this allows non-historical play, with the British offering provocative counterfactual scenarios, such as bringing Churchill into power early to end British appeasement and to prepare for war with 'Global Defense.' Even more so, radical changes to the government toward monarchist, fascist, or communist structures is possible. Both the monarchist and fascist branches allow the British to ally with Germany and gain war goals against either/or the USA and the Soviet Union. Of course, the communist sub-branch does the opposite, with leanings toward the Soviets and a policy of decolonization that pushes England into conflict with Germany and the USA.

The USA and British are curious cases that hint at missing lacunae, in that players can engage in what is often considered their most egregious acts during war, primarily the carpet bombing of German cities and the USA's use of the nuclear bomb. Any nation in *HOI4* that researches and builds long-range bombers or follows the path to nuclear weapons can use these strategies. However, the simgame offers these mechanics in an abstracted manner that functions slightly different from the overt erasure of other elements, that is, those primarily related to German war crimes. We see none of the effects of long-range bombing over cities or the full use of atomic weapons. This abstracted form of gameplay shimmies toward the uncomfortable truths of total war without allowing a player to fully engage in such simulation, while also preventing full knowledge of their devastating effects.

As mentioned earlier, a look at France's expanded focus tree reveals its potential counterfactual gameplay. Players can choose the focus 'Emergency Powers to Petain Branch' to either completely capitulate to the Germans or completely resist, the latter offering a powerful counterfactual that would have a willful France refuse any sort of appeasement of Hitler and a simulated test to see if a determined French army could challenge Germany. This resistance works through 'Strengthen the Little Entente,' not initially with the British, but with Czechoslovakia, Yugoslavia, and Romania. Such stalwart leadership could have brought the British to the table, even if they refused to back France's initial plans to resist Germany's remilitarization of the Rhineland. With Czechoslovakia joining the entente, this would have caused Germany to look eastward right away, with the danger of a new front and providing an opening for France's divisions to attack through the Rhineland.

The expanded Soviet focus tree is offered in the 'No Step Back' DLC, along with those for Poland and the Baltic nations, all of which create intriguing counterfactuals that also engage the non-historical. For example, one scenario asks how Poland could have somehow enhanced their stiff resistance after being invaded, somehow surviving against the Germans and the Russians, while at the same time ignoring Russian atrocities in Poland.

The developers structure these playable reconfigurations along varied lines, one of which is the rise of a Polish monarchy that can then find stronger ties to support its survival, especially if a player wants to imagine a counterfactual scenario that begins in 1936 and allows for Poland to prepare for the coming conflict. The Baltic States are expanded in a similar manner to how Czechoslovakia, Hungary, Romania, and Yugoslavia are detailed in the 'Death or Dishonor' DLC. These secondary nations can play a critical role by either resisting or supporting the major nations, as can Romania and its sub-branch of 'Balkan Dominance,' forming alliances to secure the region against Western or Eastern aggressors. Like the Balkan nations, the Baltic States face pressures that can affect the region, especially Poland and its ties (or troubles) with Lithuania.

These, though, are smaller in scale than the new Soviet focus tree and the historical options it allows. This simulates a reconfigured past along alternative historical lines that border on near fantasy or counterfactual scenarios that could have actually happened. The developers claim this focus tree is the largest they have ever done, with over 300 focuses (Paradox Interactive, 2021).

A look into the expansive Soviet focus tree reveals how the 'Patriotic War' continues to be used within simgames to valorize the role Russia (and Stalin) played, rather than highlighting its (and his) costly mistakes. Yet it still offers counterfactual alternatives to the narrative of Stalin as the savior of the Soviet Union, with a line in which Trotsky returns from exile or even offers a way to reconstruct the Romanov dynasty. The primary paths give more granular control over historical communist focuses under 'The Path of Marxism Leninism,' with sub-branches dedicated to Stalin as a centrist and Trotsky occupying a broader leftist position with the desire for a world-wide socialist revolution, both opposed by a right-leaning anti-Stalinist in Bukharin. A curious counterfactual would be an alternative history version that imagines a reconstituted monarchy and even a potential fascist alternative. The expansiveness of the new Soviet tree demonstrates how much the simgame has moved toward counterfactual possibilities without addressing the systematic brutality towards the Red Army and its enemies by the Soviet secret police, the Naródnyy Komissariát Vnútrennikh del (NKVD, or People's Commissariat of Internal Affairs).

A number of other DLCs provide additional focuses for key nations such as Japan in 'Waking the Tiger,' along with more refined gameplay mechanics. Japan is also a curious case in the *HOI* series, a nation that is playable without the detailed prewar history of Japan's imperialist aims that led to its aggression and war crimes. Key events such as the massacre of Nanjing (in which Japan attacked the city in 1937 and unleashed a war of terror on the Chinese civilians, with mass murder and rape being the primary crimes) are minimized. This, along with racist policies that led to the deaths of millions of non-Japanese

Asians (primarily Chinese), is a huge lacuna on the same scale as the missing Holocaust. Such elision has its own historical analogue in the West. The treatment of US prisoners of war by the Japanese was kept a secret from the US public, especially after the fall of the Philippines and the planning of the US invasion of Europe. In game, events such as the Bataan 'death march' are ignored. Historically, this suppression of the truth took place to avoid a backlash by the American public that might have shifted focus away from defeating Nazi Germany.

Furthermore, after the war, rather than American policy makers needing to integrate Japan into the Western capitalist system of liberal democracy, a task viewed with more concern than incorporating western Germany, the developers of *HOI* excise such incidents for the same reason Nazi war crimes are ignored. They would provide problematic agency for players who wish to simulate and thus glorify or fetishize such repugnant behavior. The types of horrific crimes, such as medical experiments or the enslavement of women as sex slaves for Japanese soldiers, are examples of direct policies by Imperial Japan with a historical context that find no simulation within game.[5]

## Importance of the Eastern Front

One curious result of placing so much importance on these expanded focus trees is that they refract key difficulties in how an event such as WWII was experienced by those who lived through it, and is still experienced today. We see this most clearly in how the Eastern Front is now recognized as an integral location of the war, while at the same time it presents itself as the widest lacuna to be filled outside the simgame. The German–Soviet War and its massive Eastern Front has proven to be an overlooked narrative in the popular memory of the West, although one now increasingly told, that acts as a linchpin for understanding a number of key aspects of the war, in particular why Germany attacked the Soviet Union when it did—and how it failed to claim victory.

This question has served as a primary point of inquiry for many historians interested in the Eastern Front's importance in the war. A number of answers from German *Lebensraum*, and its implications as a racist ideological solution for the liquidation of the Jews, to the need for critical resources to maintain its war effort, to a hatred of Bolshevism, or any combination, have been offered.

Moreover, Hitler's failure to find an ally in England meant his gambles that had paid off in Austria and Czechoslovakia served him less well in Poland. This earned him an unexpected enemy in a Churchill-backed England, who remained a pugnacious foe once it entered the war, even as the Soviets resisted with exponentially more losses in human lives.

Just as much, British intransigence meant Hitler had to maintain an alliance with Stalin in the German–Soviet Nonaggression Pact, with the hope that a secure Western Front would emerge. This perplexing and resistant island enemy in the West meant that attacking the Soviets would demand a two-front war, and one that would allow the looming USA to arm itself and eventually enter hostilities. Yet it would be the Soviets who bore the brunt of Germany's military might, ultimately defeating Germany with costs far beyond what the Western Allies contributed. The entire German war-effort depended on rapid success in defeating the Soviets, a need precipitated by British resistance and American rearming, but one that would provide Germany with its critical resources in fighting the coming war with the West.[6]

These historical motivators provide any number of curious counterfactual scenarios that could have affected Germany prior to its invading the Soviet Union. Turning the British into an enemy proved so unsettling to Germany, which hints at what might have happened to Germany had Churchill's defiant approach not worked. Such a fortuitous outcome as a thwarted Churchill would most likely still have led Germany to a confrontation with the Soviets as the most important conflict on the continent, but maybe one that would have happened later after Germany had built up its armed forces even more and secured additional resources.

Another counterfactual concerns the securing of the Mediterranean. This asks how a more powerful and reliable Italy could have changed the course of the war, or even (as noted earlier) what would have happened if Spain and its veteran divisions had been brought into the conflict first to seize Gibraltar and then to protect the region from any invasion. The decision by Hitler to secure the Romanian oil fields, a sphere of influence that Mussolini considered to be Italy's, could still be followed by Italy's farcical attempt to save face and take Greece, but, now with Spain's help, the diversion of German forces south would no longer be required, thereby negating the distraction and delay caused by moving German forces away from the resource prizes in the Soviet Union.

A historical account of the war in the East is a focus for professional historians because of the importance of particular battles, such as the battles of Moscow, Leningrad, Kiev, Kursk, and Stalingrad. But beyond detailing the specifics of the battles that a military historian might find critical, they also reveal aspects of the war that overtly feed into GSGs such as *HOI4*. We can see these as playable elements along a number of lines—for example, how to outfit artillery or tank divisions, how to create differing units, how to build up navies and air forces. Using these elements for strategic purposes forms the core purpose of the game. We see this most clearly when armies are used for successful mobile pincer movements, like the one that defeated General Paulus's Sixth Army west of Stalingrad in 1943.

The descriptions of Stalingrad by professional historians illuminate arguments among military historians about what caused Germany's ultimate failure in invading the Soviet Union, especially that particular battle's role. This battle can also be used to demonstrate how an event like this resonates in game, primarily because it pushed the front forward so Germany could take resources, rather than for its ideological impact on morale for either side. Such theorized questions as to the overall importance of Stalingrad encourage more research. One question asks whether Hitler insisted on taking Stalingrad as a demonstration of his will, and if his desire to defeat Stalin was a supreme symbolic act of Nazi supremacy. Or was this actually secondary to other strategic interests such as taking the oil fields to the south?

One of the more popular historians, Antony Beevor, writes:

> We can now see, with the benefit of hindsight, that the balance of power – geopolitical, industrial, economic and demographic – swung decisively against the Axis in December 1941, with the Wehrmacht's failure to capture Moscow and the American entry into the war. The psychological turning point of the war, however, would come only in the following winter with the battle for the city of Stalingrad, which, partly because of its name, became a personal duel by mass proxy. (1999: 47–48)

Beevor also argues that Hitler's notion of 'will' drove him to believe Stalingrad mattered more than practical concerns, such as outfitting his infantry with winter gear. "Hitler's mistake of believing in the power of the will" (Beevor, 1999: 42) operates in this psychological analysis of Hitler similar to Shirer's approach, as detailed earlier. It encourages clarification of abstract causes beyond a specific history of battle tactics. We can also see this broad approach to causation in biographies such as Ian Kershaw's accounts of Hitler (1999, 2000, 2008a). This widens the perspectives of understandings that compete with dominant meta-narratives, primarily those of the Allies.

Beevor's claims present the battle at Stalingrad ultimately as a personal duel between Hitler and Stalin, suggesting that Hitler was driven by delusions created by his armchair role as a general who worried over maps and flags, making disastrous decisions from afar. Others have challenged this 'myth' of Stalingrad, though, regarding it as a truly strategic critical goal for the Germans when they began their invasion. In contrast to viewing Hitler as primarily in a battle of wills with Stalin, Joel Hayward argues that "Ironically, in light of the fact that the campaign has come to be associated with the name of that city, the capture of Stalingrad was actually not a major objective. Hitler certainly considered it far less important than the Caucasus" (1998: 23).

The later refusal to lose any ground at Stalingrad, as noted in the earlier admission by Hayward of Hitler's mistakes in damning Paulus and the Sixth Army to defeat (see Chapter 4), can be viewed as critical for Germany main-taining a front that would stop a Soviet counter-offensive west—rather than being a maniacal goal of Hitler.

The meta-narrative of the war now accepts the role the Soviets played in the defeat of Germany, which makes Stalingrad a symbol for how we concep-tualize the war rather than the most critical war prize for the Germans. American perceptions have changed since the initial journalistic coverage of events in the East and the pro-Allied versions that emerged at the end of the war (and during the Cold War). This shift in professional journalism and history has challenged public memory's downplaying or outright dismissal of the contributions of the Soviets in the East.

Just as convincing is an argument that emerges when the simgame–simtext dynamic directs players to clarifying texts. This is that the ignored narrative of the Soviets has often been replaced by a sympathy (especially by Americans) for the German experience. According to Ronald Smelser and Edward J. Davies: "Those who have taken the trouble to learn about that titanic struggle [World War Two in the East], ironically enough, tend to view it, not as the agony and eventual triumph of an important ally [Soviets], but rather through the lenses of our common enemy [Germany]" (2008: 2). The authors also argue a more specific point—that postwar German officers (such as Franz Halder) influenced leading American military officials, along with other knowledge-builders and culture shapers in America, with an "interpretation of World War Two" (Smelser and Davies, 2008: 2) that was very similar to the same arguments made by Hitler himself. They argue that this view has worked its way into a general sympathy for Germany within particular sections of American culture, as seen in its media and other areas.

According to Smelser and Davies, these skewed views were bolstered by a wide range of popular memoirs from German military leaders, such as Erich von Manstein and Heinz Guderian, along with a variety of other publications from novels to books in the popular sphere (see Guderian, 2000; Manstein, 2004). These endeavors led to Americans viewing their new ally in the Cold War against the Soviets as descendants of a mostly clean Wehrmacht. Smelser and Davies even argue that some viewed the German defeat in the East as a tragedy similar to how the Confederacy's defeat in the American Civil War is often viewed with romantic nostalgia in the southern states of the USA. Such a perspective reveals how postwar American sympathy for supposedly non-Nazi Germany occludes the impact the Soviets played in Germany's defeat.

The encounter by players with simtexts that detail the German–Soviet War works against the erasure of the Soviet experience, not within formal academic study (which has provided fuller representation of the event in professional publications), but within the popular sphere. This correction is timely because a development in simgames has been advocating for this untold narrative; we see this from simgames to cinema to books, wherein the Soviet experience is increasingly foregrounded. There are just as many simtexts that offer these counternarratives in the popular sphere, with possibly even more foregrounding a valiant Germany, many of them stretching credulity. One site of contention focuses on such a group of self-published or small independently published simtexts. Among readers of English, according to Smelser and Davies (2008), these are written by popularizers who often reinforce an American romanticism of the German military rather than countering the dominant meta-narrative of Western triumph.

The authors extend their study to reading communities focused on these texts, and note that the Waffen-SS is a favorite topic; while in the simgames in this case study, such blatant Nazi representations are banned. In similar simgames across varying genres, this removal may have as much to do with sales for a wider market rather than the principle of having them banned or shamed; the simgames that present a clean Wehrmacht, though, benefit from their use as gameplay elements, conveniently also distracting from the erasure of SS units as an ignored lacuna that is discussed in this chapter. The Waffen SS, and all it stood for as a military symbol of Nazi prejudice and violence, is one of these missing pieces that is often reconfigured without the offensive symbols into clean Wehrmacht soldiers. The authors examine a few of what they call 'romancers' and 'gurus,' who fed a public interested in viewing the German military through admirable lenses. They foreground Sven Hassel's novels for a German perspective that views the Wehrmacht as heroic and admirable and Franz Kurowski's *Panzer Aces* (1992) and *Infantry Aces* (1994) as examples of this idealistic (and narrow) perspective.

These types of independent publications within the popular sphere often represent German soldiers, especially within the Wehrmacht, as idealistic heroes with uncompromising honor. Such idealism works in the same manner as simplified archetypes within literature, in this case the defenders of the Fatherland rather than soldiers complicit with the crimes of National Socialism.[7] Both extremes are totalizing reductions that remove the focus from individual stories, as best as they can be told, to generalizations with the didactic power to frame the war along certain lines, such as a grand victory for the Allies as seen through a Western perspective, or the patriotic war that cost the Soviets so much but broke the back of the Germans, or even as a war of annihilation against Jews, Slavs, and Russians.

What is problematic in totalizing reductions is what is ignored when a single idea is foregrounded. The simgame–simtext dynamic often begins with such unacknowledged lacunae, but offers a chance for wider understanding once a player moves beyond the game to simtexts that offer clarification. These, of course, may be popular texts scaffolded to tell only one part of a particular narrative, such as that of a clean Wehrmacht or a chivalrous Luftwaffe or the patriotic Soviet soldiers or Europe-saving 'best-generation' Americans. But the dynamic can just as easily confront players with more general perspectives that challenge these simplifications.

Smelser and Davies expand their analysis from independent publishers to how popularizers of the war from a German perspective found favor in "romancing communities" (Smelser and Davies, 2008: 200). They see this happening with the rise of war-gaming in the 1960s and 1970s, and connect these analog forms of war-gaming and knowledge dissemination to the radical shift provided by the internet and its democratization of information. Add to this the continued development of computer gaming and the return of interest in WWII in the 1990s, the event as a historical field has now been placed in a flourishing position within simulation gaming. These analog-and-digital games and texts offer a wide-range of activities, though, beyond hagiographic publishing and vicarious imaginings of heroism among fan clubs.

One major activity, as the authors note, was the type of counterfactual reimagining of the past focused on Stalingrad that so interests scholars such as Hayward and Beevor. But an interpretive issue emerges when the view of such a battle as Stalingrad is shifted to that of war gamers in these supposed 'romancing' communities. Referencing an early analog war game, *Streets of Stalingrad* (1979), the authors write about this battle's centrality from a strategic rather than political view:

> How did the Soviets resist the German attack and how can one reverse that outcome? What combination of arms would enable the 6th army to seize the tractor works or the grain elevator? These and other questions that romancers may have asked now could be answered. (Smelser and Davies, 2008: 189)

A less-than-helpful distinction is made here by the authors between the different types of 'romancers.' The problem is one of comparison between those communities in the decades after the war who may have romanticized the German military in analog war games with a young simgame player today who is unaware of the particulars of the battle. We see this especially in a world that is dominated by computer games in which players often have no interest in romanticizing the actual Wehrmacht, and may not even know the military differences between them and their opponents, much less the political or ideological differences between the German military's most ruthless organizations.

What can happen today, though, when new generations of players are encountering the event (such as the popular 'Stalingrad' map in *HLL*) through different forms of simgames is that many of the old icons of the past are no longer encountered at all, much less as heroes to be glorified. They may not even be part of the gamespace. Von Manstein, Guderian, Rommel, and Galland may only appear as historical names in events, if at all. The legacy of the revisionist hagiography that the authors note, so evident in novels, publications, and games in the decades that followed the war, has become a complex simulation gaming space far beyond any ideological arguments that would rehabilitate Germany's military.

Rather than suggesting that any player interested in this content is a 'romancer,' players may simply be uninformed. Granted, some may have prior interests in WWII, may certainly be conditioned by particular cultural or national sympathies to see the event through a particular frame, or may be very well acquainted with the war and how it is represented (especially the American narrative in the West or the Soviet narrative for contemporary Russians). 'Romancer' is unhelpful because of this complexity, and because the term may not always denote someone who is romancing the German military. The Soviet perspective has its own form of selective framing, as does the British with its view of the RAF and the Royal Navy. Instead, the dynamic influences players with an interest in the war beyond gaming to reconfigure it through simulation, this process being generated by playing a game and reading the texts they may encounter.

## Germany and the War of Annihilation

One distinct approach that frames how a GSG such as *HOI4* simulates counterfactual scenarios along with glaring lacunae focuses on the war in the East through the discourse of total-war 'annihilation.'

Historian Stephen G. Fritz writes that "for decades after the end of World War II, much of our understanding of the German-Soviet war came from the German perspective, for the very good reason that only German documents and archives were readily available" (2011: xix). As already mentioned, this German-centric perspective, with its memoirs of German generals ready to justify their past actions and to distance themselves from National Socialism, has led to the myth of the clean Wehrmacht. Fritz's account frames the war from the German perspective without the embrace of such romanticized elements as a guiltless German infantry.

Instead, he provides an examination through a synthesis of other sources, such as the comprehensive thirteen-volume set *Germany and the Second World War* (1990–present) by the Research Institute for Military History.[8] These volumes are written by German historians who have sought to move beyond many of the myths written, among other topics, about the German-Soviet War. Fritz's professional simtext acts as a mediating text for the many volumes in the *Germany and the Second World War* series, which he uses as a primary source of analysis. [9] His approach is to synthesize the most difficult of professional scholarship on the war in the East to argue for its importance.

Fritz clarifies how certain myths, such as the common notion of the clean and invincible Wehrmacht or the Americans' 'good' war or the role of the Battle of Britain in repelling a supposed imminent German invasion, simplify what was a series of complex events with difficult causation and, regarding the German–Soviet War, one that often misunderstands what happened in the East. He does this because, as he states, "The Second World War was not won or lost solely on the Ostfront, but it was the key—while the scale of fighting there dwarfed anything in the west" (Fritz, 2011: xxi). Fritz's monograph stands at an important place for simgame players on an interpretive journey, situated as it is between the most accessible of simtexts such as YouTube videos and the most demanding of simtexts, such as the *Germany and the Second World War* series.

Fritz clearly states in his preface that he works through these comprehensive sources to tease out the complexities that caused the war, along several "impulses—military, ideological, economic, racial, and demographic" (2011: xxii). These broad cultural frames, along with military histories, synthesize the often-disparate approaches by biographers, writers of general histories of the war, or describers of particular battles. These different levels of focus each provide particular perspectives of causation. As Fritz notes (and as mentioned earlier), the war was fought by Germany for *Lebensraum*, to counter Bolshevism, for oil, also in response to explaining the loss in WWI, and, worse, by Hitler's blaming the Jews to justify a racist ideology.

When examining the German *HOI4* focus tree for its simulation of the war in the East, there may be noted a 'horrific epicentre,' in Kershaw's thinking along with what it ignores. A player is offered a number of scenarios that allow for a wide range of play and, critically, echo key disputes that emerged after the war—but there is little of the horror. Most of these difficult areas are ignored outright, such as how to frame German citizens as culpable or not, the true nature of the Wehrmacht, and the crimes of the Luftwaffe. Throughout these organizations, the question is never asked in its war against Jews, Slavs, Bolsheviks, and so on who were National Socialist ideologues from the highest ranks through to the SS and to common soldiers. These glaring gameplay lacunae simulate an in-game Germany as detached from uncomfortable historical mechanisms that are integral to any understanding of the war at its broadest levels.

We see nothing of the radical policy toward the Jews that moved from an encouraged emigration to determined and overt prejudicial policy in 1938. Other critical events related to Hitler's challenge to the supposed "November [1918] criminals" (Fritz, 2011: 4) are missed, such as the pogrom against the Jews in Austria, *Kristallnacht*. These key precursors to the Holocaust are ignored, as is the entire false ideology of blaming the Jews as 'enemies,' for the German loss during WWI, for their supposed role in controlling world economies via plutocrats and hidden cabals, and for the coming war in Europe. These gaping lacunae avoid the difficulties of dark play and fantasies of control yet reconfigure the past through careful avoidances in such a way that even a cursory interest in the event, when looking beyond gameplay, means that players are confronted with the harsh truth of these excised elements.

The way through such material beyond gameplay presents its own sets of difficulties, especially in parsing widely differing accounts. Professional historians have sifted through the archives of texts that the Allies acquired after defeating the Germans, and these numerous records of German military activity and bureaucracy, along with the memoirs of German generals and other military leaders who survived the war, form the background for a simtext archive that frames public history and its perceptions in popular culture—and eventually in simgames. Historian Geoffrey Megargee (2006) argues that even if the German generals had to rely on memory in their account, many of them had much to hide, which proved a powerful motivator in how they recounted their roles, especially during and after Nuremberg (2006: xii). It is this published reconfiguration of the past that begins with the dubious faculty of human memory, coupled with self-interest, that informs so many simtexts outside serious academic analysis.

Approaches from professional historians such as Fritz and Megargee help to frame *HOI4*'s problematic lacunae in a way that is historically located, rather than simply to avoid the problems with playable Nazis. Megargee's argument resists a reaction that would fully separate the military histories during the German and Soviet War from the war crimes committed by the Nazis, the very parts, as noted, that are removed from simgames. Megargee claims "to bring those two halves together" (2006: xiii), an outcome as yet unrealized in simgames. This work, along with others such as Wolfram Wette's *The Wehrmacht: History, Myth, Reality* (2006), demonstrates how continued research into serious simtexts reveals lacunae as obvious missing gameplay pieces. These deficiencies may appear to negate the role such simgames have in presenting a fair rendition of the past to players; however, the dynamic emerges to fill those gaps for curious players from simulation, through interpretation, to understanding.

At the center of such lacunae, the combination of military activity with ideological violence poses problems for strategy simgames of WWII that approach their gameplay along a continuum from granularity to broad-scale control. The German perspectives of the Jews, Slavs, and Soviets, for example, serve as an example in that they waged more than a military war in the East and this is ignored in *HOI4*. While politics factors into the simgame at a number of levels, the overt misrepresentation of peoples, cultures, and so on, and the methods used to harm them are ignored—with the Jews' absence as a targeted people being the most glaring example.

Instead of simulating these most difficult elements, *HOI4* uses another mechanism to reconfigure history through triggered events that a player must respond to (or ignore). These appear in small popups with framed paragraphs that act as windows into key historical moments. Each one is a topic that can be found in any standard history textbook on WWII, along with more serious academic publications that might examine particular aspects: 'Anschluss,' 'The Anti-Comintern Pact,' 'The Tripartite Pact,' and 'The Molotov–Ribbentrop Pact' are some of the key early events for Germany. But the simgame is sophisticated enough that the actions a player takes or the results of actions by other players (or the AI) can trigger events, such as a Soviet Union that rejects the Molotov–Ribbentrop Pact.

These events move through many of the major moments of the war, each nation having their roles framed as the events trigger. For Germany, the political and cultural events that define the war beyond its military tactics are excised in a manner beyond those of the other major belligerents. The only mention of National Socialism is in the counterfactual 'Death to National Socialism,' a triggered event that occurs if a player starts a conspiracy to kill Hitler. Throughout these various events and focuses, there is no mention of Jews, their disenfranchisement, or their deportation to concentration and extermination camps.[10]

Instead, in the German focus tree, a 'Four-Year Plan' can be chosen to increase German industry prior to the war. The Siegfried Line, or Westwall, can remain an important goal, or even be bolstered with more fortifications. For example, taking the risk of militarizing the Rhineland early will earn a player improved fortifications. Likewise, the Atlantic Wall, which began in 1942, can begin to be built earlier, as long as France has fallen. There are also 'Innovations' branches that jump-start the arms race that would see Germany fielding advanced armored vehicles and aircraft. A player can also choose to focus on 'Naval Rearmament.' Other focuses, such as building Eastern fortifications for the inevitable clash with the Soviets, can be built early, or aligning with Romania and Hungary because of their location within Germany's sphere of influence, can mean finding early allies and resources. Other activities involving infrastructure such as the building of the autobahns reflect a granular narrowing of scope.

But curiously, with a 'Fascist' branch, which equates to the rise of the National Socialist party in the decade prior to the war, a focus can be made on 'Anschluss,' with no mention of its annexation goals that led to *Kristallnacht* as an early example of what was to come for the Jews. A player can focus on the German war economy with the creation of the *Reichskommissariat*, but these are described in abstract terms as giving bonuses to industry and manpower, with a huge lacuna as to the role these played in politically reorganizing entire regions (and its peoples) under Nazi ideology (and all the terror that came from this) with the *Einsatzgruppen* and other organizations of terror in the East. These broad playable focuses are abstractions of historical forces as causal mechanisms that led to the beginning of the war. They have more granularity and reflect components of each broad focus, some of which came later in the war or were never realized, but a player is able to boost them early.

The 'Air Innovations' and 'Army Innovations' branches each reflect the early German war effort that was ignored by the West. *HOI4* simulates air, sea, and land, with each branch having a major influence on a player's success. The land component offers the most functions within the game because of the core role the Wehrmacht played in the war. An air-war focus likewise provides players with early aviation innovations, both in the development of its weaponry and in strategic endeavors. These land and air focuses can also be affected by a player's political decisions, which can change how well a military branch develops, such as offering the Molotov–Ribbentrop Pact. This is enacted to allow the German war effort to benefit from increased trade in oil with the Soviet Union, along with stability from a non-aggression pact and a delay in conflict. In game, such an event creates a number of other political choices, which offers a player claims on many states in the East. Such a series of focuses presents a powerful counterfactual in the game in which Germany and the Soviets never go to war but instead form an 'Alliance with the USSR.'

Another major political choice is structured in the focus tree that follows the 'Rhineland Branch,' which allows a player to further fascist aims or take a political path that allows for major decisions, such as an 'Anti-Comintern Pact,' alliances with China and Japan, and the varieties of *Anschluss* that offer alternative approaches to Austria, Czechoslovakia, Poland, Italy, and Spain. The focus tree also provides further options, many of them with direct military outcomes, another nod towards the broad historic processes that are being offered here that directly affected military decisions, such as how to reclaim the Danzig territory in the 'Danzig or War' sub-branch, or how to maneuver 'Around [the] Maginot' line. Other political/military considerations are offered, such as the handling of Norway or even the non-historical conquering of Switzerland. The Balkans are also within the focus, as is Greece.

A player with an interest in naval warfare can bolster Germany's weak navy with a number of sub-branches, such as 'Plan Z,' an initiative to challenge British naval supremacy and one that was historically too long in the making; a player can start this focus earlier. Along with this approach, using political decisions to increase Germany's sphere of influence in order to 'Befriend' the Netherlands, Denmark, and the Nordic states is a strategy to strengthen Germany's weak navy. These major strategic choices can also be bolstered with direct military activities, such as constructing dockyards or increasing focus on a 'U-Boat Effort,' reinforcing past events within gameplay. But policies that encouraged the historical sinking of non-military vessels are ignored, or labeled as convoy raiding. Rather than filling these lacunae with consciousness-raising about the horrors of the event, such a simgame offers the mechanism of reconfiguring the past as a way to think through a curated version of the event.

The frame of reference for *HOI4* ultimately remains military strategies and the immediate tactics they encourage. Much is absent, though, from military choices to the ideological strategy that dictated their actions, such as Hitler's eventual decision to attack Poland for *Lebensraum* and later Ukraine and then the Caucasus with their prized oil fields. These 'strategic' military choices also meant the eventual wholesale eradication of Jews, Slavs, and communists after using them as forced labor, all with the ultimate goal of depopulating Eastern Europe to be settled by Germans.

The entire structure of Germany's SS police organization and its reign of terror is left out of this horrific process, especially the *Einsatzgruppen* (task forces) and the violent roles of the Gestapo and the Waffen (armed) SS in Poland and everywhere else they operated in the East, with their explicit polices of prejudicial murder. Such intelligence-oriented strategies could have been simulated in the 'La Résistance' DLC's additional game mechanics that focus on espionage if the developers had had a feasible and morally acceptable reason to do so. Instead, a player has no awareness that as German militaries pushed east an ideological murder system against civilians labeled as 'partisans' occurred with devastating effects. Rather, military and strategic activities are offered devoid of any hint of war crimes.

Instead of filling in lacunae, the simgame foregrounds interesting counter-factual scenarios. For Germany, this is clearly seen with an 'Oppose Hitler' focus; such a non-historical national focus allows a player to pursue a non-fascist game, with options for a post-civil war Germany that either follows a democratic line or a revived '*Kaiserreich*.' Either way, these choices force a player to rebuild Germany outside what actually occurred, especially in the years before what would have been Germany's push for war in Europe because of Hitler's policies.

A still expansionist Germany under a new Kaiser might focus on increasing 'Prussian Militarism' or see in Russia a looming communist threat with the

'Bulwark Against Bolshevism' sub-branch. This is removed from any of the ideological lies proclaimed by Hitler, Goebbels, and the proponents of National Socialism that maligned communists and Jews, Slavic peoples, and any non-Germans east of Germany whose land and resources were to be taken. Since such historical layers that comprise major aspects of the war's criminal effects are not playable, the game instead focuses on acceptable reconfigured scenarios, still warlike and potentially devastating.

Both the 'Revive the Kaiser' focus or maintaining democracy with the 'Re-establish Free Elections' focus allow for war-gaming scenarios without overt racist ideology and its horrific outcomes. A focus on German monarchy, rather than fascist National Socialism, would see Wilhelm II returned to Germany as its leader, problematic as this might be for Western democracies. Such a choice provides an interesting counterfactual scenario in which the perceived insults of WWI are reconfigured through the lens of a wounded monarchy, rather than through extreme right-wing fascist reactionaries. Sub-branches can be added to dedicate increasing naval focus, along with openly returning Germany to a place of world prominence. Such a counter-factual path would allow a player to imagine challenging France and England as the major European power. This can be played with the sub-branch 'Break the Anglo-French Colonial Hegemony,' a mechanic that refocuses WWII as a colonial war. This, of course, is done without the pervasive racist policies that informed National Socialist ideology.

Many strategic concerns of Hitler are also reworked, such as the conquering of European states within the German sphere of influence, along with allowing a player to eventually consider how to challenge the USA without Hitler's rhetoric against that country. Interestingly, rather than seeing Italy as an ally, a monarchist Germany allows a player to challenge fascist Italy, and even 'Assassinate Mussolini.' A number of other counterfactual sub-branches can be chosen, most of which are reconfigurations of the past devoid of its most egregious crimes.

A player can attempt to 'Rekindle Imperial Sentiment' in Austria, Hungary, and Czechoslovakia to awake a national spirit for the old Austro-Hungarian Empire. The threat to the monarchies of the world from more October Revolutions can be resisted with 'Expatriate the Communists.' This mechanic does not explain what expatriation means, other than giving bonuses to war support and increasing national spirit (in this case for the monarchy)—and that these communists flee to France. It glides over this gaping lacuna, one that might confront a player with any previous interest in the social effects of WWII on the lived experiences of those who suffered through it, or a player who reads simtexts that describe what 'expatriation' actually looked like from within cattle cars.

A monarchist focus for a player who simply wants to resist the power of a rising Soviet communist state would find alliances with the Western powers, such as the navies of England, while still planning a way to conquer nearby France. Other historical interests emerge such as control of the Baltic States, or supporting the Finns, or even of an honest offer to help the Poles resist the Soviets (rather than lies that justified invasion to take Danzig and more). These political decisions can lead to a broad 'Anti-Comintern Pact' but also to a more directed 'Anti-Soviet Pact,' which may even lead to an 'Anti-Communist Bloc.' The interesting counterfactual 'The Iberian Problem' could allow a player to remove Spain as a neutral country. The historical element of a nationalist Spain that won against the communists might not play the same way with a monarchist Germany that never supported the nationalists. What might confront such a player is a fully communist Spain, or one with victorious communist leanings.

Such choices allow a player to build an expansionist Germany and aggressively engage in a counterfactual WWII scenario that leads to alternative military conflicts. Opposing Hitler, surviving a civil war, and opting for democracy allows a player a curious counterfactual scenario that removes Germany as the primary creator of world tension. Rather than right-wing leaning fascists or monarchists, the 'Zentrum' party emerges, allowing for compromises with the military, although one that can still focus on 'The Great Red Menace.' A democratic Germany can still look for neighbors in its resistance to communism, forming a 'Central European Alliance' or a 'Danubian Membership [or] Expansion.' The main goal is to resist communism, which in a historical campaign will most likely be the largest initiator of world tension—all without the uncomfortable realities that attended the war.

Here, a sanitized democratic choice sees a number of actions that resist communism in a morally acceptable manner. This creates alliances between nations within Germany's sphere of influence from the Scandinavian countries, to the Baltic States, down to the Balkans. An 'Alliance with Poland' also forms a bulwark that allows for a preparation for war with Russia, one in which Germany leads the Allies. This proves to be one of the most imaginative reconfigured counterfactuals in the game—and, stunningly, may have serious parallels today with a contemporary Bundeswehr promised 100 billion euros in funding after Putin's invasion of Ukraine.

## Conclusion

This chapter has moved through a number of ideas both to demonstrate how a GSG such as *HOI4* simulates key military tactics and strategies of WWII, and also how it presents troubling lacunae that ignore difficult topics within the war. It acknowledges that by doing so the simgame erases important stories at the personal level of lived experiences of those who suffered, and so many of whom died. Of course, the most glaring lacuna is the removal of the Jews as the target of Hitler's Final Solution, along with German policies in Eastern Europe.

Such sanitization, though, is not so easily addressed in game, with the developers removing them from gameplay for various complex reasons. One reason foregrounded in this chapter is an avoidance of what has been referred to as dark play, along with a refusal to allow players fantasies of control. These provocative concepts within the discourse of historical game studies recognize that simgames have the potential to encourage the worst forms of simulated war crimes.

This chapter also attempts to show that the concept of 'total war' is not fully simulated because in total war the most egregious examples of war crimes occurred in the past. It looks to serious simtexts for clarification on such unplayable elements. Early popular simtexts provide an example of how historians captured the war in tactical, strategic, and ideological terms. It looks to even more demanding simtexts in the professional sphere, to demonstrate how such simtexts clarify the most complex of questions, such as the culpability of common Germans.

It ends with a detailed analysis of *HOI4*'s national focuses to demonstrate how counterfactual play is encouraged, along with how missing lacunae become clear through the simgame–simtext dynamic. It focuses most of its detailed analysis on the German National Focus Tree, especially in how *HOI4* approaches the devastating German–Soviet War. It argues that while this has been overlooked, the European war in the East is increasingly becoming a part of the metanarrative of the war; and rather than Western triumphalism being the most readily available narrative, the Soviet contribution is recognized for its importance.

This is critical in accepting Germany's role in which so many lives were lost, especially those unmentioned Jewish victims that *HOI4* ignores.

# Conclusion

In this book, I explore the simgame–simtext dynamic. I show the relationship between players, games, and texts, one that asks for an interpretive posture that adds clarity to an event, in this case, WWII. Each of the areas under investigation, shooters, simulators, and strategies, exemplify how players interested in gameplay tactics and strategy look outside gameplay for clarification, beginning an interpretive journey that may start in the popular sphere with YouTube videos or other accessible online sources and in some cases end in the most professionally produced publications by recognized historians.

I have structured this book so that the first two chapters theorize the dynamic along a number of pathways. I begin by viewing players as latent interpreters when engaging in serious simgames, rather than in the more prevalent arcade-like versions. It is at this curious moment that I shimmy with interdisciplinary steps through a number of humanistic fields, such as literary studies, at home as it is with the articulation of imaginary worlds. I translate this controlling literary idea into the simulated imaginary. Rather than reading novels and imagining the settings, we have digital simulations and their convincing gameworlds. We have agential players, and it is to this agency we must look for the transformative dynamo at work in this new mode. With such a player in mind, I foreground the emerging power of VR over 2D screens to increase the experience of these simulated worlds. I also theorize how the digital acts as a prime mover for this dynamic, the very language of the computer revolution.

In these initial chapters, I also reveal the type of problems that emerge when we interpret how digital computer games approach an event such as WWII. We see myths reinforced in simgames, especially those of national pride for the victors who still heroically symbolize their machines of war. It is to the imaginary, then, that I add the idea of the reconfigured past in simulation games; this process of providing historical gameplay is coupled with areas that defy simulation. These form two theoretical axes that work through my methodology of looking for the reimagined and reconfigured past in games. These are that simgames offer curious experiences of the past with differing degrees of accuracy and authenticity, while they also ignore the most difficult areas by creating glaring gameplay lacunae.

To this end, I offer the idea of a phenomenological gameworld, a game space where particular experiences occur differently in shooters, simulators, and strategies. Again, it is here I move from literature and its well-trodden theories of how subject formation occurs through the encounter with fictions, to an archive of analog and digital simtexts that augment gameplay. We see these in popular and professional histories, along with fictions of the war, technical descriptions of the machines of war, and works by professional historians that offer the most challenges to players. Taken together, these simtexts exist as artifacts of popular memory as much as academic productions. I also argue that this dynamic of games and texts works through the remediation of elements from literature and cinema to games, with agential play offering a powerful new mode of experience for players. And it is on this experience I focus my analysis in each case study, especially to show how each offers its particular inflection of simulated play—and what each excludes.

I begin the central chapters of the book with shooters, yet shooters and simulators share many aspects, especially those related to player experience. Both narrow the POV of the player—whether that be a soldier with feet planted firmly on the ground in shooters or the cockpit as a containing space in simulators. These provide a close subjective experience, which is pointedly focused compared with the broad scale of the final chapter, which discusses strategies. The shooter, then, is where I begin because it is a very popular game genre, with WWII now providing two serious simgames that I analyze: *HLL* and *PS*.

I frame my analysis of these games by arguing that time and space in shooters, such as precursor simgames including *BF1* or the WWI game *BtW*, provide a curated type of gameplay experience, one that reframes trauma away from the lived experiences of soldiers in actual war towards what is possible in a simulation. Yet, I argue, even as they fail to address the true experience of war, serious simgame shooters function as a type of playable memorial, especially in how they present maps as curated snapshots of the war. Alongside these maps, I theorize the categories of roles and equipment as core mechanisms for how the past is reconfigured.

In vehicle simulators, I look for an intensification of the experience found in shooters. I offer the flight simulators *IL2:GB* and the WWII modules of *DCS* as examples of how VR reconfigures the past into powerful gameworlds where the experience of flying deadly aircraft approximates aspects of air combat—without fully replicating it. I detail a brief history of VR to show where we are today with such powerful peripherals. These provide a type of immersion I define as having immediacy and presence far beyond what is offered by a 2D screen. These simulate the cockpit as a mediating space between the player and the digital gameworld. The past, I argue, is reconfigured within the simulated imaginary, not for training purposes, but to provide a reconfigured experience. The dynamic, then, emerges as a way to clarify gameplay success, and also as a way to clarify the past for those intrepid players who are willing to look.

Throughout the book and primarily in this chapter, I offer the example of the British Spitfire and German BF 109 as symbols of nationalism, but also as primary gameplay mechanisms for WWII flight simulators. These feature in a few simtext memoirs that I examine, reflecting how historical elements related to these aircraft, and others, can be simulated—and what elements cannot. The memoirs function as simtexts that clarify the gameplay of *IL2* and *DCS*, especially in how these simgames' single-player and multiplayer modes function. I examine these modes to show the sort of experiences a player will have, and how they relate to a reconfigured past.

The final chapter of this book focuses on strategies, in particular the GSG *HOI4*. This type of simgame reveals the difference in scope from the earlier case studies, with strategies widening beyond individual soldiers or pilots to governments and the forces that led to the war. Yet, as I argue, *HOI4* excludes elements of dark play and fantasies of control, what I call gameplay lacunae. Playable Nazis, the Holocaust, war crimes, and so on find no home in such a simgame—and rightly so, even if such erasure risks the problem of forgetfulness.

It is to this central topic I devote this chapter's analysis, especially in how *HOI4* offers interesting counterfactual scenarios even as it excises so much of what defines the war. I look to a few examples of professional histories to reveal what a curious player might find in such simtexts. They offer all sorts of strategies and tactics that nations used during the war; these, then, can become the counterfactual scenarios that *HOI4* does an excellent job in simulating. These simtexts, though, also reveal the material that finds no simulation in game. In particular, I follow Kershaw's observation that the war in the East was the 'epicentre of horror' and look to how simgames are increasingly recognizing the importance of the German–Soviet War as an underrepresented metanarrative both in the Western imagination and in simgames, and also that so much of what happened in this epicentre is completely missing from simgame play.

To this end, I work through several key playable nations and look to their national focuses as a way to understand what counterfactuals are available for play, along with what is ignored. I end the chapter with a detailed examination of Germany's national focus tree, a core gameplay mechanic that provides the previous mentioned analysis. It reveals several widely divergent counterfactuals, such as the early removal of Hitler, yet it barely mentions National Socialism, has no mention of the Jews, and completely erases the political policies and crimes that followed the invading Germans east into the Soviet Union.

I argue finally that these absences may point players to simtexts full of misinformation about the war as much as they might provide some form of consciousness-raising awareness of the past. Similarly, lacunae in simgames are excised by developers for valid reasons, even if they risk much in removal. I argue that with the continued improvement of VR technologies we may have to revisit this topic, especially if such lacunae begin to be simulated by independent developers or modders. If so, we will have moved from experiencing curated but effective simulations of the past to experiencing, at best, true acknowledgment of the horrors and destruction of war and, at worst, gratuitous reveling in wartime atrocity.

# Notes

## 1. Theorizing Simulation

1   See *BF:1942* (2002), *BF:1943* (2009), *BF:V* (2018); *CoD* (2003), *CoD:2* (2005), *CoD:3* (2006), *CoD:World at War* (2008), *CoD:WWII* (2017).

2   For example, its aircraft, the aces, and the crews all figure prominently in serious combat flight simulators such as *IL2*. Aircraft manuals from the RAF exist that explain how to operate a Spitfire. Personal memoirs of actual fighter pilots provide insights into tactics, such as how the Luftwaffe adopted formation tactics from the fighter ace Werner Mölders' experiences during the Spanish Civil War.

## 2. Simtexts: Reimagining the Past

1   For my use of 'gameworld,' see how Don Ihde reworks the idea of a phenomenological 'lifeworld' (1990).

2   Grossman's *Stalingrad* was originally titled *For a Just Cause* (1952).

3   See Chapter 5 for how the myth of the clean Wehrmacht has been challenged by accounts of what happened in on the Eastern Front.

4   For a full list, see the Jewish Heritage Center resource at https://www.jhcwc.org /list-of-recommended-holocaust-films/.

5   See TVB's *War and Destiny* (2007), HBO's *The Pacific* (2010), and ZDF's *Unsere Mütter, unsere Väter* (*Generation War*, 2013).

6   See the miniseries *Istrebiteli* (*The Attackers*, 2013) for a Russian perspective of the air war in the East. The publishers of the simgame *War Thunder* (2013), Gaijin, crowd-funded the film *28 panfilovtsev* (*Panfilov's 28 Men*, 2016). This dramatizes the resistance put up by Russian infantry who were defending Moscow against German tank attacks.

7   See https://www.youtube.com/playlist?list=PLAn5xS7gOumkzOosH2JAwHKgjOS1 QLQBb for interviews with 1C Games developers and their challenges in modeling aircraft.

## 3. Simgames: Shooters

1   See https://twitter.com/Battlefield/status/999444760921300992.

2   See http://www.companyofheroes.com/blog/2014/12/16/the-battle-of-the-bulge-an
-infographic, which provides an infographic on the Battle of Bulge and https://www
.youtube.com/watch?v=HE-NBUYYstY, in which the developer and a historian provide
an example of a simtext. Other examples taken from this article are http://graviteam
.com/games/GTOS.html?action=history and https://www.eugensystems.com/steel
-division-normandy-44-division-of-the-week-101st-airborne-us/.

3   See Jenkins (2008).

4   *EN* has also recently released a Battle of Stalingrad map, while *HLL* has done the
same for Remagen and Kharkov.

5   See https://hellletloose.fandom.com/wiki/Stalingrad for a description of key
locations.

6   See https://4experience.co/portfolio-item/vr-storytelling-world-war-ii/ for an example.

7   See https://www.parliament.uk/about/living-heritage/transformingsociety/private-lives
/yourcountry/collections/churchillexhibition/churchill-the-orator/human-conflict/.

8   For an early look at *CoD* (2002), see Gish (2010). On reenactments, see Rejack (2007).

9   See https://time.com/4583817/remembering-pearl-harbor-virtual-reality/.

10  Compare with the cinematic dramatization in *The Longest Day* (1962).

11  This hearkens back to earlier mods of *BF2* (2005), such as the 'Forgotten Hope 2'
mod (2009), and its detailed depictions of the environs.

12  See a *Reddit* post that superimpose both *HLL* and *PS* maps. https://www.reddit.com
/r/HellLetLoose/comments/huxdm8/carentan_comparison_map/?utm
_source=share&utm_medium=ios_app&utm_name=iossmf

13  See https://youtu.be/w_I29ev-sFQ for a video of Carentan as it is today; and https://
youtu.be/vpzMSVGqGgg for how well *Band of Brothers* captured the town.

14  See https://youtu.be/-4Z_eXfFLu8 (accessed: March 2023).

## 4. Simgames: Simulators

1   Volume 2 is currently in early access.

2   As of the revision of this chapter in the late winter of 2023, the *CloD* developers have
begun VR testing.

3   This advance can be seen in the February 2023 release of the PSVR2. The technology
uses eye tracking to only render a small portion of a screen in high resolution. This
reduces the amount of processing power because the non-rendered areas of the screen
are blurred with lower resolution (but not noticed by the eye).

4   See https://authentikit.org.

5   See 'Mixed Reality + fully physical fighter jet cockpit simulator: The best implementation of XR/MR' https://www.youtube.com/watch?v=F4yKM_FgMOE&t=11s

6   See   https://www.1news.co.nz/2021/01/25/gabe-newell-says-brain-computer-interface-tech-will-allow-video-games-far-beyond-what-human-meat-peripherals-can-comprehend/. Here, the head of Valve, Gabe Newell, talks about VR and brain–computer interfaces.

7   See Clark (2010), as well as Lakoff and Johnson (1999).

8   See *Hurricane* (2018).

9   See Franz Stigler's account in *A Higher Call* (2012).

10   See Chapter 5 on the myth of the 'clean' Wehrmacht.

11   The Mark-1b changed its machine guns to only four, but added two 20 mm cannons.

12   The famous military-aviation phrase "Beware of the Hun in the sun" reflects this principle (the 'Hun' being a pejorative term used by the British in WWI that recast the Germans in the role of modern Attilas).

13   This is described in the introduction PDF to the campaign.

14   This can be found when purchasing the campaign.

15   Normandy has just been released during the revision of his manuscript in the fall of 2022.

16   See the manual at https://tacticalairwar.com/, and the 'Our History' section.

17   As of the time of revising this chapter in the early winter of 2023, they are also experimenting with limited co-op missions set a specific times, another example of serious multiplayer gameplay.

18   The manual is in a navigational header on the main TAW website that links to a Google.doc file, accessed January 23, 2022.

19   This is another penalty that is sometimes changed through experimentation to see what works best for both players and TAW's demanding server ethos.

20   See http://seowhq.net/seowwiki-en/index4875.html?title=Main_Page, and also https://sourceforge.net/projects/seow.

21   Author note:  I know this because I went through this procedure in the Spring of 2019. I flew in Spitfire MJ627 at Biggin Hill, which operated and got a 109 kill over Arnhem in 1944.


## 5. Simgames: Strategies

1   See https://store.steampowered.com/stats/, accessed May 31, 2020.

2   See the young protagonists in Doerr's *All The Light We Cannot See* (2014, Chapter 2) or any of the large host of Vasily Grossman's *For a Just Cause* (1952) (also titled *Stalingrad*) and *Life and Fate* (1959).

3   See Bachrach and Luckert (2009) for an example of how Germany used propaganda techniques leading up to the war. Also see Cull (1995) for how the British used

propaganda to sway an ally. For Soviet propaganda, see Berkhoff (2012). For how Hollywood influenced American perceptions, see Donald (2017). For Japanese use, see Kushner (2005).

4   For a recent dramatization of these events see Netflix's *Munich: The Edge of War* (2022).

5   See Tanaka (1996) for a seminal work on Japanese war crimes that tries to understand the reasons beyond reliance on tradition or some unique difference in the psychology of the Japanese. For more recent work, see Wilson et al. (2017) and Jacob (2018).

6   This broad perspective is primarily taken from Smelser and Davies (2008, and Fritz 2011) but reflects commonly held understanding of the event.

7   For the Soviets, it is the patriotic comrade fighting for the motherland; see Berkhoff (2012).

8   These are written in German, with ten volumes so far in English.

9   See the Oxford University Press website for a description of the series: https:// global.oup.com/academic/content/series/g/germany-and-the-second-world-war-gsww /?cc=us&lang=en&, accessed February 23, 2023. See Bibliography for full reference details.

10  See the official Paradox Wiki on the events: https://hoi4.paradoxwikis.com/German _events.

# References

Aarseth, Espen J. 1997. *Cybertext: Perspectives on Ergodic Literature*. Baltimore, MD: Johns Hopkins University Press. https://doi.org/10.56021/9780801855788 2004. "Genre Trouble: Narrativism and the Art of Simulation." In *First Person: New Media as Story, Performance, and Game*. Cambridge and New York: MIT Press.

Abrams, M. H. 1958. *The Mirror and the Lamp: Romantic Theory and the Critical Tradition*. New York: Norton.

Agnew, Vanessa, Jonathan Lamb, and Juliane Tomann, eds. 2019. *The Routledge Handbook of Reenactment Studies: Key Terms in the Field*. New York: Routledge. https://doi.org /10.4324/9780429445637-1.

Alber, Jan. 2011. *Why Study Literature?* Aarhus and Bristol, CT: Aarhus University Press.

Allison, Tanine. 2010. "The World War II Video Game, Adaptation, and Postmodern History." *Literature/Film Quarterly* 38 (3): 183–93.

Aly, Götz, and Susanne Heim. 2003. *Architects of Annihilation: Auschwitz and the Logic of Destruction*. Translated by A. G. Blunden. Princeton, NJ: Princeton University Press.

Ambrose, Stephen A. 1992. *Band of Brothers: E Company, 506th Regiment, 101st Airborne from Normandy to Hitler's Eagle's Nest*. New York and London: Simon & Schuster.

Apperley, Tom. 2018. "Counterfactual Communities: Strategy Games, Paratexts and the Player's Experience of History." *Open Library of Humanities* 4 (1): 15. https://doi.org/10.16995/olh.286.

Applebaum, Anne. 2020. "Putin's Big Lie." *The Atlantic*. January 5, 2020. https://www.theatlantic .com/ideas/archive/2020/01/putin-blames-poland-world-war-ii/604426/.

Arendt, Hannah. 1979. *The Origins of Totalitarianism*. New York and London: Harcourt, Brace.

Bachrach, Susan, and Steven Luckert. 2009. *State of Deception: The Power of Nazi Propaganda*. Washington, DC and New York: US Holocaust Memorial Museum.

Beevor, Antony. 1999. *Stalingrad: The Fateful Siege: 1942–1943*. New York: Penguin Books. 2014. *The Second World War*. London: Orion Publishing Co.

Berkhoff, Karel C. 2012. *Motherland in Danger: Soviet Propaganda during World War II*. Cambridge, MA: Harvard University Press. https://doi.org/10.4159/harvard.9780674064829.

Berry, David M., ed. 2012. *Understanding Digital Humanities*. Houndmills and New York: Palgrave Macmillan.

Black, Jeremy. 2008. *What If?* London: Social Affairs Unit.

Blank, Ralf, Jorg Echternkamp, Karola Fings, Jurgen Forster, Winfried Heinemann, Tobias Jersak, Armin Nolzen, and Christoph Rass. 2008. *Germany and the Second World War: Volume IX/I: German Wartime Society 1939–1945: Politicization, Disintegration, and the Struggle for Survival*. Translated by Derry Cook-Radmore. Oxford: Clarendon Press.

Bolter, J. David, and Richard. Grusin. 1999. *Remediation Understanding New Media*. Cambridge, MA: MIT Press. https://doi.org/10.1108/ccij.1999.4.4.208.1.

Boog, Horst, Jurgen Forster, Joachim Hoffman, Ernst Klink, Rolf-Dieter Muller, and Gerd R. Ueberschar. 2015. *Germany and the Second World War: Volume IV: The Attack on the Soviet Union*. Translated by Ewald Osers. Illustrated ed. Oxford and New York: Clarendon Press.

Boog, Horst, Gerhard Krebs, and Detlef Vogel. 2006. *Germany and the Second World War: Volume VII: The Strategic Air War in Europe and the War in the West and East Asia, 1943-1944/5*. Illustrated ed. Oxford: Clarendon Press.

Boog, Horst, Werner Rahn, Reinhard Stumpf, and Bernd Wegner. 2015. *Germany and the Second World War: Volume VI: The Global War*. Translated by Derry Cook-Radmore. Illustrated ed. Oxford and New York: Oxford University Press.

Brickhill, Paul. 1954. *Reach for the Sky: The Story of Douglas Bader*. London: Collins.

Brode, Douglas. 2020a. *From Hell to Hollywood: An Encyclopedia of World War II Films Volume 1*. Albany, GA: BearManor Media. 2020b. *From Hell to Hollywood: An Encyclopedia of World War II Films Volume 2*. Albany, GA: BearManor Media.

Buchheim, Lothar-Günther. 1973. *Das Boot Roman*. Munich: Dtv.

"Campaigns." 2021. IL-2 Sturmovik: Great Battles. https://il2sturmovik.com/store/campaigns/.

Carbonell, Curtis D. 2019. *Dread Trident: Tabletop Role-Playing Games and the Modern Fantastic*. Liverpool: Liverpool University Press. https://doi.org/10.3828/liverpool/9781789620573.001.0001

Champion, Erik. 2015. *Critical Gaming: Interactive History and Virtual Heritage*. Farnham: Routledge. https://doi.org/10.4324/9781315574981

Chapman, Adam. 2013. "Is Sid Meier's Civilization History?" *Rethinking History* 17 (3): 312–32. https://doi.org/10.1080/13642529.2013.774719. 2016. "It's Hard to Play in the Trenches: World War I, Collective Memory and Videogames." *Game Studies* 16 (2). http://gamestudies.org/1602/articles/chapman. 2018. *Digital Games as History*. New York and London: Routledge.

Chapman, Adam, and Jonas Linderoth. 2015. "Exploring the Limits of Play: A Case Study of Representations of Nazism in Games." In *The Dark Side of Game Play: Controversial Issues in Playful Environments*, edited by Torill Elvira Mortensen, Jonas Linderoth, and Ashley M. L. Brown. Routledge. https://doi.org/10.1080/13642529.2013.774719

Charmley, John. 1993. *Churchill: The End of Glory : A Political Biography*. New York: Harcourt.

Churchill, Winston S. 1990. *Memoirs of the Second World War: An Abridgment of the Six Volumes of The Second World War with an EPILOGUE by the Author on the Postwar Years Written for This Volume*. Reissue ed. London: Houghton Mifflin Harcourt.

Clark, Andy. 2010. *Supersizing the Mind: Embodiment, Action, and Cognitive Extension*. Oxford: Oxford University Press. https://doi.org/10.1007/s11098-010-9598-9

Copplestone, Tara Jane. 2016. "But That's Not Accurate: The Differing Perceptions of Accuracy in Cultural-Heritage Videogames between Creators, Consumers and Critics." *Rethinking History* 21 (3): 415–38. https://doi.org/10.1080/13642529.2017.1256615

Cowley, Robert, ed. 1999. *What If?: Eminent Historians Imagine What Might Have Been*. New York: Putnam. 2005. *What If? 2: Eminent Historians Imagine What Might Have Been*. New York: Berkley.

Crawford, Chris. 1984. *The Art Of Computer Game Design: Reflections Of A Master Game Designer*. Berkeley, CA: Osborne/McGraw-Hill.

Cull, Nicholas John. 1995. *Selling War: The British Propaganda Campaign Against American "Neutrality" in World War II*. New York: Oxford University Press. https://doi.org/10.2307/2945249

Daugbjerg, Mads. 2019. "Battle." In *The Routledge Handbook of Reenactment Studies: Key Terms in the Field*, edited by Vanessa Agnew, Jonathan Lamb, and Juliane Tomann. New York: Routledge, 2020. https://doi.org/10.4324/9780429445637.

Deist, Wilhelm, Manfred Messerschmidt, Hans-Erich Volkmann, and Wolfram Wette, eds. 2015. *Germany and the Second World War: Volume I: The Build-up of German Aggression*. Translated by P. S. Falla, Dean S. McMurry, and Ewald Osers. Illustrated ed. Oxford and New York: Clarendon Press.

Deleuze, Gilles, and Claire Parnet. 2007. *Dialogues II*. Translated by Hugh Tomlinson and Barbara Habberjam. Revised ed. New York: Columbia University Press.

Dibbs, John, and Tony Holmes. 2016. *Spitfire: The Legend Lives On*. 80th ed. Oxford: Osprey Publishing.

Dick, Philip K. 1962. *The Man In the High Castle*. New York: G. P. Putnam's Sons.

Doerr, Anthony. 2014. *All the Light We Cannot See*. New York and London: Scribner.

Donald, Ralph. 2017. *Hollywood Enlists!: Propaganda Films of World War II*. Lanham, MD: Rowman and Littlefield.

Echternkamp, Jorg. 2014. *Germany and the Second World War: Volume IX/II: German Wartime Society 1939–1945: Exploitation, Interpretations, Exclusion*. Oxford: Oxford University Press.

Erll, Astrid. 2005. "Literature, Film, and the Mediality of Cultural Memory." In *Media and Cultural Memory / Medien Und Kulturelle Erinnerung*, edited by Astrid Erll and Ansgar Nünning, 2005 ed. Vol. 3. Berlin and Boston, MA: De Gruyter. https://doi.org/10.1515/9783110922639.

Erll, Astrid, and Ansgar Nünning, eds. 2005. *Media and Cultural Memory/ Medien Und Kulturelle Erinnerung*. 2005 ed. Vol. 3. Berlin and Boston, MA: De Gruyter. https://doi.org/10.1515/9783110922639.

Evans, R. 2002. *Telling Lies About Hitler: The Holocaust, History and the David Irving Trial*. London: Verso.

Ferguson, Niall. 1997. *Virtual History: Alternatives And Counterfactuals*. New York: Basic Books.

Follett, Ken. 1979. *Eye of the Needle*. New York and Berkeley, CA: Arbor House. 2002. *Jackdaws*. New York: Penguin Books.

Frieser, Karl-Heinz, Klaus Schmider, Klaus Schönherr, Gerhard Schreiber, Krisztián Ungváry, and Bernd Wegner. 2017. *Germany and the Second World War. Volume VIII: The Eastern Front 1943–1944: The War in the East and on the Neighbouring Fronts*. Translated by Barry Smerin and Barbara Haider-Wilson. Oxford: Oxford University Press.

Fritz, Stephen G. 2011. *Ostkrieg: Hitler's War of Extermination in the East*. Lexington: University Press of Kentucky.

Galland, Adolf. 1954. *The First and the Last: The Rise and Fall of the German Fighter Forces 1938–1945*. Translated by Mervyn Savill. New York: Henry Holt and Company.

Galloway, Alexander R. 2006. *Gaming: Essays on Algorithmic Culture*. Electronic Mediations 18. Minneapolis: University of Minnesota Press.

Genette, Gerard, and Richard Macksey. 1997. *Paratexts: Thresholds of Interpretation*. Translated by Jane E. Lewin. Cambridge and New York: Cambridge University Press.

Gish, Harrison. 2010. "Playing the Second World War: Call of Duty and the Telling of History." *Eludamos. Journal for Computer Game Culture* 4 (2): 167–80. https://doi.org/10.7557/23.6042

Glantz, David, and Jonathan M. House. 2009. *To the Gates of Stalingrad: Soviet-German Combat Operations, April–August 1942*. Illustrated ed. Lawrence: University Press of Kansas.

Goldhagen, Daniel Jonah. 1997. *Hitler's Willing Executioners: Ordinary Germans and the Holocaust*. New York: Vintage.

Grass, Günter. 1962. *The Tin Drum*. Edited by Ralph Manheim. New York: Pantheon.

Grossman, Vasily. 2006. *Life and Fate*. Translated by Robert Chandler. London: Vintage Classics. 2019. *Stalingrad*. Translated by Robert Chandler. New York: NYRB Classics.

Guderian, H. 2000. *Panzer Leader*. New York: Penguin Books.

Hampton, Dan. 2015. *Lords of the Sky: Fighter Pilots and Air Combat, from the Red Baron to the F-16*. New York: William Morrow Paperbacks.

Harris, Robert. 1992. *Fatherland*. New York: Random House.

Hartmann, Stephan. 2005. "The World as a Process: Simulations in the Natural and Social Sciences." Preprint, August. http://philsci-archive.pitt.edu/2412/

Hayward, Joel S. A. 1998. *Stopped at Stalingrad: The Luftwaffe and Hitler's Defeat in the East, 1942–1943*. Revised ed. Lawrence: University Press of Kansas.

Hellbeck, Jochen, ed. 2016. *Stalingrad: The City That Defeated the Third Reich*. Translated by Christopher Tauchen. Illustrated ed. New York: Public Affairs.

Heller, Joseph. 1962. *Catch-22*. New York: Dell Publishing.

Hemingway, Ernest. 1929. *Farewell to Arms*. New York: Scribner. 1940. *For Whom the Bell Tolls*. New York: The Blakiston Co.

Higgins, Jack. 1975. *The Eagle Has Landed*. New York: Henry Holt & Co.

Hitler, Adolf, 1925-1927. *Mein Kampf*. Munchen: Verlag Franz Eher Nachfolger,,

Huizinga, Johan. 1949. *Homo Ludens: Study of the Play Element in Culture*. London and Boston, MA: Routledge.

Hume, Kathryn. 1985. *Fantasy and Mimesis: Responses to Reality in Western Literature*. New York: Routledge. https://doi.org/10.2307/1771923

Humphreys, Paul, and Cyrille Imbert, eds. 2012. *Models, Simulations, and Representations*. Routledge Studies in the Philosophy of Science 9. New York: Routledge.

Huntemann, Nina B., and Matthew Thomas Payne, eds. 2009. *Joystick Soldiers: The Politics of Play in Military Video Games*. New York: Routledge.

Ihde, Don. 1990. *Technology and the Lifeworld: From Garden to Earth*. Bloomington: Indiana University Press.

Jacob, Frank. 2018. *Japanese War Crimes during World War II: Atrocity and the Psychology of Collective Violence*. Santa Barbara, CA: Praeger.

Jenkins, Henry. 2008. *Convergence Culture: Where Old and New Media Collide*. Revised ed. New York: NYU Press.

Jones, James. 1962. *The Thin Red Line*. London: Sceptre.

Juul, Jesper. 2011. *Half-Real: Video Games between Real Rules and Fictional Worlds*. Cambridge, MA: MIT Press.

Kapell, Matthew William, and Andrew B. R. Elliott, eds. 2013. *Playing with the Past: Digital Games and the Simulation of History*. New York: Bloomsbury Academic.

Kempshall, C. 2015. *The First World War in Computer Games*. Basingstoke and New York: Palgrave Pivot. https://doi.org/10.1057/9781137491763

Kershaw, Ian. 1999. *Hitler: 1889–1936 Hubris*. New York and London: W.W. Norton & Company. 2000. *Hitler: 1936–1945 Nemesis*. New York and London: W.W. Norton & Co Inc. 2008a. *Hitler: A Biography*. New York and London: W.W. Norton & Company. 2008b. *Hitler, the Germans, and the Final Solution*. Jerusalem and New Haven, CT: International Institute for Holocaust Research, Yad Vashem, and Yale University Press.

Kotkin, Stephen. 2015. *Stalin: Paradoxes of Power, 1878–1928*. London: Penguin Books. 2017. *Stalin: Waiting for Hitler, 1929–1941*. London: Penguin Books.

Kroener, Bernhard R., Rolf-Dieter Muller, and Hans Umbreit. 2000. *Germany and the Second World War: Volume V/I: Organization and Mobilization of the German Sphere of Power*. Translated by Ewald Osers, John Brownjohn, Patricia Crampton, and Louise Willmott. Oxford: Oxford University Press. 2015. *Germany and the Second World War: Volume V/II: Organization and Mobilization in the German Sphere of Power: Wartime Administration, Economy, and Manpower Resources 1942-1944/5*. Translated by Derry Cook-Radmore. Illustrated ed. Oxford and New York: Clarendon Press.

Kushner, Barak. 2005. *The Thought War: Japanese Imperial Propaganda*. Annotated ed. Honolulu: University of Hawaii Press.

Kylander, Johan. 2006. *In Pursuit: A Pilot's Guide to Online Air Combat*. Stockholm: Pilot Press.

Lakoff, George, and Mark Johnson. 1999. *Philosophy in the Flesh: The Embodied Mind and Its Challenge to Western Thought*. New York: Basic Books.

Lipstadt, Deborah E. 2006. *History on Trial: My Day in Court with a Holocaust Denier*. New York: Ecco.

Liu, Alan. 2004. *The Laws of Cool: Knowledge Work and the Culture of Information*. Chicago: University Of Chicago Press. https://doi.org/10.7208/chicago/9780226487007.001.0001

MacLean, Alistair. 1967. *Where Eagles Dare*. 3rd ed. London: Collins.

Maier, Klaus A., Horst Rohde, Bernd Stegemann, and Hans Umbreit. 1991. *Germany and the Second World War: Volume II: Germany's Initial Conquests in Europe*. Translated by Dean S. McMurry and Edward Osers. Oxford: Oxford University Press.

Mailer, Norman. 1948. *The Naked and the Dead*. New York: Holt, Rinehart and Winston.

Makos, Adam, and Larry Alexander. 2012. *A Higher Call: An Incredible True Story of Combat and Chivalry in the War-Torn Skies of World War II*. Illustrated ed. New York: Berkley Caliber.

Manstein, Erich. 2004. *Lost Victories: The War Memoirs of Hitler's Most Brilliant General*. St. Paul, MN: Zenith Press.

McCall, Jeremiah. 2020. "The Historical Problem Space Framework: Games as a Historical Medium." *Game Studies* 20 (3). http://gamestudies.org/2003/articles/mccall.

McEwan, Ian. 2003. *Atonement*. New York: Anchor Books.

Megargee, Geoffrey P. 2006. *War of Annihilation – Combat and Genocide on the Eastern Front, 1941*. Lanham, MD: Rowman and Littlefield.

Feist, Uwe, Norman E. Harms, and Mike Dario. 1978. *The Fighting 109: A Pictorial History of the Messerschmitt Bf 109 in Action*. Newton Abbot: Doubleday.

Milburn, Colin. 2018. *Respawn: Gamers, Hackers, and Technogenic Life*. Experimental Futures: Technological Lives, Scientific Arts, Anthropological Voices. Durham, NC: Duke University Press. https://doi.org/10.1215/9781478002789

Mortensen, Torill Elvira, Jonas Linderoth, and Ashley ML Brown, eds. 2015. *The Dark Side of Game Play: Controversial Issues in Playful Environments*. New York and London: Routledge. https://doi.org/10.4324/9781315738680

Murray, Janet H. 1998. *Hamlet on the Holodeck: The Future of Narrative in Cyberspace*. Cambridge, MA: MIT Press.

Murray, Williamson, and Allan R Millett. 2009. *War to Be Won: Fighting the Second World War, 1937–1945*. Cambridge, MA: Harvard University Press.

Okerstrom, Dennis R. 2015. *Dick Cole's War: Doolittle Raider, Hump Pilot, Air Commando*. Columbia: University of Missouri.

Olick, Jeffrey K., Vered Vinitzky-Seroussi, and Daniel Levy, eds. 2011. *The Collective Memory Reader*. New York: Oxford University Press.

Ondaatje, Michael. 1993. *The English Patient*. New York: Vintage Books.

Orwell, George. 1949. *Nineteen Eighty-Four : A Novel*. New York: Harcourt, Brace.

O'Shaughnessy, Nicholas. 2016. *Selling Hitler: Propaganda and the Nazi Brand.* London: Hurst. 2017. *Marketing the Third Reich: Persuasion, Packaging and Propaganda.* London and New York: Routledge.

Owen, David. 2015. *Dogfight: The Supermarine Spitfire and the Messerschmitt BF 109.* Barnsley: Pen & Sword Aviation.

Paradox Interactive, dir. 2021. *Hearts of Iron IV: No Step Back | Soviet Focus Tree.* https://www .youtube.com/watch?v=LiMEwLq_g00.

Pelt, Robert Jan Van. 2016. *The Case for Auschwitz: Evidence from the Irving Trial.* Bloomington: Indiana University Press.

Pfister, Eugene. 2020. "'Man Spielt Nicht Mit Hakenkreuzen!'" In *Historia Ludens: The Playing Historian,* edited by Alexander von Lünen, Katherine J. Lewis, Benjamin Litherland, and Pat Cullum.New York and London: Routledge. https://doi.org/10.4324/9780429345616-17

Price, Alfred. 2012. *Spitfire: Pilots' Stories.* Stroud: The History Press.

Pynchon, Thomas. 1987. *Gravity's Rainbow.* New York: Penguin Books.

Ramsay, Debra. 2020. "Liminality and the Smearing of War and Play in Battlefield 1." *Game Studies* 20 (1). http://gamestudies.org/2001/articles/ramsay.

Ramsay, Stephen. 2011. *Reading Machines: Toward an Algorithmic Criticism.* Topics in the Digital Humanities. Urbana: University of Illinois Press. https://doi.org/10.5406/illinois /9780252036415.001.0001

Rejack, Brian. 2007. "Toward a Virtual Reenactment of History: Video Games and the Recreation of the Past." *Rethinking History* 11 (3). https://www.tandfonline.com/doi/abs/10.1080 /13642520701353652.

Rigney, Ann. 2005. "The Dynamics of Remembrance: Texts Between Monumentality and Morphing." In *Media and Cultural Memory / Medien Und Kulturelle Erinnerung,* edited by Astrid Erll and Ansgar Nünning, 2005 ed. Vol. 3. Berlin and Boston, MA: De Gruyter. https://doi.org/10.1515/9783110922639.

Rudel, Hans Ulrich. 2012. *Stuka Pilot.* Illustrated ed. Edinburgh: Black House Publishing.

Sabin, Philip. 2012. *Simulating War: Studying Conflict through Simulation Games.* London: Bloomsbury Academic.

Said, Edward W. 1979. *Orientalism.* New York: Vintage. 1994. *Culture and Imperialism.* New York: Vintage.

Saler, Michael. 2012. *As If: Modern Enchantment and the Literary PreHistory of Virtual Reality.* Oxford and New York: Oxford University Press.

Salvati, Andrew J. 2020. "Fantasies of Control: Modding for Ethnic Violence and Nazi Fetishism in Historical Strategy Games." In *Historia Ludens: The Playing Historian,* edited by Alexander von Lünen, Katherine J. Lewis, Benjamin Litherland, and Pat Cullum. New York and London: Routledge.

Schlink, Bernhard. 1997. *The Reader.* Translated by Carol Brown Janeway. New York: Vintage.

Schreiber, Gerhard, Bernd Stegemann, and Detlef Vogel. 1995. *Germany and the Second World War: Volume III: The Mediterranean, South-East Europe, and North Africa, 1939–1941, From Italy's*

*Declaration of Non-Belligerence to the Entry of the US into the War.* Translated by Dean S. McMurry, Ewald Osers, and Louise Wilmott. Oxford and New York: Oxford University Press.

Schwab, Klaus. 2017. *The Fourth Industrial Revolution.* New York: Crown Business.

Shaw, Robert L. 1985. *Fighter Combat: Tactics and Maneuvering.* 7th ed. Annapolis, MD: Naval Institute Press.

Shirer, William L. 1960. *Rise and Fall of the Third Reich.* New York and London: Simon & Schuster.

Shull, Michael S., and David E. Wilt. 1996. *Hollywood War Films, 1937–1945: An Exhaustive Filmography of American Feature-Length Motion Pictures Relating to World War II.* Jefferson, NC: McFarland Publishing.

Smelser, R., and E. Davies. 2008. *The Myth of the Eastern Front: The Nazi-Soviet War in American Popular Culture.* Cambridge: Cambridge University Press.

Smicker, Josh. 2009. "Future Combat, Combating Futures: Temporalities of War Video Games and the Performance of Proleptic Histories." In *Joystick Soldiers: The Politics of Play in Military Video Games*, edited by Nina B. Huntemann and Matthew Thomas Payne. New York: Routledge.

Snyder, Timothy. 2010. *Bloodlands: Europe between Hitler and Stalin.* New York: Basic Books.

Stenros, Jaakko, and Markus Montola, eds. 2010. *Nordic Larp.* Stockholm: Fea Livia.

Suid, Lawrence H. 2002. *Guts and Glory: The Making of the American Military Image in Film.* Revised ed. Lexington: The University Press of Kentucky.

"Tactical Air War." 2021. https://tacticalairwar.com/.

Tanaka, Yuki. 1996. *Hidden Horrors: Japanese War Crimes in World War II, Second Edition.* New York: Routledge.

Toliver, Raymond, and Trevor Constable. 1970. *The Blond Knight of Germany: A Biography of Erich Hartmann.* Blue Ridge Summit, PA: Tab Aero.

Tournier, Michel. 1973. *The Ogre.* New York: Dell.unmerged(9046). 2011. "No Gulags, Gas, Concentration Camps, Holocaust or Swastikas! If in Doubt, Ask a Mod." Paradox Interactive Forums. April 6, 2011. https://forum.paradoxplaza.com/forum/threads/no-gulags -gas-concentration-camps-holocaust-or-swastikas-if-in-doubt-ask-a-mod.529860/.

Uricchio, William. 2005. "Simulation, History, and Computer Games." In *Handbook of Computer Game Studies*, edited by Joost Raessens and Jeffrey Goldstein. Cambridge, MA: MIT Press.

van Creveld, Martin. 2013. *Wargames: From Gladiators to Gigabytes.* Cambridge and New York: Cambridge University Press. https://doi.org/10.1017/CBO9781139579872

van den Heede, Pieter. 2020. "'Experience the Second World War Like Never Before!' Game Paratextuality between Transnational Branding and Informal Learning ('¡Experimenta La Segunda Guerra Mundial Como Nunca Antes!' La Paratextualidad de Los Videojuegos Entre El Branding Transnacional y El Aprendizaje Informal )." *Journal for the Study of Education and Development* 43 (3): 606–51. https://doi.org/10.1080/02103702.2020.1771964.

van den Heede, Pieter, Kees Ribbens, and Jeroen Jansz. 2018. "Replaying Today's Wars? A Study of the Conceptualization of Post-1989 Conflict in Digital 'War' Games." *International Journal of Politics, Culture, and Society* 31 (3): 229–50. https://doi.org/10.1007/s10767-017-9267-5.

Vonnegut, Kurt. 1969. *Slaughterhouse-Five*. New York: Delacorte.

Wackerfuss, Andrew J. 2013. "'This Game of Sudden Death' : Simulating Air Combat of the First World War." In *Playing with the Past : Digital Games and the Simulation of History*, edited by Matthew William Kapell and Andrew B. R. Elliott. London: Bloomsbury Academic. https://doi.org/10.5040/9781628928259.

Wainwright, A. Martin. 2014. "Teaching Historical Theory through Video Games." *The History Teacher* 47 (4): 579–612. 2019. *Virtual History: How Videogames Portray the Past*. London and New York: Routledge.

Walker, Shaun. 2019. "Polish PM Furious at Putin Rewriting History of Second World War." *The Guardian*, December 30, 2019, sec. World news. https://www.theguardian.com/world/2019/dec/30/polish-pm-furious-at-putin-rewriting-history-of-second-world-war.

Watanabe, Rikyu and Grinsell, Robert. 1980. *Messerschmitt Bf 109*. London: Jane's

Wellum, Geoffrey. 2002. *First Light*. London; New York: Viking.

Welsh, Timothy J. 2016. *Mixed Realism: Videogames and the Violence of Fiction*. Electronic Mediations 50. Minneapolis: University of Minnesota Press.

Wette, Wolfram. 2006. *The Wehrmacht: History, Myth, Reality*. Cambridge, MA: Harvard University Press.

Wilson, Sandra, Robert Cribb, Beatrice Trefalt, and Dean Aszkielowicz. 2017. *Japanese War Criminals: The Politics of Justice After the Second World War*. New York: Columbia University Press.

Winters, Dick, and Cole C. Kingseed. 2008. *Beyond Band of Brothers: The War Memoirs of Major Dick Winters*. New York: Dutton Caliber.

Zimmerman, Eric, and Katie Salen. 2003. *Rules of Play: Game Design Fundamentals*. Cambridge, MA: MIT Press.

# Index